Lecture Notes in Computer Science 6481

Commenced Publication in 1973
Founding and Former Series Editors:
Gerhard Goos, Juris Hartmanis, and Jan va

Services Science

Subline of Lectures Notes in Computer Science

Subline Editors-in-Chief

Subline Editorial Board

Elisabetta Di Nitto   Ramin Yahyapour (Eds.)

Towards
a Service-Based Internet

Third European Conference, ServiceWave 2010
Ghent, Belgium, December 13-15, 2010
Proceedings

 Springer

Volume Editors

Elisabetta Di Nitto
Politecnico di Milano, Dipartimento di Elettronica e Informazione
Piazza Leonardo da Vinci 32, 20133 Milano, Italy
E-mail: dinitto@elet.polimi.it

Ramin Yahyapour
Technische Universität Dortmund, IT & Medien Centrum
August-Schmidt-Str. 12, 44227 Dortmund, Germany
E-mail: ramin.yahyapour@udo.edu

Library of Congress Control Number: 2010940293

CR Subject Classification (1998): C.2, D.2, H.4, H.3, C.2.4, H.5

LNCS Sublibrary: SL 2 – Programming and Software Engineering

ISSN   0302-9743
ISBN-10   3-642-17693-3 Springer Berlin Heidelberg New York
ISBN-13   978-3-642-17693-7 Springer Berlin Heidelberg New York

springer.com

© Springer-Verlag Berlin Heidelberg 2010
Printed in Germany

Typesetting: Camera-ready by author, data conversion by Scientific Publishing Services, Chennai, India
Printed on acid-free paper   06/3180   5 4 3 2 1 0

Preface

The ServiceWave conference series is committed to being the premier European forum for researchers, educators and industrial practitioners to present and discuss the most recent innovations, trends, experiences and concerns in software services (or the "Future of the Internet of Service") and related underlying infrastructure technologies. ServiceWave fosters the creation of cross-community scientific excellence by gathering industrial and academic experts from various disciplines such as business process management, distributed systems, grid and cloud computing, networking, service science and software engineering.

ServiceWave 2010 was the third edition of the series. The first edition was held in Madrid in 2008 and the second one in Stockholm in 2009, in conjunction with the International Conference on Service-Oriented Computing (ICSOC 2009). ServiceWave 2010 took place in the lovely city of Ghent in Belgium, during December 13–15, 2010.

This year again, the program featured a rich selection of quality contributions. The strict review process yielded an acceptance rate of about 30%. Out of 49 submissions, the Program Committee selected 15 research papers for presentation at the conference and its publication as full papers in this volume. Reviews were performed by at least three members of the Program Committee.

The accepted papers cover a broad range of subjects related to service-oriented architectures and the underlying cloud infrastructure. Thus, this volume contains contributions in the areas of:

- Cloud computing
- Service adaptation and identification
- Service identification and adaptation
- Infrastructures and middleware
- Applications and mashups
- Engineering of service-oriented applications

In addition to the scientific track, the joint ServiceWave, FIA and FIRE call for demonstrations received 31 submissions, of which 24 were accepted for presentation in Ghent, resulting in an acceptance rate of 77%. Authors had to submit a two-page extended abstract as well as a short video of the actual demonstration. Reviewers found videos extremely helpful in forming an opinion about the scope and maturity of each demo. The accepted demonstrations cover a wide spectrum of technology and application domains. Papers were rejected mainly because of either a lack of innovative content, i.e., the system demonstrated was similar to existing commercial or open source offerings, or the demo was about a system that was not yet built, typically submitted too early by projects in their first year. Authors of the latter type of proposal were encouraged to re-submit a demonstration proposal next year.

The Chairs would like to take this opportunity to express their gratitude to
the members of the Program Committee for their valuable help in guaranteeing
a high-quality conference. We would also like to thank all contributors.

October 2010   Elisabetta Di Nitto and Ramin Yahyapour
                                            Scientific Programme Co-chairs

                                        Jennifer Peréz and Julien Vayssière
                                            Demonstration Co-chairs

Organization

General Chair

Thierry Priol   INRIA, France

Program Committee Chairs

Elisabetta Di Nitto   Politecnico di Milano, Italy
Ramin Yahyapour   Dortmund University of Technology, Germany

Industry Program Chairs

Marquart Franz   Siemens, Germany
Stefano De Panfilis   Engineering, Italy

Workshop Chairs

Michel Cezon   INRIA, France
Yaron Wolfsthal   IBM Haifa Research Lab, Israel

Demonstration Chairs

Jennifer Pérez   Technical University of Madrid, Spain
Julien Vayssière   Smart Services CRC, Australia

Organizing Committee

Veronique Pevtschin   Engineering, Italy (Coordination)
Sophie Debeck   NESSI
Marco Müller   University of Duisburg-Essen, Germany
Barbara Pirillo   NESSI
Vanessa Stricker   University of Duisburg-Essen, Germany

Scientific Program Committee

Marco Aiello	University of Groningen, The Netherlands
Walter Binder	University of Lugano, Switzerland
Pascal Bisson	Thales, France
Manuel Carro	Universidad Politécnica de Madrid, Spain
Stefano De Panfilis	Engineering I.I., Italy
Schahram Dustdar	Technical University of Vienna, Austria
Erik Elmroth	Umea University, Sweden
Ioannis Fikouras	Ericsson, Sweden
Howard Foster	Imperial College, UK
Wolfgang Gerteis	SAP, Germany
Maritta Heisel	University of Duisburg-Essen, Germany
Paola Inverardi	University of L'Aquila, Italy
Valerie Issarny	INRIA, France
Borka Jerman-Blazic	Jozef Stefan Institute, Slovenia
Jean-Marc Jézéquel	University of Rennes 1, France
Zoltan Juhasz	University of Pannonia and MTA SZTAKI, Hungary
Dimka Karastoyanova	University of Stuttgart, Germany
Arto Karila	Helsinki Institute of Information Technology, Finland
Patricia Lago	VU University of Amsterdam, The Netherlands
Philippe Lalanda	Universitè de Grenoble, France
Ignacio Llorente	Universidad Complutense de Madrid, Spain
Nikolay Mehandjiev	University of Manchester, UK
Andreas Metzger	University of Duisburg-Essen, Germany
Werner Mohr	Nokia Siemens Networks, Germany
Christine Morin	INRIA, France
Christos Nikolaou	University of Crete, Greece
Dimitri Papadimitriou	Alcatel-Lucent, Belgium
Michael Parkin	Tilburg University, The Netherlands
Marco Pistore	FBK, Trento, Italy
Pierluigi Plebani	Politecnico di Milano, Italy
Ita Richardson	Lero, Ireland
Collette Rolland	University of Paris, France
Fabrizio Silvestri	CNR, Italy
Ian Sommerville	St. Andrews University, UK
George Spanoudakis	City University, UK
Wolfgang Theilmann	SAP, Germany
Yaron Wolfsthal	IBM Haifa, Israel
Andreas Wombacher	University of Twente, The Netherlands
Eugenio Zimeo	University of Sannio, Italy
Andrea Zisman	City University, UK

Scientific Program External Reviewers

Françoise Andre
Olivier Barais
Benoit Baudry
Vanessa Bembenek
Lianne Bodenstaff
David Breitgand
Viktoryia Degeler
Ando Emerencia
Christoph Fehling
Qing Gu
Daniel Henriksson
Francisco Hernandez
Waldemar Hummer
Dragan Ivanovic

Raman Kazhamiakin
Freddy Lecue
Wubin Li
Khaled Mahbub
Philippe Massonet
Syed Naqvi
Alexander Nowak
Per-Olov Ostberg
Maryam Razavian
Onn Shehory
Danilo Squatarroni
Petter Svard
Usman Wajid
Adrian Waller

Demonstration Program Committee

Claudio Bartolini	HP Labs, USA
Markus Brunner	NEC, Germany
Zeta Dooly	Waterford Institute of Technology, Ireland
Keith Duddy	Queensland University of Technology, Australia
Alexander Gluhak	University of Surrey, UK
Michael Goedicke	University of Duisburg-Essen, Germany
Miguel Jimenez	Technical University of Madrid, Spain
André Ludwig	University of Leipzig, Germany
Norman May	SAP, Germany
Ingo Weber	UNSW, Australia

Table of Contents

Applications and Mashups

Engineering of Service Oriented Applications

Demonstrations

Service Provisioning on the Cloud: Distributed Algorithms for Joint Capacity Allocation and Admission Control

Danilo Ardagna[1], Carlo Ghezzi[1], Barbara Panicucci[1],
and Marco Trubian[2]

[1] Politecnico di Milano, Dipartimento di Elettronica e Informazione, Italy
[2] Università degli Studi di Milano, Dipartimento di Scienze dell'Informazione, Italy

Abstract. Cloud computing represents a new way to deliver and use services on a shared IT infrastructure. Traditionally, IT hardware and software were acquired and provisioned on business premises. Software applications were built, possibly integrating off-the-shelf components, deployed and run on these privately owned resources. With service-oriented computing, applications are offered by service providers to clients, who can simply invoke them through the network. The offer specifies both the functionality and the Quality of Service (QoS). Providers are responsible for deploying and running services on their own resources. Cloud computing moves one step further. Computing facilities can also be delivered on demand in the form of services over a network. In this paper we take the perspective of a Software as a Service (SaaS) provider whose goal is to maximize the revenues from end users who access services on a pay-per-use basis. In turn, the SaaS provider exploits the cloud, which provides an Infrastructure as a Service (IaaS), where the service provider dynamically allocates hardware physical resources.

This paper presents a distributed algorithm for run-time management of SaaS cloud systems that jointly addresses the capacity allocation and admission control of multiple classes of applications providing an heuristic solution which closely approximates the global optimal solution.

1 Introduction

Computing systems are becoming increasingly virtual. We come from a world where applications were entirely developed by organizations for their own use, possibly using components and/or platforms developed by third parties, but in the end deployed and run on the organizations' own IT facilities. We are moving into a world in which *Software as a Service* (SaaS) may be discovered by looking into registries and directly used from clients, or composed by service providers to form new services. Services are delivered and run by independent providers over the network. Clients simply invoke them remotely. In principle, service composition may occur dynamically, without concerning the user, who only cares about the global Quality of Service (QoS) that the composition assures, which in turn depends on the QoS that the integrated services assures. We are therefore

E. Di Nitto and R. Yahyapour (Eds.): ServiceWave 2010, LNCS 6481, pp. 1–12, 2010.
© Springer-Verlag Berlin Heidelberg 2010

moving from a setting where a single owner was in charge (and in control) of the whole system to a situation where multiple stakeholders are involved. The added complexity of the new setting, however, is largely compensated by the advantages in terms of higher reuse and easier software evolution.

The SaaS paradigm discussed above promotes a view of virtual components that one may compose to create additional virtual components that provide added-value functionality. Recent advances in cloud computing are pushing into another dimension of virtuality. Cloud computing is an emerging paradigm that aims at streamlining the on-demand provisioning of flexible and scalable services accessible through the Internet [9]. The main idea is to supply users with on-demand access to computing or storage resources and charge fees for their usage. In these models, users pay only for the resources they utilize and they can access software applications SaaS, hardware physical resources (Infrastructure as a Service – IaaS) or tools for the development and deployment of cloud-based applications (Platform as a Service – PaaS).

The adoption of cloud computing is attractive: users obtain the benefits of the infrastructure without having to implement and administer it directly and they can add or remove capacity, almost instantaneously, and only pay for what they actually use. Moreover, cloud computing is potentially environment friendly: By reducing the number of hardware components and replacing them with cloud computing systems we may reduce energy costs for running and cooling hardware.

In this paper we take the perspective of a SaaS provider. Providers need to comply with QoS requirements, specified in Service Level Agreement (SLA) contracts, which determine the revenues and penalties on the basis of the achieved performance level. At the same time, providers want to maximize the revenues from SLAs, while minimizing the cost of use of resources supplied by an IaaS provider. In this framework our aim has been to develop a distributed algorithm for run-time management of SaaS cloud systems that jointly addresses the capacity allocation and admission control of multiple classes of applications. The problem has been modelled as a non-linear programming problem and solved with decomposition techniques. The solution takes into account the SaaS provider's revenues, the IaaS cost, and the end users' QoS requirements specified in terms of the response time of individual requests. Experimental results show that we can determine an heuristic solution for the provider's net profit in few seconds, which closely approximates the global optimal solution.

The remainder of the paper is organized as follows. Section 2 introduces the problem under study. Section 3 describes our reference framework and formulates the joint capacity allocation and admission control problem. The experimental results in Section 4 demonstrate the quality and efficiency of our solutions. Other approaches proposed in the literature are discussed in Section 5. Conclusions are finally drawn in Section 6.

2   Problem Statement

As we stated, our goal is to support an SaaS provider who uses cloud computing facilities to offer services, according to the IaaS paradigm. We assume that a

SaaS provider offers multiple transactional Web services (WSs) and each service represents a different application. The hosted WSs can be heterogeneous with respect to resource demands, workload intensities and QoS requirements, and will be modelled as independent WS classes.

An SLA contract, associated with each WS class, is established between the SaaS provider and the end users. It specifies the QoS levels the SaaS provider must meet while responding to end user requests, as well as the corresponding pricing scheme. We adopt the pricing model presented in [2] and assume that the SaaS provider gains full revenues from the requests served within a response time threshold specified in the SLA contracts. Otherwise, the provider incurs in a loss of the revenue. Applications are hosted in virtual machines (VMs) which are provided on demand by an IaaS provider. We make the simplifying assumption that each VM hosts a single Web service application. Multiple VMs implementing the same WS class can run in parallel. In that case, we further assume that the running VMs are homogeneous in terms of RAM and CPU capacity and evenly share the incoming workload. Furthermore, services can be located on multiple sites (see Figure 1). For example, if we consider Amazon's Elastic Compute Cloud (EC2) [3] as an IaaS provider, EC2 allows to dynamically deploy VMs on four data centers located around the world.

IaaS providers usually charge software providers on a hourly basis [3]. Hence, the SaaS has to face the problem of determining every hour the optimal number of VMs for each WS class in each IaaS site in order to maximize the revenues from SLAs, while minimizing infrastructural costs. Note that with the current technology starting up a new VM takes at most a couple of minutes and hence starting and stopping virtualized instances do not add any significant overhead.

The SaaS performs resource allocation on the basis of a prediction of future WS workloads [1,6]. The SaaS needs also an estimate of the future performance of each VM in order to determine future SLA violations for each WS class. In this way the SaaS provider can determine the optimal number of VMs to be allocated to each WS class, i.e., capacity allocation (CA), as well as the number of requests effectively served for each class, i.e., admission control (AC), that maximize the worldwide net profits. The optimal joint CA and AC policies will be implemented by the local managers every hour.

3   Distributed Optimization Framework

3.1   System Model and Notation

Hereafter we introduce the model of the cloud computing system under study. Let us assume that the IaaS provider (see Figure 1) has a set I of sites, while the SaaS runs a set of WS classes K. We assume that in each IaaS site, VMs are homogeneous in terms of their computing capacity, which will be denoted by C_i. This simplification may be easily removed. In fact, even in the case of heterogeneous VMs, IaaS providers have a limited set of available configurations, say m, and therefore an IaaS site with heterogeneous VMs can be modelled as m sites with homogeneous VMs.

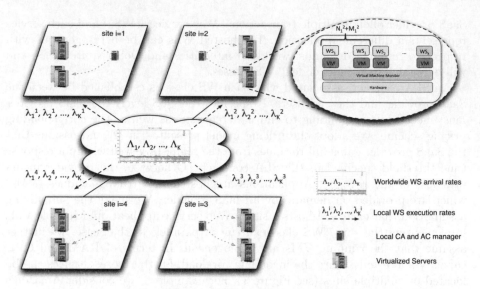

Fig. 1. Cloud system reference framework

In our model, we consider response time and VM utilization as QoS resource metrics. As discussed in Section 2, if the response time of a WS class k is above a fixed threshold $\overline{R}_k$, the SLA is violated and there will be no revenue for the provider. Otherwise, there will be a revenue ω_k^i, for each request k serviced at site i. In order to avoid the performance instability common to systems running close to saturation, we also introduce an upper-bound ρ_k, up to which the utilization of VMs allocated to WS class k is planned.

Furthermore, we assume that a SaaS provider can establish two different contracts with an IaaS provider. Namely, it may be possible to access VMs on a pure *on-demand* basis and the SaaS provider will be charged on a hourly basis (see e.g., Amazon EC2 *on-demand* pricing scheme, [3]). Otherwise, it may be possible to pay a fixed annual *flat* rate for each VM and then access the VMs on a pay-per-use basis with a fee lower than the pure *on-demand* case (see e.g., Amazon EC2 reserved instances pricing scheme, [3]). The time unit cost (e.g., \$ per hour of VM usage) for the use of *flat* VMs at site i is denoted by $\overline{c}^i$, while the cost for VMs *on demand* will be denoted by $\hat{c}^i$, with $\overline{c}^i < \hat{c}^i$.

The SaaS provider's goal is to determine the number of *flat* VMs to be allocated to WS class k at site i, N_k^i, the number of *on demand* VMs to be allocated to class k at site i, M_k^i, and the rate of WS class k executed at site i, λ_k^i, in order to satisfy the prediction Λ_k for the worldwide arrival rate of class k request (see Figure 1) for the next control time horizon T (e.g., one hour), in order to maximizing the net revenues. We will denote with N^i the number of *flat* VMs available at site i.

The decision variables of our optimization problem are N_k^i, M_k^i, and λ_k^i. For the sake of clarity, the notation adopted in this paper is summarized in Table 1.

Table 1. Problem parameters and decision variables

System Parameters

I	Set of IaaS geographically distributed sites
K	Set of WS request classes
T	Control time horizon
N^i	Number of *flat* VMs available at site i
C^i	Capacity of VMs at site i
Λ_k	Prediction for the worldwide arrival rate of class k for the next control time horizon
μ_k	Maximum service rate of a capacity 1 VM for executing class k requests
ω_k^i	SaaS revenue for a single WS class k request executed at site i with the QoS level specified in the SLA
$\bar{c}^i$	Time unit cost for *flat* VMs at site i
$\hat{c}^i$	Time unit cost for *on demand* VMs at site i
R_k^i	Response time for executing a single WS class k request at site i
$E[R_k^i]$	Average response time for executing WS class k request at site i
$\overline{R}_k$	Response time threshold guaranteed for WS class k requests
ρ_k	Utilization upper bound for the VMs allocated to class k

Decision Variables

λ_k^i	Rate of class k request executed at site i
N_k^i	Number of *flat* VMs allocated for class k request at site i
M_k^i	Number of *on demand* VMs allocated for class k request at site i

In our model, the SLA is defined by considering the response time for executing individual WS requests at each site. In particular, as it will be discussed in the next section, we express the revenue in terms of the probability distribution of response times, therefore focusing on the performance observed by individual user requests, instead of average performance.

In the following we will model each WS class hosted in a VM as an M/G/1 queue [8], as done in [14,13,2] and we assume that requests are served according to the processor sharing scheduling discipline, which is common among Web service containers. Under these hypotheses, an upper bound on the probability that the response time of a class k request at site i, R_k^i, exceeds a threshold $\overline{R}_k$ can be expressed in terms of the average response time of a request to a WS of class k at site i, $E[R_k^i]$ as $P[R_k^i > \overline{R}_k] \leq e^{-\frac{\overline{R}_k}{E[R_k^i]}}$, [13].

Assuming that the load is evenly shared among the VMs supporting WS class k, the average response time for executing class k request at site i is $E[R_k^i] = \frac{1}{C_i\mu_k - \frac{\lambda_k^i}{N_k^i + M_k^i}}$, then we get:

$$P[R_k^i > \overline{R}_k] \leq e^{-(C_i\mu_k - \frac{\lambda_k^i}{N_k^i + M_k^i})\overline{R}_k},$$

and therefore $P[R_k^i \leq \overline{R}_k] \geq 1 - e^{-(C_i\mu_k - \frac{\lambda_k^i}{N_k^i + M_k^i})\overline{R}_k}$.

3.2   Joint Capacity Allocation and Admission Control Problem

The objective is to determine the joint capacity allocation and admission control strategy to cooperatively maximize the worldwide net profit for the next control time horizon T. A lower bound of the worldwide net profit is given by:

$$\sum_{k \in K} \sum_{i \in I} (\omega_k^i \, \lambda_k^i \, (1 - e^{-(C_i \, \mu_k - \frac{\lambda_k^i}{N_k^i + M_k^i}) \, \overline{R}_k})) \, T - \sum_{i \in I} \overline{c}^i \sum_{k \in K} N_k^i - \sum_{i \in I} \hat{c}^i \sum_{k \in K} M_k^i,$$

that is, the revenues minus the costs. Note that the pricing model can be extended taking into account monetary penalties for requests exceeding the time limit by changing only the ω_k^i coefficient in the objective function. Moreover, since the (average) utilization for the resources allocated to class k, at each site i is $\frac{\lambda_k^i}{C_i \, \mu_k \, (N_k^i + M_k^i)}$, to entail that the overall utilization of system resources dedicated to serve class k requests is below the planned threshold ρ_k, we must have $\frac{\lambda_k^i}{C_i \, \mu_k \, (N_k^i + M_k^i)} < \rho_k$, hence $\lambda_k^i < \rho_k \, C_i \, \mu_k \, (N_k^i + M_k^i)$.

If we let $\gamma_k^i = \rho_k \, C_i \, \mu_k$, the utilization condition becomes:

$$\lambda_k^i < \gamma_k^i \, (N_k^i + M_k^i). \tag{1}$$

In the formulation of the joint capacity allocation and admission control problem, we also need to account for the flow balance constraint for each class k, ensuring that the total requests executed is less than or equal to the predicted incoming workload:

$$\sum_{i \in I} \lambda_k^i \le \Lambda_k. \tag{2}$$

Finally we need to guarantee that at most N^i *flat* VMs are allocated for class k requests at site i:

$$\sum_{k \in K} N_k^i \le N^i. \tag{3}$$

We can now state the joint capacity allocation and admission control problem as:

(P)

$$\max \sum_{k \in K} \sum_{i \in I} (\omega_k^i \, \lambda_k^i \, (1 - e^{-(C_i \, \mu_k - \frac{\lambda_k^i}{N_k^i + M_k^i}) \, \overline{R}_k})) \, T - \sum_{i \in I} \overline{c}^i \sum_{k \in K} N_k^i - \sum_{i \in I} \hat{c}^i \sum_{k \in K} M_k^i$$

subject to constraints (1), (2), (3) and $\lambda_k^i, N_k^i, M_k^i \ge 0, \forall k \in K, i \in I$.

Note that in the formulation of the problem we have not imposed variables N_k^i, M_k^i to be integer, as in reality they are. In fact, requiring variables to be integer makes the solution much more difficult. We therefore decide to deal with continuous variables, actually considering a relaxation of the real problem. However, preliminary experimental results have shown that if the optimal values of the variables are fractional and they are rounded to the closest integer solution, the gap between the solution of the real integer problem and the relaxed one is very small, justifying the use of a relaxed model. Furthermore, we can always choose a rounding to an integer solution which preserves the feasibility and the corresponding gap in the objective function is a few percentage points.

Problem (P) is a general nonlinear optimization problem, and we exploit decomposition procedures to solve it. Decomposition techniques support a distributed protocol for the joint capacity allocation and admission control in which each site solves its problem using both local information and information received from other sites. In particular, as discussed in the following, we develop an iterative method and at each iteration λ_k^i is the only information that will be shared among sites. Our decomposition technique is founded on duality theory in optimization, [7].

The optimization problem (P) is concave (in fact the eigenvalues of the objective function are non positive) with affine constraints, hence strong duality holds, i.e., the optimal values of the primal problem (P) and its dual are equal [7]. This allows us to solve the primal via the dual. To this end we first note that, using Lagrangian relaxation, we are able to separate problem (P) into $|I|$ subproblems that can be solved in parallel by each site. The idea is to remove the constraints that link the variables, namely coupling constraints (2). For each of these constraints, a multiplier $r_k \geq 0$ is defined and the corresponding relaxed problem is [7]:

(PR)
$$\mathcal{L}(r) = \max \sum_{k \in K} \sum_{i \in I} (\omega_k^i \, \lambda_k^i \, (1 - e^{-(C_i \, \mu_k - \frac{\lambda_k^i}{N_k^i + M_k^i}) \overline{R}_k})) \, T - \sum_{i \in I} \overline{c}^i \sum_{k \in K} N_k^i +$$

$$- \sum_{i \in I} \hat{c}^i \sum_{k \in K} M_k^i - \sum_{k \in K} (\sum_{i \in I} \lambda_k^i - \Lambda_k) \, r_k,$$

subject to (1), (3) and $\lambda_k^i, N_k^i, M_k^i \geq 0, \forall k \in K, i \in I$.

Note that all constraints appearing in problem (PR) are the same as in (P), except for constraints (2) that have been relaxed.

For a given vector of multipliers r, the dual decomposition results in solving at each site i, the following sub-problem:

(SUB_i)
$$\max \sum_{k \in K} (\omega_k^i \, T \, (1 - e^{-(C_i \, \mu_k - \frac{\lambda_k^i}{N_k^i + M_k^i}) \overline{R}_k}) - r_k) \, \lambda_k^i - \overline{c}^i \sum_{k \in K} N_k^i - \hat{c}^i \sum_{k \in K} M_k^i + \sum_{k \in K} \Lambda_k \, r_k$$

subject to (1), (3) and $\lambda_k^i, N_k^i, M_k^i \geq 0, \forall k \in K$.

To define the dual function $\mathcal{L}_i(r)$, we consider, for all i, the optimal value of (SUB_i) for a given r. The dual problem is then given by:

(D) $\min_r \mathcal{L}(r) = \sum_i \mathcal{L}_i(r)$.

The dual problem admits decentralized solution and it can be solved by using a sub-gradient method ([7]): Given an initial vector $r(0)$, at each iteration the multipliers are updated by each site as:

$$r_k(t + 1) = r_k(t) - \alpha_t \left(\Lambda_k - \sum_{i \in I} \lambda_k^i \right), \tag{4}$$

where t is the iteration index and α_t is determined using an expression of the form:

$$\alpha_t = a_t \frac{(\mathcal{L}(r(t)) - LB(t))}{\sum\limits_{k \in K} (\sum\limits_{i \in I} \lambda_k^i - \Lambda_k)^2},$$

with $0 < a_t < 2$ and $LB(t)$ being a lower bound of the optimal dual value at the t-th iteration. Note that the term in the denominator of the step-size formula is the sum of squared "violations" of the constraint we have relaxed.

To obtain the lower bound, we determine the objective function value of (P) in a feasible solution obtained as follows: (i) we consider an even distribution of the incoming workload among the sites, (ii) at each site, the number of *flat* VMs is split among the WS classes, and finally (iii) the number of *on demand* VMs is evaluated in order to provide an average utilization less or equal to a given threshold (see Algorithm 1 step 1). Then, at each iteration, in order to speed up the convergence of the iterative procedure, the lower bound is updated by evaluating the objective function of (P) at the current solution, if it is feasible, otherwise, the values of the current λ_k^i violating the flow balance constraint (2), are reduced proportionally to the percentage of violation (steps 7-14 of Algorithm 1). The entire procedure is stopped when the gap between the current value of the relaxed problem (PR), providing an upper bound of the optimal value of (P), and the lower bound is less than a given threshold (Algorithm 1 step 21).

In this distributed algorithm, the sites act independently in their own self-interest solving $(SUB)_i$, maximizing their revenues. Each site only needs the information of λ_i^k of the previous iteration, in order to update the values of the Lagrange multipliers r_k and the upper and lower bounds. Therefore, the proposed optimization schema requires that each site broadcasts the new computed value λ_i^k at each iteration. However, since the number of physical IaaS providers sites is limited (e.g., Amazon EC2 is located in only four physical locations [3]), then the overhead introduced by the optimization protocol (which is also performed periodically every T time unit) is limited. The performance of the distributed algorithm will be discussed in the next section.

4   Experimental Results

To evaluate the effectiveness of our joint CA and AC algorithm we have applied it to a variety of system and workload configurations. All tests have been performed on VMWare virtual machine based on Ubuntu 9.10 server running on an Intel Nehalem dual socket quad-core system with 32 GB of RAM. The virtual machine has a physical core dedicated with guaranteed performance and 4 GB of memory reserved. To evaluate the efficiency of the proposed algorithm, we have used a large set of randomly generated instances. The number of cloud sites $|I|$ has been varied between 20 and 60, the number of request classes $|K|$ between 100 and 1000. We would like to remark that, even if the number of cloud sites is small in reality (e.g., four for Amazon), we consider up to 60 sites, since we

> **input** : Λ_k, N^i, C^i, μ_k, ρ_k
> **output**: N_k^i, λ_k^i, M_k^i
> 1 Let $\alpha := 1$; $N_k^i := \frac{N^i}{|K|}$, $\lambda_k^i = \frac{\Lambda_k}{|I|}$, $M_k^i = max(\frac{\lambda_k^i}{C^i \mu_k \rho_k} - N_k^i, 0)$; Let $UB = 0$
>   and LB the objective function value of (P); $r_k^i := 0$;
> 2 $STOP$=false;
> 3 **while** *not STOP* **do**
> 4   **for** $i \in I$ **do**
> 5   *Solve (SUB$_i$)*; Let N_k^i, λ_k^i, M_k^i the solution; Let UB the function
>   value; Broadcast λ_k^i;
> 6   **end**
> 7   **for** $k \in K$ **do**
> 8   **if** $\sum_{i \in I} \lambda_k^i > \Lambda_k$ **then**
> 9   **for** $i \in I$ **do**
> 10 $\hat{\lambda}_k^i := \lambda_k^i \frac{\Lambda_k}{\sum_{i \in I} \lambda_k^i}$;
> 11   **end**
> 12
> 13   **end**
> 14   **end**
> 15   Update LB (objective function value of (P) evaluated with $\hat{\lambda}_k^i$) if better
> 16   **for** $k \in K$ **do**
> 17 $r_k := max(0, r_k - \alpha \frac{UB - LB}{\sum_{k \in K}(\Lambda_k - \sum_{i \in I} \lambda_k^i)^2} (\Lambda_k - \sum_{i \in I} \lambda_k^i))$;
> 18   **end**
> 19   Update α;
> 20   **if** $(UB - LB)/LB <$ precision threshold OR the maximum number of
>   iterations is reached **then**
> 21   STOP=true;
> 22   **end**
> 23 **end**
> 24 **return** N_k^i, λ_k^i, M_k^i;

Algorithm 1. Joint CA and AC procedure

assumed that VMs are homogeneous, and heterogeneous VMs can be modeled
by replicating sites with homogeneous VMs. The utilization upper bound for the
VMs allocated to class k, ρ_k, has been set equal to 0.6. The maximum service
rate of a capacity one VM for executing class k requests, μ_k, has been varied
uniformly in (0.1,1), as in [2]. In the stopping criterion, we have used the relative
gap between the current value of the relaxed problem (PR), which provides an
upper bound of the optimal value of (P), and the lower bound. Furthermore,
the algorithm exits when the maximum number of iterations (300 in the current
evaluation) is reached. The experimental tests have been stopped when the gap
was less than 1%, 3% or 5%. We reached the maximum number of iterations
limits in 5 instances out of 4,500. Table 2 reports, for problem instances of
different sizes, the computational time in seconds as well as the network time to

Table 2. Algorithm 1 Execution Time

	Precision					
	1%		3%		5%	
$(|K|,|I|)$	Comp. Time	Net. Time	Comp. Time	Net. Time	Comp. Time	Net. Time
(100,20)	0.0047	4.2	0.0048	3.3	0.0048	2.7
(100,40)	0.0041	4.8	0.0041	3.7	0.004	2.9
(100,60)	0.0043	5.4	0.0045	3.9	0.0046	3.3
(500,20)	0.0907	8.1	0.0894	5.7	0.089	5.1
(500,40)	0.0904	9.6	0.0944	6.9	0.0933	6
(500,60)	0.0952	9.6	0.0932	7.2	0.0907	6
(1000,20)	0.1932	12	0.192	7.2	0.191	5.4
(1000,40)	0.2171	9	0.2145	5.7	0.2119	4.8
(1000,60)	0.2249	15.6	0.2077	9.9	0.2023	5.1

broadcast, at each iteration, the new rate of request for class k, at site i, λ_k^i. The computational time assumes that at each iteration sub-problems are solved in parallel at the IaaS provider sites, while the network time considers an average end-to-end delay for the data transfer among IaaS sites equal to $300ms$ which is the worst case delay we measured among the four Amazon EC2 sites during a one week experiment.

In Figure 2 we compare the network and computational times for different numbers of class requests. Results show that the computation time is negligible with respect to network time. For the problem instances of maximum size and at the highest accuracy level the overall Algorithm 1 execution time is lower than $20s$, demonstrating the effectiveness of our approach.

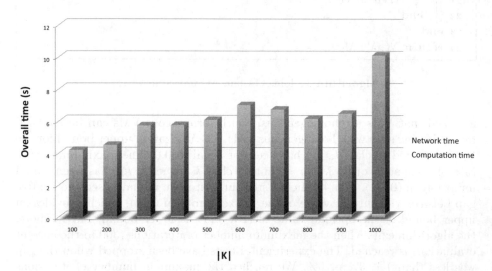

Fig. 2. Computation and Network times for $|I| = 60$ with Varying Number of WS Classes at 3% Precision

5 Related Work

With the development of autonomic computing systems, dynamic resource allocation techniques received a great interest both within industry and academia. The solutions proposed can be classified as centralized and distributed. In a centralized approach, a dedicated entity is in charge of establishing resource allocation, admission control or load balancing for the autonomic system and has a global knowledge of the resources state in the whole network [5,16].

Centralized solutions are not suitable for geographically distributed systems, such as the cloud or, more generally, massively distributed systems [4,12,10], since no entity has global information about all of the system resources. The communication overhead required to share the resource state information is not negligible and the delay to collect state information from remote nodes could lead a centralized resource manager to very inaccurate decisions due to dynamic changes in system conditions, as well as resource consumption fluctuations or unexpected events [12].

Distributed resource management policies have been proposed to govern geographically distributed systems that cannot implement centralized decisions and support strong interactions among the remote sites [4]. Distributed resource management is very challenging, since one node's decisions may inadvertently degrade the performance of the overall system, even if they greedily optimize the node' s performance. Sometimes, local decisions could lead the system even to unstable oscillations [11]. It is thus difficult to determine the best control mechanism at each node in isolation, so that the overall system performance is optimized. Dynamically choosing when, where, and how to allocate resources and coordinating the resource allocation accordingly is an open problem and is becoming more and more relevant with the advent of clouds [10].

One of the first contributions for resource management in geographically distributed systems has been proposed in [4], where novel autonomic distributed load balancing algorithms have been proposed. In distributed streaming networks, [12] proposed a joint admission control and resource allocation scheme, while [17] proposed optimal scheduling techniques. Scheduling in streaming systems faces the problem that the incoming workload would far exceed system capacity much of the time. Other researchers In the distributed resource management area are currently exploring ideas borrowed from the biological world [15].

To the best of our knowledge this is the very first contribution that proposes an analytical solution to the joint capacity allocation and admission control for SaaS cloud systems, also providing a-priory global optimality guarantees.

6 Conclusions

We proposed a distributed algorithm for the joint admission control and capacity allocation of SaaS cloud systems maximizing the net worldwide profits associated with multiple WS classes. The cost model includes the IaaS costs and revenues which depend on the achieved level of performance of individual WS requests. In contrast to previous proposals, we developed a scalable analytical solution to the problem providing a-priori fixed optimality guarantees. Future work will extend the validation of our solution currently based on simulation by performing experiments in real cloud environments and performing a comparison with the heuristics adopted by SaaS and IaaS providers for the run time cloud management.

References

1. Abraham, B., Ledolter, J.: Statistical Methods for Forecasting. John Wiley and Sons, Chichester (1983)
2. Almeida, J.M., Almeida, V.A.F., Ardagna, D., Cunha, I.S., Francalanci, C., Trubian, M.: Joint admission control and resource allocation in virtualized servers. J. Parallel Distrib. Comput. 70(4), 344–362 (2010)
3. Amazon Inc. Amazon Elastic Cloud, http://aws.amazon.com/ec2/
4. Andreolini, M., Casolari, S., Colajanni, M.: Autonomic request management algorithms for geographically distributed internet-based systems. In: SASO (2008)
5. Ardagna, D., Panicucci, B., Trubian, M., Zhang, L.: Energy-Aware Autonomic Resource Allocation in Multi-tier Virtualized Environments. IEEE Trans. on Services Computing (to appear)
6. Bennani, M., Menascé, D.: Resource Allocation for Autonomic Data Centers Using Analytic Performance Models. In: IEEE Int'l Conf. Autonomic Computing Proc. (2005)
7. Bertsekas, D.: Nonlinear Programming. Athena Scientific (1999)
8. Bolch, G., Greiner, S., de Meer, H., Trivedi, K.: Queueing Networks and Markov Chains. J. Wiley, Chichester (1998)
9. Dikaiakos, M.D., Katsaros, D., Mehra, P., Pallis, G., Vakali, A.: Cloud Computing: Distributed Internet Computing for IT and Scientific Research. IEEE Internet Computing 13(5), 10–13 (2009)
10. Erdogmus, H.: Cloud computing: Does nirvana hide behind the nebula? IEEE Softw. 26(2), 4–6 (2009)
11. Felber, P., Kaldewey, T., Weiss, S.: Proactive hot spot avoidance for web server dependability. In: IEEE Symposium on Reliable Distributed Systems, pp. 309–318 (2004)
12. Feng, H., Liu, Z., Xia, C.H., Zhang, L.: Load shedding and distributed resource control of stream processing networks. Perform. Eval. 64(9-12), 1102–1120 (2007)
13. Liu, Z., Squillante, M.S., Wolf, J.: On maximizing service-level-agreement profits. In: Proc. 3d ACM Conf. on Electronic Commerce (2001)
14. Menascé, D.A., Dubey, V.: Utility-based QoS Brokering in Service Oriented Architectures. In: IEEE International Conference on Web Services Proceedings, pp. 422–430 (2007)
15. Nitto, E.D., Dubois, D.J., Mirandola, R., Saffre, F., Tateson, R.: Self-aggregation techniques for load balancing in distributed systems. In: SASO (2008)
16. Urgaonkar, B., Pacifici, G., Shenoy, P.J., Spreitzer, M., Tantawi, A.N.: Analytic modeling of multitier Internet applications. ACM Transaction on Web, 1(1) (January 2007)
17. Wolf, J.L., Bansal, N., Hildrum, K., Parekh, S., Rajan, D., Wagle, R., Wu, K.-L., Fleischer, L.: SODA: An optimizing scheduler for large-scale stream-based distributed computer systems. In: Issarny, V., Schantz, R. (eds.) Middleware 2008. LNCS, vol. 5346, pp. 306–325. Springer, Heidelberg (2008)

TwoSpot: A Cloud Platform for Scaling Out Web Applications Dynamically

Andreas Wolke and Gerhard Meixner

University of Applied Sciences Augsburg
Department of Informatics
Friedberger Str. 2a, 86161 Augsburg, Germany
Andreas.Wolke@live.com, Gerhard.Meixner@hs-augsburg.de

Abstract. Cloud computing is an emerging technology with a high impact on the operation and development of applications. Scalable web applications in particular can benefit from the advantages of Platform-as-a-Service solutions as they simplify development and maintenance. Unfortunately most of these offerings are a kind of one-way road as they lock the applications in the platform and vendor. This paper describes the TwoSpot platform we have developed to provide broader access to the advantages of Platform-as-a-Service and Infrastructure-as-a-Service functionalities by applying open and standards-based technologies.

Keywords: cloud computing, platform-as-a-service, horizontal scalability, web applications.

1 Introduction

Cloud computing has emerged into a significant technology to run and develop a broad range of application types. Especially web applications are predestinated to make use of cloud computing offers as they perfectly match their benefits: scalability, simplicity and a pay per use pricing model with low upfront investments [6]. But as the term cloud computing still seems undefined the cloud computing offerings are rather different. A large part can be classified as Infrastructure-as-a-Service (IaaS) [10]. This type is mainly advertised by Amazon with its EC2 cloud and uses virtualization technology to provide the customer with virtual machines [10]. The huge advantage of IaaS over typical hosting services is the pay per use pricing model which allows the customer to rent and pay any number of virtual machines for only a short period of time (typically one hour or more) [6].

But IaaS does not solve the difficulties of developing software which efficiently uses a large number of machines. Platform-as-a-Service (PaaS) offerings address exactly this disadvantage. They provide a software platform as the basis for developing and running applications. The platform itself takes care of scaling the applications [8]. Usually it also includes mostly proprietary services like logging, databases, memcaching or search functions [10] easing the development.

In this paper we describe our research on the PaaS software platform TwoSpot. Our goal is to combine existing and open technologies to build a new software platform which runs on virtual machines typically offered by IaaS providers.

E. Di Nitto and R. Yahyapour (Eds.): ServiceWave 2010, LNCS 6481, pp. 13–24, 2010.
© Springer-Verlag Berlin Heidelberg 2010

2 Objectives

The TwoSpot platform is specifically designed for web applications and represents a software platform which can run lots of applications in parallel based on a large set of physical or virtual machines. The platform should automatically scale the applications in a horizontal fashion. For this reason not only the application and platform but also the underlying services like database, caching or user and session services must be scalable. The horizontal scalability therefore is a strong criterion for selecting software components and designing the TwoSpot architecture. As the platform is in charge of automatically scaling the web applications it also must provide facilities to measure the application performance and spread the applications over multiple machines.

One frequently mentioned disadvantage [9, 5, 8] of existing PaaS offerings is the so called vendor lock-in. It describes a scenario where an application, written for one platform cannot easily be migrated to another one, even if the target platform uses the same technology e. g. Java. The TwoSpot platform should reduce the vendor lock-in while relying on existing standards and decoupling the platform from the application as far as possible. Also TwoSpot is developed as an open source project, which means, applications can use its software stack but are not locked into a specific vendor to operate them. Despite the efforts to reduce the vendor lock-in, TwoSpot is not designed with legacy applications in mind. We choose this approach in order not to be limited in the choices of technology.

Currently there are only a few open-source PaaS implementations available. One of these is the Joyent Smart [7] platform which aims to be a competitor to the Google App Engine and relies on proprietary APIs. Another one is the AppScale [4] platform which aims to execute Google App Engine applications elsewhere than the Google infrastructure. TwoSpot pursues similar goals as both of them, but is built to support applications written in different programming languages while paying attention on existing software standards. Furthermore its architecture is highly modular in order to simplify further research in the fields of security aspects, monitoring, pricing and scaling mechanisms.

3 Architecture Overview

The TwoSpot architecture bears resemblance to the architecture of the Google App Engine [11] and consists of four major components: Frontend as a reverse proxy which accepts and distributes incoming HTTP requests over the Work Servers; AppServer as an application container; Controller to manage all AppServers on a single machine; Master which makes decisions in respect to load balancing. Additionally a scalable file server and a scalable database system are required to allow applications storing data. The communication paths between the components are shown in Fig. 1. It is critical that all components may be deployed on their own machine, but also on a single machine together.

Each incoming HTTP request is handled by the Frontend which analyzes the Request and forwards it to a Work Server. Each TwoSpot application is identified by a string called AppId which is encoded in front of the domain name of the request URL using the DNS wildcard mechanism. All requests directed to a Work Server are handled by the Controller which then forwards them to an appropriate AppServer.

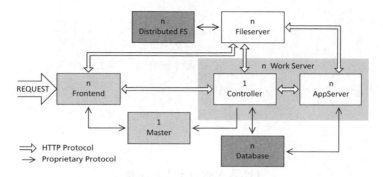

Fig. 1. TwoSpot Architecture Components

Therefore it also extracts the AppId of the URL. The AppServer finally handles the request and creates a HTTP response which is passed back to the browser.

4 Work Server

There can be multiple Work Servers which eventually execute the applications in processes called AppServers. An AppServer represents the application server for TwoSpot applications. Its software stack (shown in Fig. 2) is built to support different programming languages which are all running on top of the Java Virtual Machine. For example Python applications are supported using the Jython library and a WSGI bridge (Web Server Gateway Interface) to Jetty. The goal is to provide a standardized runtime environment for each implemented programming language.

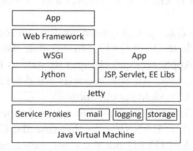

Fig. 2. Application Stack

The AppServer is started by the Controller using notably two program arguments: AppId and a port number. Its bootstrapping process foremost downloads the application archive from the fileserver and extracts it. The archive's file structure is almost identical to the file structure of Java Web Application Archives (WAR) but additionally contains an application descriptor. This describes important configuration settings for the AppServer and most importantly specifies the programming language used by the application. Regardless of the programming language the WAR file structure is always used to store the application files. After the application archive and descriptor have been processed the corresponding application stack and the application are launched.

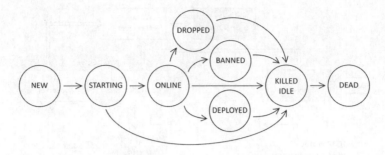

Fig. 3. AppServer Lifecycle

Each machine is managed by exactly one Controller. Like the Frontend it implements an HTTP proxy which delegates all requests to appropriate AppServers running on the same machine. The Controller automatically starts a new AppServer if it receives a HTTP request for an application which is not running. For the scaling out purpose one application is typically managed by multiple Controllers while running on multiple machines. When the Controller starts a new application it also creates a new lifecycle to manage its AppServer (see Fig. 3). Initially the lifecycle's state is NEW which immediately transits into STARTING. A background thread is in charge of starting and stopping AppServer processes. When a lifecycle transits into STARTING a new job is scheduled which then starts the AppServer process. As soon as the AppServer has been started the lifecycle's state is changed to ONLINE. On the other hand if the AppServer fails or cannot be contacted by the Controller, the lifecycle's state is changed to KILLED and a kill job is scheduled. As soon as the kill job is done the lifecycle's state is changed to DEAD and eventually removed by another background thread.

Once the Controller receives a deployment notification for an application it updates the corresponding lifecycle to DEPLOYED. In this state the Controller does not delegate new requests to the AppServer and changes its state to KILLED as soon as it has processed all running requests. All new requests are delegated to a new AppServer instance which executes the updated application.

For the sake of load balancing (described in section 8) the lifecycle's state may also be changed to DROPPED or BANNED. In this case the Controller almost behaves identically to the state DEPLOYED but does not start a new AppServer. Instead it blocks all incoming requests for a predefined time.

The Controller additionally implements various platform services which can be used by the applications using an RPC protocol. Currently various services like a logging service and a storage service are implemented. Each service is published by means of a proprietary but language independent protocol based on Google ProtoBuf and is typically used by the AppServers. They in turn provide a simplified service interface for the application. The services are not implemented within the AppServer in order to reduce its memory footprint, startup time and to increase the security of the platform.

5 Master and Frontend

The Master registers its IP address within the Apache ZooKeeper service, which is a central configuration and synchronization service. As soon as a Controller recognizes that entry it starts sending management data about itself and all its managed AppServers to the Master. The data are transferred using the UDP protocol and Google ProtoBuf to encode the messages. It is not necessary for the Master to receive each management data package, therefore no further actions to detect and prevent the loss of UDP messages are taken. This approach makes the Master very robust to network and machine errors and does not put any constraints on the programming language used to communicate with the Master.

The Frontend is basically a reverse proxy which delegates all HTTP requests to a Controller. It therefore extracts the AppId of each request using the URL and determines a target Controller. This is done by checking an internal cache. In case of a cache miss it calls the Master which then exploits the management data. The Master therefore analyzes all available data, selects one or more appropriate Controllers using a load balancing algorithm (see section 8) and returns them to the Frontend which finally adds them to the cache.

In both cases multiple Controller addresses may be returned for a given AppId. The Frontend applies a simple load balancing algorithm to distribute the load over all Controllers returned by the Master or Cache. In order to change the number of Controllers assigned to one application the cache entries time out after a predefined period. To prevent the Frontend from overloading multiple Frontends could be load balanced using a hardware or software load balancer like DNS round robin.

6 Security Aspects

TwoSpot implements multiple mechanisms to protect the applications from each other. Every deployed application is treated as potentially harmful. As a consequence each application is executed within its own AppServer process and address space. Furthermore the AppServer takes advantage of the Java Security Architecture and implements a security policy with a very limited set of permissions. This prohibits applications from accessing system resources like the file system or networking functionality.

The described approach protects applications from interfering with each other directly but does not provide a protection against Denial-of-Service attacks or application errors. As an example one application may process a CPU intensive task which takes a long time and slows down other applications running on the same machine. To address this situation the AppServer monitors the processing time for each HTTP request. It terminates itself if the request processing takes too long. This also causes all running requests to terminate. The Controller recognizes that and responds to all terminated requests with a HTTP error. This behavior is very unlikely but unfortunately Java does not provide a mechanism which forces the request processing thread to terminate [13]. We decided that stability and security of the platform are more important than the correct execution of the remaining requests.

Another security mechanism addresses huge file uploads and downloads which may lead to a bandwidth bottleneck. This mechanism is implemented within the Controller to terminate all requests and responses transferring more data than allowed.

As described in section 4 applications may access various platform services. These services are largely implemented inside the Controller which publishes them using a proprietary RPC protocol. The security manager prevents applications from using network services directly. Hence the AppServer provides proxy implementations residing inside a protection domain which is granted a greater set of permissions. In addition each proxy implementation uses privileged blocks thereby it could be used by application codes with less permissions. The applications now use these proxies to access the platform services.

The Controller also provides privileged services to administrate the platform. These services may only be used by some predefined applications. The proxy implementations therefore pass a security token with each privileged service call which authenticates the application. This token is generated by the Controller and passed as a program argument while starting the AppServer. It therefore can check if the token is valid and the service call is admissible.

TwoSpot uses the HBase database which does not implement any security mechanisms. For the sake of performance all application data are stored in one huge HBase table which additionally increases vulnerability. By reason of performance and security we implemented a storage service which operates between HBase and the JDO implementation used to access the database. This storage service too depends on the security token mentioned above and protects applications from accessing foreign data.

7 Storing Data

TwoSpot provides a storage service which is used by the platform itself and could be used by applications to store any type of data. As the applications cannot access the file system, the storage service remains as the only possibility to store data persistently.

Typically web applications use relational databases but as these are mostly inappropriate for scaling out systems built of cheap server hardware [1] we searched for alternative storage solutions. Some promising ones we found are: Apache Cassandra, Apache HBase, Hypertable and MongoDb. The listed solutions are categorized as Non-SQL databases and have in common that they provide a very limited set of functionality, especially if it comes to transactions and their ACID properties (Atomicity, Consistency, Isolation, Durability). One reason for this is that the solutions follow the BASE concept (Basically Available, Soft-state, Eventual consistency) and underlie the CAP theorem [3] (Consistency, Availability, Tolerance to network Partitions) due to their distributed nature. The theorem states that a system can only have two out of the three CAP properties. This is often a disadvantage if existing applications which rely on relational databases have to be migrated. But as stated in section 2 we do ignore the requirements of legacy applications and focus on new applications. That is why we have chosen to use a Non-SQL storage solution in favor of its scalability and availability. Actually we are using Apache HBase which behaves like the Google Bigtable storage solution.

We decided to use Java Data Objects (JDO) as the interface between the application and the storage solution. The advantage of JDO over Java Persistence API or alternative solutions like Hibernate is that it is datastore-agnostic. This is very important as the Non-SQL storage solutions do not provide an SQL interface, features of a relational database and even do not store data in the fashion of a relational database. Furthermore JDO is an open standard which helps decoupling the applications from proprietary platform APIs.

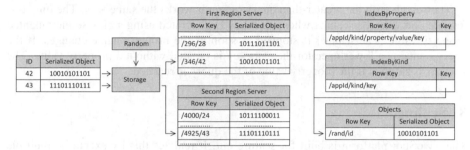

Fig. 4. Distributed Storage of Objects   **Fig. 5.** HBase Table Design

In order to use JDO we created a new storage layer which interacts between the JDO implementation and HBase. This storage layer is implemented in a similar fashion as Google uses in its App Engine Datastore [2]. One huge HBase table named *Objects* is used, which stores all persistable objects in the form of serialized byte data. As the storage layer does not implement any security mechanisms, it is crucial that it be independent to Java class files which could contain malicious code. Therefore the serialization process must not rely on the provided Java serialization mechanism. Another advantage of this is that the storage service is not just limited to Java clients.

Each table row of an HBase table must provide a unique row key for identification which is also used to sort the rows in an ascending ordering. The storage layer assigns a row key starting with a random value to each object stored in the *Objects* table. This distributes the objects uniformly over the entire row key namespace and all HBase region servers which resembles a horizontal scaling of the data (see Fig. 4).

HBase does not provide a query language like SQL which could be used to retrieve serialized objects. Instead it provides a scan operation which returns all rows from a given start row up to a given stop row. Similar to the Google App Engine Datastore [12] this operations are used to realize simple SQL-like queries. Therefore multiple index tables are introduced which are all used in the same fashion. As an example, the *IndexByProperty* table acts as an index (see Fig. 5) and enables processing queries comparing an object property against a given value using the typical operators: equals, greater and lower.

When updating or creating an object all its properties and values are extracted by deserializing it within the storage layer. This is possible as the object's schema is embedded within each serialized object. For each property a new index row in the *IndexByProperty* table is created. Its row key is a combination of the AppId, object kind, property name, property value and the row key of the object in the *Objects* table: (appId/kind/property name/property value/row key). Since HBase sorts all rows in an ascending order by the row key, all rows with the same AppId, object kind, property name and property value are stored in one coherent block.

To search all objects with a property value equal to a given value a new row key is created using the known values from the query: AppId, kind, property name and property value. The object's row key remains unset. Now the scan operation is used in combination with this start key to fetch all rows until the fetched property values change. Then the key column of each fetched index row is extracted and used to lookup the serialized objects in the *Objects* table (see Fig. 5).

The search with the greater-than query operator works the same way. The only difference concerns the scanner whose start key is generated using a bitwise incremented property value. The scanner is stopped as soon as the property name changes. If the query contains a lower operator the start key is created without a property value. The scanner is stopped if the property value of the query is reached.

8 Scaling

The TwoSpot platform is built for scaling out. It realizes this by executing multiple instances of an application on different machines. Depending on the application load TwoSpot must either start new AppServers if the application load increases or terminate them if the application load decreases.

As described earlier the Master decides which Controllers should handle the requests for an application and therefore is responsible for scaling out. It takes this decision based on a simple load algorithm which ranks each Controller based on its performance data: Number of running applications, CPU usage, memory load, requests per second and a flag which the Controller or AppServer activates if it is under high load. In the first step the algorithm determines all Controllers which are already running the requested application and adds them to a list. The algorithm ranks all remaining Controllers if the list is empty or mostly contains overloaded Controllers. This is done by multiplying each performance data value with a predefined weight and creating the sum of the weighted performance data values. The best ranked Controller is then added to the list which is finally returned to the Frontend. As the Controllers automatically start new AppServers, the Master does not have to instruct them explicitly while assigning an application. The Frontend caches the list entries and distributes the load uniformly across all Controllers using a queue based approach. The cache entries time out after a predefined time or if the connection with the Controller fails. This allows changes in the assignments between applications and Controllers.

The platform has to shutdown AppServers if the load decreases. This is handled by the Controllers independently. Each Controller runs a set of so called balancing processors. A balancing processor implements an algorithm which evaluates each running AppServer and decides whether it should be terminated.

We have implemented multiple balancing processors. The first one searches for AppServers which did not handle a request during the last minutes. If such an AppServer is found the processor changes the lifecycle to DROPPED. This causes the Controller to respond all requests for this application with the HTTP error code 801 during the next few seconds. The Frontend recognizes this error and redirects the requests to another Controller or returns a 503 HTTP error to the client if the redirect fails. This mechanism suppresses a restart of the AppServer just after it has been stopped intentionally.

The second balancing processor searches for AppServers which are underloaded. These are using less than 1/3 of the request processing threads in average. If the balancing processor detects such an AppServer it checks if other Controllers are managing an AppServer for the application by using the ZooKeeper service. In this case the balancing processor changes the lifecycle's state to DROPPED.

The last balancing processor is only active if the Controller is under a high load. The balancing processor then determines the AppServer with the lowest load and changes its lifecycle state to BANNED. As long as the Controller is under a high load the balancing processor continues to remove AppServers until only one remains. The behavior of the BANNED state is very similar to the DROPPED state but with an increased timeframe in which the application requests are blocked for.

In summary the scaling mechanisms used to start and stop AppServers are implemented both within the Master and the Controller. The Master is in charge of triggering new AppServers to be started if the load increases. In contrast the Controllers try to shutdown unnecessary AppServers in order to reduce their load and free resources. Both interests are contrary causing an automatic adjustment of the number of running AppServers.

The described scaling technique may potentially lead into various oscillation scenarios. We counteract these by setting the threshold for stopping applications much greater than for starting new ones as AppServers are only stopped if they are definitely unused. Also they have to run for a couple of minutes until a balancing processor can shut them down. Furthermore one Controller cannot restart an application immediately after it has been terminated. Finally it is important that there are always enough Controllers and machines available which is assumed by the scaling mechanisms.

Another important aspect of scaling is the handling of user session data. As described earlier each request is delegated to a Controller by the Frontend. The Frontend does not support sticky sessions which means that the client browser is not stuck with a specific Controller and AppServer. In such a situation session handling becomes increasingly difficult as the data of each user session have to be available to each AppServer running the application.

Various approaches exist for session clustering. For example session data may be serialized to a central file system or the database. In this case each request has to read and write all session data from and to the database. This will put the database under a very high load. Another approach is the in-memory-replication of session data. With this approach an AppServer multicasts all session data changes to all other AppServers executing the same application. This approach scales up to a certain amount of machines but depends on the size of the session data. It is also very complex and therefore error-prone, especially when implemented in a system like TwoSpot which regularly starts and stops AppServers.

Since we put a focus on scalability we have decided not to provide a mechanism which handles session data in the AppServer's memory and therefore do not assign users to a specific application instance. As a result each request handler has to be stateless. The Controller provides access to a user service which could be used to cover user sessions. It handles user logins and stores a session-id in the storage service and a browser cookie. The applications can query the user service to acquire just the username for the current request. This can then be used by the application to manage the users session data in the storage service.

9   Tests

We deployed TwoSpot using 13 machines of an IaaS provider. Eight machines were configured with 512MB memory and were guaranteed 1/32 of two 2GHz quad core processors. The other five machines were configured with 1024MB memory and 1/16 of the processors. The machines were interconnected with a gigabit Ethernet adapter. HBase with default configuration settings was deployed on the five 1024MB machines. Another machine was dedicated to run the HBase and TwoSpot master process. Yet another machine was configured with the TwoSpot Frontend and the TwoSpot fileserver. We used a single machine to run Apache JMeter which generates the load for the platform. The remaining five machines where dedicated to the Controller and AppServer processes.

In order to test the platform we chose three simple applications. The Portal application is a web application dedicated to manage TwoSpot users and applications. GWiki is a very simple wiki implementation. Finally, the Guestbook application is a basic implementation of an online guestbook. The Portal and GWiki applications both comprise a Servlet which zip-compresses 512Kb and 1024Kb of random data. It is executed by each JMeter test in order to stress the CPU. It should be noted that the processor capacity depends on the Hypervisor which supports CPU bursting. This means a VM can utilize the CPU fully if no other VM on the same physical machine requests the CPU.

In order to test the applications under a high load we first created a test plan for each application by browsing the application and recording the user session. We then executed the test plan within a loop which in turn was executed by multiple threads. Initially three threads were used and another three threads were added every five seconds which simulates an increasing number of users.

During test execution each processed request was recorded. Based on the logs we investigated two metrics: First, we computed the average number of requests completed for each five second interval. Second, we calculated the average response time for all requests which have been started in a five second interval. We executed each test five times and calculated the average and standard deviation across all test runs. The results are shown in Fig. 6.

Both the Portal and GWiki application are able to process more requests per second as the load increases. The Guestbook application only scales for about 60 users. Beyond the number of finished requests does not increase with the load. The reason for this behavior is the start page which displays the ten latest guestbook entries. This page executes storage requests using a very small segment of an index table. This is located on a single HBase region server, which is thus queried by each request. As soon as this region server gets overloaded the application cannot scale any further.

One possible solution of such a situation is to use a cache. The Guestbook application may cache the start page and update the cache entry after a certain time. New guestbook entries may also be written to the storage and the cache. Thus, new entries would also be visible immediately. This situation illustrates that applications may not scale if they are written in an inefficient manner.

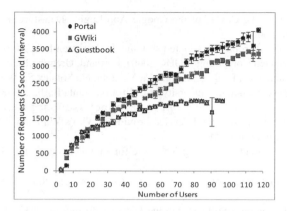

Fig. 6. Number of Processed Requests over the Number of Users

Furthermore the graph shows random drops in performance. For one reason these occur if new instances of an application are started. The Frontend then immediately redirects request to the new instance, which has to start the application first. Therefore the requests are delayed. HBase region splits are another cause of performance impacts. They cause segments of the database to be unavailable for which reason the application has to wait until they are available again.

10   Conclusion and Future Work

We have described TwoSpot, a PaaS cloud platform which is built to run scalable web applications based on a set of virtual machines. The complete architecture has been designed while carefully paying attention on its scalability and open standards but ignoring the requirements of legacy applications. This led to an exceptional architecture which differs from typical platform architectures in multiple critical points. Nevertheless we were able to build a fully functional prototype which showed promising results in early scalability tests.

Now we are in the process of further optimizing scalability and performance. One optimization approach is to preload AppServers without applications. This could speed up the startup time of applications. The applications could also profit from the provisioning of a distributed cache solution. Another optimization concerns the load balancing process in the Frontend which should take the startup time and load of AppServers as well as the complexity of requests into account. The storage implementation also requires further work in order to provide a mechanism for importing and exporting data in a reusable format. Furthermore the Master needs to interact with the underlying IaaS provider in order to efficiently control the number and size of the provided VMs.

References

1. Atwood, T.: Cost and Scalability in Vertical and Horizontal Architectures. Implications for Database and Application Layer Deployments. Technical White Paper. Sun Microsystems (2004), http://www.sun.com/servers/wp/docs/cost_scalability.pdf

2. Barrett, R.: Under the Covers of the Google App Engine Datastore. In: Google I/O, San Francisco, CA (2008)
3. Brewer, E.: Towards robust distributed systems. In: Nineteenth ACM Symposium on Principles of Distributed Computing (PODC 2000), Portland, Oregon (2000)
4. Chohan, N., Bunch, C., Pang, S., Krintz, C., Mostafa, N., Soman, S., Wolski, R.: AppScale Design and Implementation. University of California, Santa Barbara (2009), http://www.cs.ucsb.edu/~ckrintz/papers/appscale2009-02TR.pdf
5. Garvin, J.: Perceptions of Cloud Service Providers. Who's Who and Where in the Cloud. Evans Data Corporation (2009)
6. Grossman, R.L.: Cloud Computing. The Case for Cloud Computing. IT Professional 11(2), 23–27 (2009)
7. Joyent Smart Platform, http://www.joyent.com/products/joyent-smart-platform/
8. Lawton, G.: Developing Software Online With Platform-as-a-Service Technology. Computer 41(6), 13–15 (2008)
9. Leavitt, N.: Is Cloud Computing Really Ready for Prime Time? Computer 42(1), 15–20 (2009)
10. Lenk, A., Klems, M., Nimis, J., Tai, S., Sandholm, T.: What's Inside the Cloud? An Architectural Map of the Cloud Landscape. In: CLOUD 2009: Proceedings of the 2009 ICSE Workshop on Software Engineering Challenges of Cloud Computing, pp. 23–31. IEEE Computer Society, Washington (2009)
11. Levi, A.: From Spark Plug to Drive Train: Life of an App Engine Request. In: Google I/O, San Francisco, CA (2009)
12. Ryan, B.: Google App. Engine. How Index Building Works. Google (2008), http://code.google.com/intl/de-DE/appengine/articles/index_building.html
13. Overview (Java Platform SE 6), http://java.sun.com/javase/6/docs/api/

Simulating Autonomic SLA Enactment in Clouds Using Case Based Reasoning

Michael Maurer[1], Ivona Brandic[1], and Rizos Sakellariou[2]

[1] Vienna University of Technology, Distributed Systems Group,
Argentinierstraße 8, 1040 Vienna, Austria
{maurer,ivona}@infosys.tuwien.ac.at
[2] University of Manchester, School of Computer Science, U.K.
rizos@cs.man.ac.uk

Abstract. With the emergence of Cloud Computing resources of physical machines have to be allocated to virtual machines (VMs) in an on-demand way. However, the efficient allocation of resources like memory, storage or bandwidth to a VM is not a trivial task. On the one hand, the Service Level Agreement (SLA) that defines QoS goals for arbitrary parameters between the Cloud provider and the customer should not be violated. On the other hand, the Cloud providers aim to maximize their profit, where optimizing resource usage is an important part. In this paper we develop a simulation engine that mimics the control cycle of an autonomic manager to evaluate different knowledge management techniques (KM) feasible for efficient resource management and SLA attainment. We especially focus on the use of Case Based Reasoning (CBR) for KM and decision-making. We discuss its suitability for efficiently governing on-demand resource allocation in Cloud infrastructures by evaluating it with the simulation engine.

Keywords: Cloud Computing, Autonomic Computing, Service Level Agreement, Case Based Reasoning, Knowledge Management, Resource Management.

1 Introduction

The emergence of Cloud Computing – a computing paradigm that provides computing power as a utility – raises the question of dynamically allocating resources in an on-demand way. The resources that Cloud Computing providers should allocate for the customers' applications can be inferred from so called *Service Level Agreements* (SLAs). SLAs contain *Service Level Objectives* (SLOs) that represent Quality of Service (QoS) goals, e.g., storage $\geq 1000GB$, bandwidth $\geq 10Mbit/s$ or response time $\leq 2s$, and penalties that have to be paid to the customer if these goals are violated. Consequently, on the one hand Cloud providers face the question of allocating enough resources for every application. On the other hand, however, they have to use resources as efficiently as possible: one should only allocate what is really needed.

E. Di Nitto and R. Yahyapour (Eds.): ServiceWave 2010, LNCS 6481, pp. 25–36, 2010.

This work is embedded in the *Foundations of Self-governing ICT infrastructure* (FoSII) project [3]. The *FoSII* project aims at developing an infrastructure for autonomic SLA management and enforcement. Besides the already implemented *LoM2HiS* framework [12] that takes care of monitoring the state of the Cloud infrastructure and its applications, the knowledge management (KM) system presented in this paper represents another building block of the FoSII infrastructure. [11] proposes an approach to manage Cloud infrastructures by means of Autonomic Computing, which in a control loop monitors (M) Cloud parameters, analyzes (A) them, plans (P) actions and executes (E) them; the full cycle is known as MAPE [15]. According to [14] a MAPE-K loop stores knowledge (K) required for decision-making in a knowledge base (KB) that is accessed by the individual phases. This paper addresses the research question of finding a suitable KM system (i.e., a technique of how stored information should be used) and determining how it interacts with the other phases for dynamically and efficiently allocating resources.

In [19] we have argued for the use of *Case Based Reasoning* (CBR) as KM technique, because it offers a natural translation of Cloud status information into formal knowledge representation and an easy integration with the MAPE phases. Moreover, it promises to be scalable (as opposed to e.g., Situation Calculus) and easily configurable (as opposed to rule-based systems). Related work has not observed the usage of CBR nor has it evaluated different KM techniques in Cloud environments. Yet, evaluating the KM system on a real environment is not a trivial task, because Cloud infrastructures usually are huge data centers consisting of hundreds of PMs and even more VMs. Thus, a first step is to simulate the impact of autonomic management decisions on the Cloud infrastructure to determine the performance of the KM decisions.

The main contribution of this paper is the formulation of a CBR-based approach for the decision making in the MAPE cycle (in particular the analysis and planning phases) of an autonomic SLA enactment environment in Clouds. Furthermore, we design, implement and evaluate a generic simulation engine for the evaluation of CBR. With proper interfaces the engine can be used for the evaluation of other decision making techniques. Finally, we carry out an initial evaluation of the approach to assess the suitability of CBR for resource-efficient SLA management.

The remainder of this paper is organized as follows: Section 2 gives a brief overview of related work. Section 3 describes the Cloud Infrastructure we are simulating and explains the autonomic management system of FosII. While Section 4 explains the idea of the simulation engine, Section 5 provides a detailed view of its implementation and details of the adaptation of CBR. Finally, we present the evaluation of CBR as KM technique by the simulation engine in Section 6 and conclude in Section 7.

2 Related Work

Firstly, there has been some considerable work on optimizing resource usage while keeping QoS goals. These papers, however, concentrate on specific subsystems of Large Scale Distributed Systems, as [17] on the performance of memory systems, or only deal with one or two specific SLA parameters. Petrucci [21] or Bichler [10] investigate one general resource constraint and Khanna [7] only focuses on response time and throughput. A quite similar approach to our concept is provided by the Sandpiper framework [22], which offers black-box and gray-box resource management for VMs. Contrary to our approach, though, it plans reactions just after violations have occurred. Additionally, none of the presented papers uses a KB for recording past action and learning.

Secondly, there has been work on KM of SLAs, especially rule-based systems. Paschke [20] et al. look into a rule based approach in combination with the logical formalism ContractLog. It specifies rules to trigger after a violation has occurred, but it does not deal with avoidance of SLA violations. Others inspected the use of ontologies as KBs only at a conceptual level. [18] viewed the system in four layers (i.e., business, system, network and device) and broke down the SLA into relevant information for each layer, which had the responsibility of allocating required resources. Again, no details on how to achieve this have been given. Bahati et al. [9] also use policies, i.e., rules, to achieve autonomic management. As in the other papers, this work deals with only one SLA parameter and a quite limited set of actions, and with violations and not with the avoidance thereof. Our KM system allows to choose any arbitrary number of parameters that can be adjusted on a VM.

Thirdly, compared to other SLA management projects like SLA@SOI [6], the FoSII project in general is more specific on Cloud Computing aspects like deployment, monitoring of resources and their translation into high level SLAs instead of just working on high-level SLAs in general service-oriented architectures.

3 FoSII Overview

In this section we describe the basic design of the Cloud infrastructure being simulated and the autonomic management cycle used in the FoSII project.

3.1 FoSII's Autonomic Cycle and Monitoring

As shown in Figure 1 the FoSII infrastructure is used to manage the whole life-cycle of self-adaptable Cloud services [11]. The management is governed by a *MAPE* cycle, whose components will be explained in this subsection. As part of the Monitor phase of the MAPE cycle, the host monitor sensors continuously monitor the infrastructure resource metrics and provide the autonomic manager with the current resource status. The run-time monitor sensors sense SLA violation threats based on predefined threat thresholds. *Threat thresholds* (TTs) as explained in [5] are more restrictive thresholds than the SLO values. The generation of TTs is far from trivial and should be retrieved and updated by the KM system, and only at the beginning be configured manually. Violation threats are then forwarded to the KB together with monitoring information that represents a current snapshot of the system.

Since monitoring VMs retrieves values like `free_disk` or `packets_sent`, but we are more interested in SLA parameters like storage or bandwidth, there has

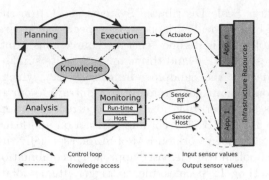

Fig. 1. FoSII infrastructure

to be a mapping between these low level metrics and high level SLAs. This is achieved by the already mentioned highly scalable framework *LoM2HiS* [12].

After an SLA violation threat has been received by the KM during the *Analysis* phase, it has to decide which reactive action has to be taken in order to prevent the possible violation. The *Plan* phase is divided into two parts: phase *Plan I* cares about mapping actions onto PMs and managing the PMs (levels (ii) and (iii) in Subsection 3.2). Phase *Plan II* then is in charge of planning the order and timing of the actions with the additional goal of preventing oscillations, i.e., increasing and decreasing the same resources for several times. Finally the actions are executed (*Execution* phase) with the help of actuators.

3.2   FoSII's Infrastructure and Knowledge Management Use Case

We assume that customers deploy applications on an IaaS Cloud infrastructure. SLOs are defined within an SLA between the customer and the Cloud provider for every application. Furthermore, there is a 1:1 relationship between applications and VMs. One VM runs on exactly one PM, but one PM can host an arbitrary number of VMs with respect to supplied vs. demanded resource capacities. After allocating VMs with an initial capacity (by estimating initial resource demand) for every application, we continuously monitor actually used resources and re-allocate resources according to these measurements. Along with the process of re-allocating VM resources, the VMs have to be deployed to PMs, a VM possibly migrated from one PM to another or PMs turned on/off. Thus, one is dealing with autonomic management on three levels with respect to the following order: (i) VM resource management, (ii) VM deployment, (iii) PM management. This paper will focus on level (i). As far as level (ii) is concerned, deploying VMs on PMs with capacity constraints minimizing consumed energy by the PMs (also taking into account the costs of booting PMs and migrating VMs) can be formulated into a *Binary integer problem* (BIP), which is known to be NP-complete [16]. The proof is out of scope for this paper, but a similar approach can be seen in [21]. As realistic Cloud environments consist of many VMs and PMs, this can be considered as a real problem in practice.

Table 1. Cases of (non-) SLA violations using the example of storage

Provided (1)	Utilized (2)	Agreed (3)	Violation?
500 GB	400 GB	$\geq 1000GB$	NO
500 GB	510 GB	$\geq 1000GB$	YES
1000 GB	1010 GB	$\geq 1000GB$	NO

Consequently, heuristics have to be found to approach this problem within reasonable time. Level (iii) considers turning on/off PMs or modifying CPU frequency.

For level (i) we need to define how the measured, provided and agreed values interrelate. An example is provided in Table 1. At first, we deal with the measured value (1), which represents the amount of a specific resource that is currently used by the customer. Second, there is the amount of allocated resource (2) that can be used by the customer, i.e., that is allocated to the VM which hosts the application. Third, there is the SLO agreed in the SLA (3). A violation therefore occurs, if less is provided (2) than the customer utilizes (or wants to utilize) (1) with respect to the limits set in the SLA (3). Considering Table 1 we can see that rows 1 and 3 do not represent violations, whereas row 2 does represent an SLA violation.

4   Description of the Simulation Engine

The goal of the simulation engine is to evaluate the quality of a KM system with respect to the number of SLA violations and the utilization of the resources. Furthermore, the simulation engine serves as an evaluation tool for any KM technique in the field of Cloud Computing, as long as it can implement the two methods of the KB management interface:

1. `public void receiveMeasurement(int slaID, String[] provided,`
   `       String[] measurements, List<String> violations);` and
2. `public Action recommendAction(int slaID);`.

The parameter `slaID` describes the ID of the SLA that is tied to the specific VM, whose provided and measured values are stored in the arrays `provided` and `measurements`, respectively. The list `violations` contains all SLA parameters

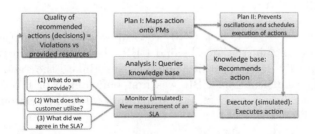

Fig. 2. MAPE cycle in FoSII

being violated for the current measurements. The method `receiveMeasurement` inputs new data into the KB, whereas the method `recommendAction` outputs an action specific to the current measurement of the specified SLA.

The simulation engine traverses parts of the MAPE-cycle as can be seen in Figure 2 and described in Subsection 3.1. The Monitoring and Executor part are simulated, Analysis I and the KB are implemented using CBR. Plan phases I and II are currently not considered within the simulation engine; the focus of the engine is to solve the question of how to correctly allocate resources for VMs before deploying them to PMs. Possible reactive actions have to be pre-defined and are – for the Analysis phase – tied to parameters that can directly be tuned on a VM: Increase/Decrease storage/bandwidth/memory etc. by 10%/20% etc., or do nothing.

As far as the measurements are concerned, a sensor is "installed" for every VM parameter that should be measured. The simulated Monitor component simultaneously asks the sensors for the current value of their VM parameter. Sensors can be implemented completely modularly and independently. An example sensor implementation is explained in the following: For the first measurement, it randomly draws a value from a Gaussian distribution with $\mu = \frac{SLO}{2}$ and $\sigma = \frac{SLO}{8}$, where SLO describes the SLO threshold set for the current VM parameter. Then, it randomly draws a trend up or down and a duration the trend is going to last. Now, as long as the trend lasts, it increases (trend up) or decreases (trend down) the measured value for every iteration by any percentage uniformly distributed in the interval $[iBegin\%, iEnd\%]$. After the trend is over, a new trend and a new duration of the trend are selected. By doing this, we achieve a set of measurement data, where values do not behave just randomly, but follow a certain trend for a period of time that is a-priori unknown to the KM. As the intensity of the trend varies for every iteration, we deal with both, slow developments and rapid changes.

The simulation engine is iteration-based, meaning that in one iteration the MAPE cycle is traversed exactly once. In reality, one iteration could last from some minutes to about an hour depending on the speed of the measurements, the length of time the decision making takes, and the duration of the execution of the action, like for example migrating a resource intensive VM to another PM.

5   Implementation of CBR-Based Knowledge Management

In this section we describe how CBR was implemented within the simulation engine. We first explain the idea behind CBR, then define when two cases are similar, and finally derive a utility function to estimate the "goodness" of an action in a specific situation. CBR was first built ontop of FreeCBR [4], but is now a completely independent Java framework taking into account, however, basic ideas of FreeCBR.

5.1   CBR Overview

Case Based Reasoning is the process of solving problems based on past experience [8]. In more detail, it tries to solve a *case* (a formatted instance of a problem) by looking for similar cases from the past and reusing the solutions of these cases to solve the current one. In general, a typical CBR cycle consists of the following phases assuming that a new case was just received:

1. Retrieve the most similar case or cases to the new one.
2. Reuse the information and knowledge in the similar case(s) to solve the problem.
3. Revise the proposed solution.
4. Retain the parts of this experience likely to be useful for future problem solving. (Store new case and found solution into KB.)

In this paragraph we formalize language elements used in the remaining paper. Each SLA has a unique identifier *id* and a collection of SLOs. SLOs are predicates of the form

$$SLO_{id}(x_i, comp, \pi_i) \text{ with } comp \in \{<, \leq, >, \geq, =\}, \tag{1}$$

where $x_i \in P$ represents the parameter name for $i = 1, \ldots, n_{id}$, π_i the parameter goal, and *comp* the appropriate comparison operator. Additionally, action guarantees that state the amount of penalty that has to be paid in case of a violation can be added to SLOs, which is out of scope in this paper. Furthermore, a case c is defined as

$$c = (id, m_1, p_1, m_2, p_2, \ldots, m_{n_{id}}, p_{n_{id}}), \tag{2}$$

where *id* represents the SLA id, and m_i and p_i the measured (m) and provided (p) value of the SLA parameter x_i, respectively.

A typical use case for the evaluation might be: SLA id $= 1$ with SLO_1 ("Storage", $\geq$, 1000, ag_1) and SLO_1 ("Bandwidth", $\geq$, 50.0, ag_1), where ag_1 stands for the appropriate action guarantee to execute after an SLO violation. A simple case that would be received by a measurement component could therefore look like $c = (1, 500, 700, 20.0, 30.0)$. A result case $rc = (c^-, ac, c^+, utility)$ includes the initial case c^-, the executed action ac, the resulting case c^+ measured some time interval later (one iteration in the simulation engine) and the calculated *utility* described in Section 5.3.

5.2   Similarity Measurement between Two Cases

In order to retrieve similar cases already stored in the database to a new one, the similarity of two cases has to be calculated. However, there are many metrics that can be considered.

The problem with Euclidean distance, for instance, is due to its symmetric nature that it cannot correctly fetch whether a case is in a state of over- or under-provisioning. Additionally, the metric has to treat parameters in a normalized way so that parameters that have a larger distance range are not

over-proportionally taken into account than parameters with a smaller difference range. (E.g., if the difference between measured and provided values of
parameter A always lie between 0 and 100 and of parameter B between 0 and
1000, the difference between an old and a new case can only be within the same
ranges, respectively. Thus, just adding the differences of the parameters would
yield an unproportional impact of parameter B.)

This leads to the following equation whose summation part follows the principle of semantic similarity from [13]:

$$d(c^-, c^+) = \min(w_{id}, |id^- - id^+|) + \sum_{x \in P} w_x \left| \frac{(p_x^- - m_x^-) - (p_x^+ - m_x^+)}{max_x - min_x} \right|, \quad (3)$$

where $w = (w_{id}, w_{x_1}, \ldots, w_{x_n})$ is the weight vector; w_{id} is the weight for non-
identical SLAs; w_x is the weight, and max_x and min_x the maximum and minimum values of differences $p_x - m_x$ for parameter x. As can easily be checked,
this indeed is a metric also in the mathematical sense.

Furthermore, the match percentage mp of two cases c^- and c^+ is then calculated as

$$mp(c^-, c^+) = \left(1 - \frac{d(c^-, c^+)}{w_{id} + \sum_x w_x}\right) \cdot 100. \quad (4)$$

This is done because the algorithm does not only consider the case with the
highest match, but also cases in a certain percentage neighborhood (initially set
to 3%) of the case with the highest match. From these cases the algorithm then
chooses the one with the highest utility. By calculating the match percentage,
the cases are distributed on a fixed line between 0 and 100, where 100 is an
identical match, whereas 0 is the complete opposite.

5.3   Utility Function, Utilization and Resource Allocation Efficiency

To calculate the utility of an action, we have to compare the initial case c^- vs.
the resulting final case c^+. The *utility function* is composed by a violation and
a utilization term weighed by the factor $0 \leq \alpha \leq 1$:

$$utility = \sum_{x \in P} violation(x) + \alpha \cdot utilization(x) \quad (5)$$

Higher values for α give more importance to the utilization of resources, whereas
lower values to the non-violation of SLA parameters. We further note that $c(x)$
describes a case only with respect to parameter x. E.g., we say that a violation
has occurred in $c(x)$, when in case c the parameter x was violated.

The function *violation* for every parameter x is defined as follows:

$$violation(x) = \begin{cases} 1, & \text{No violation occurred in } c^+(x), \text{ but in } c^-(x) \\ 1/2, & \text{No violation occurred in } c^+(x) \text{ and } c^-(x) \\ -1/2 & \text{Violation occurred in } c^+(x) \text{ and } c^-(x) \\ -1 & \text{Violation occurred in } c^+(x), \text{ but not in } c^-(x) \end{cases} \quad (6)$$

For the *utilization* function we calculate the utility from the used resources in comparison to the provided ones. We define the distance $\delta(x,y) = |x - y|$, and utilization for every parameter as

$$utilization(x) = \begin{cases} 1, & \delta(p_x^-, m_x^-) > \delta(p_x^+, u_x^+) \\ -1, & \delta(p_x^-, m_x^-) < \delta(p_x^+, u_x^+) \\ 0, & \text{otherwise.} \end{cases} \quad (7)$$

We get a utilization utility of 1 if we experience less over-provisioning of resources in the final case than in the initial one, and a utilization utility of -1 if we experience more over-provisioning of resources in the final case than in the initial one.

If we want to map utilization, u, and the number of SLA violations, v, into a scalar called *resource allocation efficiency* (RAE), we can achieve this by

$$RAE = \begin{cases} \frac{u}{v}, & v \neq 0 \\ u, & v = 0, \end{cases} \quad (8)$$

which reflects our evaluation goals. High utilization leads to high RAE, whereas a high number of SLA violations leads to a low RAE, even if utilization is in normal range. This can be explained by the fact that having utilization at a maximum - thus being very resource efficient in the first place - does not pay if the SLA is not fulfilled at all.

6   Evaluation of CBR

This section first describes which initial cases are fed into CBR and then evaluates how CBR behaved over several iterations.

As a first step, the KB has to be filled with some meaningful initial cases. This was done by choosing one representative case for each action that could be triggered. For our evaluation the SLA parameters *bandwidth* and *storage* (even though not being tied to them in any way – we could have also named them, e.g., *memory* and *CPU time*) were taken into consideration resulting into 9 possible actions "Increase/Decrease bandwidth by 10%/20%", "Increase/Decrease storage by 10%/20%", and "Do nothing".

Taking storage for example, we divide the range of distances for storage St between measured and provided resources into five parts as depicted in Figure 3. We choose some reasonable threshold for every action as follows: If $p_{St} - m_{St} = -10$ then action "Increase Storage by 20%" as this already is a violation; if $p_{St}^- - m_{St} = +50$ then action "Increase Storage by 10%" as resources are already scarce but not so problematic as in the previous case; if $p_{St} - m_{St} = +100$ then action "Do nothing" as resources are neither very over- nor under-provisioned; if $p_{St} - m_{St} = +200$ then action "Decrease Storage by 10%" as now resources are over-provisioned; and we set action "Decrease Storage by 20%" when we are over the latest threshold as then resources are extremely over-provisioned. We choose the values for our initial cases from the center of the respective intervals. Ultimately, for the initial case for the action, e.g., "Increase Storage by 20%" we take the just mentioned value for storage and the "Do nothing" value for bandwidth. This leads to $c = (id, 0, -10, 0, 7.5)$, and because only the differences between the values matter, it is equivalent to, e.g., $c = (id, 200, 190, 7.5, 15.0)$.

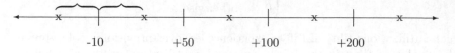

-10   +50   +100   +200

Fig. 3. How to choose initial cases using the example of storage

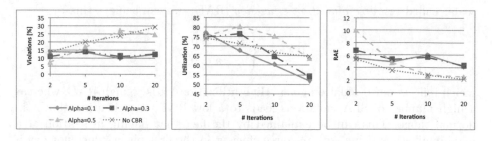

Fig. 4. SLA violations   **Fig. 5.** Utilization   **Fig. 6.** RAE

The CBR implementation is evaluated by comparing the outcome of the simulation running with the autonomic manager and without it. At the beginning, we configure all VMs exactly equally with 80% of the storage SLO value and 2/3 of the bandwidth SLO value provided. Then, we execute 2, 5, 10 and 20 iterations with values for α being 0.1, 0.2, 0.3, 0.4, 0.5, 0.6 and 0.8 (cf. Eq. 5). We omit values 0.2 and 0.4 in the evaluation because their outcomes do not differ enough from the values shown, and all values > 0.5, because they reveal unacceptable high SLA violation rates. After the iterations we calculate the percentage of occurred SLA violations in respect to all possible SLA violations (cf. Fig. 4), the resource utilization (cf. Fig. 5) and the RAE (cf. Fig. 6). Running without the autonomic manager means that we will leave the configuration of the VMs as they are and effect no actions due to changing demands. We set the weights $w = (1, 1, 1)$. In Figures 4 and 5 we see that the number of SLA violations and resource utilization heavily depend on the factor α. Lower values for α clearly prefer to avoid SLA violations, whereas higher ones emphasize on resource utilization. We also see that with $\alpha \in \{0.1, 0.3\}$ up to more than half of the SLA violations can be avoided. However, fewer SLA violations result in lower resource utilization, as more resources have to be provided than can actually be utilized. Another point that can be observed, is that after a certain amount of iterations the quality of the recommended actions decreases. This is probably due to the fact that the initial cases get more and more blurred when more cases are stored into CBR, as all new cases are being learned and there is no distinction being made between "interesting" and "uninteresting" cases. Nevertheless, when we relate SLA violations and resource utilization in terms of RAE, CBR methods for $\alpha \in \{0.1, 0.3\}$ are up to three times better than the default method. Summing up, the simulation shows that learning did take place and that CBR is able to recommend right actions for many cases, i.e., to correctly handle and interpret the measurement information that is based on a random distribution not known to CBR.

7 Conclusion

This paper presents a first attempt to create a KM system for Cloud Computing. To evaluate such systems, a KM technique-agnostic simulation engine that simulates monitoring information and executing actions on VMs in a Cloud environment has been developed. Furthermore, we implemented a CBR style knowledge base and evaluated it. The results are both encouraging and exhibit needs for further improvement. On the one hand they show that CBR reduces the number of SLA violations and increases RAE compared to a static approach. On the other hand, we can subsume two points that have to be leveraged: (i) learning techniques have to be ameliorated (step 4 in subsection 5.1) in order to maintain the high quality of the cases in the knowledge base; (ii) fine-tuning the similarity function should help to choose the most dangerous parameters with higher precision. One of the limitations of CBR is that for every parameter, the parameter space has to be divided into different areas corresponding to specific actions as in Fig. 3. This, however, could be also used for a rule-based approach, where these areas are specified with thresholds that can be learned using the utility function defined in Section 5.3. In CBR, the learning of these spaces inherently and implicitly takes place, but it would be interesting for a rule-based approach to compare whether an explicit learning or definition of the thresholds could bring a benefit to the RAE of the system. Therefore, the evaluation of other KM techniques with this simulation engine is our ongoing work. We want to compare the performance of CBR with a rule-based approach using Drools [2] and a default logic based approach based on DLV [1] in order to determine the most appropriate knowledge management method for Cloud computing.

Acknowledgments. The work described in this paper is supported by the Vienna Science and Technology Fund (WWTF) under grant agreement ICT08-018 Foundations of Self-Governing ICT Infrastructures (FoSII) and by COST-Action IC0804 on energy efficiency in large scale distributed systems.

References

1. (DLV) - The DLV Project - A Disjunctive Datalog System, http://www.dbai.tuwien.ac.at/proj/dlv/
2. Drools, http://www.drools.org
3. (FOSII) - Foundations of Self-governing ICT Infrastructures, http://www.infosys.tuwien.ac.at/linksites/fosii

4. FreeCBR, http://freecbr.sourceforge.net/
5. IT-Tude: SLA monitoring and evaluation,
   http://www.it-tude.com/sla-monitoring-evaluation.html
6. SLA@SOI, http://sla-at-soi.eu/
7. Application Performance Management in Virtualized Server Environments (2006),
   http://dx.doi.org/10.1109/NOMS.2006.1687567
8. Aamodt, A., Plaza, E.: Case-based reasoning: Foundational Issues, Methodological
   Variations, and System Approaches (1994)
9. Bahati, R.M., Bauer, M.A.: Adapting to run-time changes in policies driving autonomic management. In: ICAS 2008: Proceedings of the 4th Int. Conf. on Autonomic
   and Autonomous Systems. IEEE Computer Society, Washington (2008)
10. Bichler, M., Setzer, T., Speitkamp, B.: Capacity Planning for Virtualized Servers.
    Presented at Workshop on Information Technologies and Systems (WITS), Mil-
    waukee, Wisconsin, USA (2006)
11. Brandic, I.: Towards self-manageable cloud services. In: Ahamed, S.I., et al. (eds.)
    COMPSAC (2), pp. 128–133. IEEE Computer Society, Los Alamitos (2009)
12. Emeakaroha, V.C., Brandic, I.: Maurer, M., Dustdar, S.: Low level metrics to high
    level SLAs - LoM2HiS framework: Bridging the gap between monitored metrics and
    SLA parameters in cloud environments. In: The 2010 High Performance Computing
    and Simulation Conference in conjunction with IWCMC 2010, Caen, France (2010)
13. Hefke, M.: A framework for the successful introduction of KM using CBR and
    semantic web technologies. Journal of Universal Computer Science 10(6) (2004)
14. Huebscher, M.C., McCann, J.A.: A survey of autonomic computing—degrees, mod-
    els, and applications. ACM Comput. Surv. 40(3), 1–28 (2008)
15. Jacob, B., Lanyon-Hogg, R., Nadgir, D.K., Yassin, A.F.: A practical guide to the
    IBM Autonomic Computing toolkit. IBM Redbooks (2004)
16. Karp, R.M.: Reducibility among combinatorial problems. In: Miller, R.E.,
    Thatcher, J.W. (eds.) Complexity of Computer Computations: Proc. of a Symp.
    on the Complexity of Computer Computations, pp. 85–103. Plenum Press, New
    York (1972)
17. Khargharia, B., Hariri, S., Yousif, M.S.: Autonomic Power and Performance Man-
    agement for Computing Systems. Cluster Computing 11(2), 167–181 (2008)
18. Koumoutsos, G., Denazis, S., Thramboulidis, K.: SLA e-negotiations, enforcement
    and management in an autonomic environment. Modelling Autonomic Communi-
    cations Environments, pp. 120–125 (2008)
19. Maurer, M., Brandic, I., Emeakaroha, V.C., Dustdar, S.: Towards knowledge man-
    agement in self-adaptable clouds. In: IEEE 2010 Fourth International Workshop of
    Software Engineering for Adaptive Service-Oriented Systems, Miami, USA (2010)
20. Paschke, A., Bichler, M.: Knowledge representation concepts for automated SLA
    management. Decision Support Systems 46(1), 187–205 (2008)
21. Petrucci, V., Loques, O., Mossé, D.: A dynamic optimization model for power and
    performance management of virtualized clusters. In: e-Energy 2010: Proceedings of
    the 1st International Conference on Energy-Efficient Computing and Networking,
    pp. 225–233. ACM, New York (2010)
22. Wood, T., Shenoy, P., Venkataramani, A., Yousif, M.: Sandpiper: Black-box and
    gray-box resource management for virtual machines. Computer Networks 53(17),
    2923–2938 (2009)

Service Identification Methods: A Systematic Literature Review

Qing Gu* and Patricia Lago

Department of Computer Science, VU University Amsterdam, The Netherlands

Abstract. Many service identification methods (SIMs) have been proposed to support the determination of services that are appropriate for use in an SOA. However, these SIMs vary in terms of analysis objectives, identification procedures and service hierarchies. Due to the heterogeneity of the SIMs, practitioners often face the difficulty of choosing a SIM that copes with available resources and fits their needs. To gain a holistic view of existing SIMs and to support the selection of the right SIM, in this paper we present the results of a systematic literature review. A total number of 237 studies were examined, of which 30 studies were selected as primary studies. From these studies, we identified different types of inputs, outputs and processes used by the existing SIMs. Based on these results, we created a matrix which can be used in three different ways for practitioners to select among alternative SIMs.

1   Introduction and Research Questions

Service-oriented architecture (SOA) is an architectural enabler for quick response to business changes and effective reuse of software assets [1]. In an on-demand world, many enterprises have adopted SOA in order to gain competitive power [1]. A key factor that determines whether an enterprise really can benefit from adopting SOA is the design of services, including the scope of functionality a service exposes to meet business needs, and the boundaries between services to achieve maximum reusability and flexibility [2].

In the design of services, service identification (SI) is a significant task aiming at determining (based on available resources) services that are appropriate for use in an SOA. Many service identification methods (SIMs) have been proposed from both academia and industry. However, these SIMs differ significantly, ranging from source code extraction to business domain analysis, from bottom-up to top-down strategy and from ontology-based process to guideline-driven process. Accordingly, the inputs and outputs of these approaches vary as well. Some approaches start with business process whereas some others start with domain knowledge (e.g. goals and strategies); some approaches focus on business services whereas others focus on software services.

* The research leading to these results has received funding from the European Community's Seventh Framework Programme FP7/2007-2013 under grant agreement 215483 (S-Cube).

E. Di Nitto and R. Yahyapour (Eds.): ServiceWave 2010, LNCS 6481, pp. 37–50, 2010.
© Springer-Verlag Berlin Heidelberg 2010

Given many SIMs, a common question that practitioners face is how to select the most appropriate SIM that copes with the available resources and fits their needs [2]. Some enterprises, for instance, not only have well defined business process models in place but also well documented goals, business partners and enterprise capabilities (e.g. IT resources) to support its business process. For them, a SIM that takes all of this information into account will be more suitable than those identifying services only based on e.g. business processes.

Despite the comparisons (e.g. [3,4]) presented so far, none systematically searches for all the existing SIMs. As a result, a holistic overview of extant SIMs is missing. Moreover, the criteria used in the existing comparison frameworks cover many aspects, including economic, business, and technical aspects. However, a comparison of the basic elements (such as the inputs, outputs and processes) of the SIMs is currently missing. When selecting SIMs one often starts questioning what is required for using certain SIMs, what can be expected from them and how to carry them out, before addressing other requirements. Without such an overview of the basic elements of SIMs, the selection of SIMs becomes more complicated. Accordingly, the following research questions arise:

- *RQ1: What are the existing SIMs?*
- *RQ2: How do the SIMs differ? This can be elaborated into: RQ2.a what types of inputs do the SIMs start from? RQ2.b what types of services do the SIMs produce? RQ2.c what types of strategies and techniques are used by the SIMs?*

To answer these research questions, we decided to conduct a systematic literature review, which are particularly powerful in collecting and analyzing existing work. It can maximize the chance to retrieve complete data sets and minimize the chance of bias and summarizing the existing evidence [5]. In the remainder of the paper, Sec. 2 reports on the review results; Sec. 3 presents an input-output matrix that aids the selection of SIMs; and Sec. 4 concludes the paper.

2   The Results of the Review

To conduct the review, we followed the guidelines suggested in [5][1]. In the first step, we obtained 237 articles whose titles or abstracts contain the keywords specified in our search query. After applying the selection criteria, 38 articles were identified as *primary studies* that are relevant for review. By further reviewing their related work (motivated by the fact that an article presenting a SIM most likely discusses other SIMs as related work), we identified 11 more primary studies. Among these two lists of primary studies, 19 articles are duplicates and hence resulting 30 articles as identical primary studies.

---

[1] Due to the space limitation, we do not present the review protocol that we followed. Interested readers are referred to www.few.vu.nl/~qgu/SIMReviewProtocol.pdf for details, including the specified search query, selected electronic libraries, and strategies for data extraction data synthesis.

2.1 RQ1 What Are the Existing SIMs?

Each primary study presents one SIM and we have identified 30 SIMs altogether. An overview of the SIMs is given in Table 7. As we can see, SIM S1 and SIM S2 (hereafter labeled as S1 and S2) are the pioneering SIMs presented in 2004. The increasing number of SIMs being proposed in the last three years (6 in 2007, 9 in 2008 and 9 in 2009) reveals its increasing importance in the service engineering field.

Most of the SIMs have certain form of validation as shown in Table 7. The best way to validate a method is to put it into practice. Two primary studies describe the experience in using their methods in real life *projects*. Another way of validation is to experiment a SIM in *case studies*, which was adopted by 13 studies. In order to improve their usability, 6 primary studies provide *examples* in explaining how to use the proposed SIMs. For judging their quality, 4 primary studies *evaluate* the method in terms of e.g. survey or comparison. Only five primary studies do not discuss any validation of the proposed SIMs.

2.2 RQ2.a What Are the Different Types of Inputs?

We examined each primary study and extracted information about the input of the SIMs. We found that many SIMs start from the same type of information. For instance, legacy source code and existing software application or components are both existing software assets but in different forms. In the same vein, a collection of business models, requirements, strategies and organizational structures are all about the domain knowledge of an enterprise but describing specific enterprise elements. By comparing the inputs and classifying the ones that share the same type of information, we identified seven types of inputs. These types of inputs and the SIMs that use them are summarized in Table 1.

The classification of the inputs shows that the resources used by SIMs often have a different scope. For instance, types *data, feature* and *use case* are more specific than *application domain* or *business process* in that the former can be

Table 1. Types of inputs used in the SIMs

Type of input	Description	SIM	Total
Business process	A collection of related tasks or activities to fulfill a specific business requirement	S3,S10,S12,S15, S16,S17,S23, S24,S25,S26,	10
Application domain	A collection of models or documents that describe the various aspects of an application domain, including enterprise goals or mission, business rules, business processes, business entities, organization structures, etc.	S1,S7,S8,S9, S14,S22	6
Legacy system	Existing software assets of an enterprise. It can be software systems, source code, or the architecture of the existing systems	S4,S5,S20,S27	4
Mix	A mix of type legacy system and other types	S2,S13,S21,S30	4
Data	The information that is processed, exchanged, or produced by business processes	S6,S29	2
Feature	A set of distinctive attributes or characteristics of software systems	S18,S19	2
Use case	A sequence of business functions that human actors benefit from	S11,S28	2

derived from the latter. The number of SIMs using each type of input shows that fewer methods start with more specific or technical information.

Most of the SIMs start from business processes and enterprise level information, taking both the business and its context into consideration. This is in line with the fact that service-oriented design intends to realize software re-use through large grained services especially meant to create business value.

Legacy system is another type of input and is used by four SIMs, as shown in Table 1. These SIMs take a bottom-up approach to examine the architecture (e.g. S5) or source code (e.g. S27) of the existing systems for identifying services.

As we can see, most of the SIMs are either based on domain knowledge at the enterprise level (*top*) or existing systems (*bottom*). When adopting SOA, enterprises rarely start from scratch; instead, very often they need to migrate their existing systems while creating additional services to address new business requirements. Only four SIMs take a meet-in-middle approach to identify services based on a combination of legacy systems and other information type *Mix*, such as domain analysis in S2 and business process models in S30. This low number is contradictory to the comparison of service analysis approaches reported in [3], which pointed out that most approaches postulate a meet-in-the middle strategy. The cause for this contradiction lies in the fact that in our review we selected *only* the SIMs that provide detailed description of the methods. In [3] such a criterion does not apply and many approaches that only conceptually discuss their SI strategies have been selected for comparison. It has been admitted by the authors in [3] that many approaches do fail to go into detail. Despite of the equal importance of existing software assets and business requirements, only few SIMs provide enough guidance on how to take into account both of them.

2.3   RQ 2.b What Are the Different Types of Services Being Produced?

In this section, we discuss the outputs of the SIMs, including the *types of services* produced and how these services are described (*output format*).

Types of services. The general goal of SIMs is to identify services that are valuable, either from business or IT perspective. Each individual SIM has a specific goal in identifying specific types of services. For instance, some SIMs target at services that represent business processes whereas others focus on identifying services that bridge the gap between business services and IT infrastructure. By studying, comparing and synthesizing the data about the objectives of the services produced by the SIMs, we identified 6 types of services that have been explicitly discussed, summarized in Table 2 (note that a SIM may identify multiple types of services).

From a business perspective, we can see that 21 SIMs result in *business services* representing businesses processes, and 12 result in *data services* for business entities. Both of these two types of services are business-related. Because of the nature of services (i.e exposing business functions), it is quite understandable that a large number of SIMs focus on business.

Table 2. Types of outputs produced by the SIMs

Type of output	Description	SIM	Total
Business process service (BS)	A service that has the business logic or represents a business process, including task services, process services.	S3,S7,S8,S9,S10,S11,S12, S13,S14,S15,S17,S18,S19, S21,S22,S23,S24,S25,S26, S28,S29	21
Data service (DS)	A service that represents business centric entities, including information services, entity services	S6,S7,S8,S9,S13,S15,S16, S17,S21,S22,S24,S25	12
Composite Service (CS)	A composition of multiple services.	S7,S8,S11,S12,S13,S14, S15,S17,S21,S25,S28,S29	12
IT service (IS)	A service that represents technology specific functionalities, including application services, software services, utility services and infrastructure services.	S3,S7,S8,S9,S10,S13, S17,S22,S24	9
Web service (WS)	A service that is implemented using the web service technology. This type is orthogonal to the other types	S1,S2,S4,S5,S20,S30	7
Partner service (PS)	A service that is offered to external partners.	S3,S16,S17,S26,S29	5

On the other hand, it is worth noticing that the numbers of SIMs for identifying *IT services* and *partner services* is relatively low and lower than we expected. Business-IT alignment is recognized as a research challenge [6] and the need of integrating technical architecture (e.g. IT infrastructure, data models) with business architecture (e.g. business models, organizational structure) has been widely agreed [1,2]. As shown in Table 2, all 9 SIMs that do consider IT services also identify business services and more importantly, they pay specific attention to the integration of business and IT. This alignment should, in our opinion, be supported by all the SIMs, which points out a gap in those SIMs lacking support for IT services.

As for *partner services*, we see that only 5 SIMs lead to services that explicitly consider their service providers (SPs) and consumers (SCs). Services are designed, developed, provided, maintained and owned by SPs. The task of SCs is to discover and compose services fulfilling their needs. SI for SPs entails how to identify services that are potentially useful to others. For SCs, it, instead, entails how to identify services for integration purposes. Because of this difference, a SIM should explicitly indicate which role it supports. Unfortunately, most of the SIMs fail to highlight this difference. Despite that the separation of SPs and SCs is considered as one of the main characteristics of SOA, these two roles are often not explicitly considered in service engineering in general, as found by a survey of SOA methodologies that we reported in [7].

Further, 7 SIMs explicitly aim at identifying *web services* without describing any of the types described above. That is why we regard web service as a special type, orthogonal to the others. Interestingly, nearly all of these SIMs (except for S1) rely on legacy systems.

Types of output format. Different SIMs also describe the identified services in multiple ways and in multiple levels of detail. Some SIMs describe their output in terms of a list of services with short descriptions; whereas some others illustrate their output in terms of a model describing the relation between services and sometimes with other artifacts of the system. To understand better the outputs of the SIMs, we analyzed the ways that the SIMs describe their identified services. As a result, five different ways of describing services have been identified, as summarized in Table 3.

Table 3. Ways of describing outputs produced by the SIMs

Output for-mat	Description	SIM	Total
Informal service specification	Specify the identified services with a list of terms, such as service description, input, output, etc	S22,S7,S21,S29,S6,S9, S11,S18,S19,S25,S28	11
Service model	Model the identified services in terms of diagrams, illustrating the service landscape	S3,S8,S10,S12,S13, S14,S16,S24	8
Formal service specification	Describe the identified services using standard language, such as WSDL	S2,S15,S20,S26	4
Service implementation	Implement the identified services	S4,S5,S27,S30	4
A list of services	List the identified services with several key elements, such as name, operation, etc)	S1,S17,S23	3

From Table 3 we can see that many identified services are described in *informal service specification*. However, different SIMs often use different terms for specifying the identified services. For instance, in S11 services are specified in detail using many terms including functional and non-function description, and technique-related aspects, such as operations and standards. In S6, however, services are specified only in terms of their operation and in/out messages. Some SIMs describe their output using only *a list of services*, without entering their details. While we do not enter the merit of one or the other approach, we observe that there is no unified way for describing services.

A *service model* is used by 8 SIMs, with the purpose of illustrating the relation between the identified services (e.g. S8) and the relation between services and their providers (e.g. S16). Thanks to its power of illustrating relations, a service model is extremely useful for describing composite services (CSs) and partner services (PSs). As shown in the overview of the SIMs (given in Table 7), only 5 (out of 12) SIMs identifying CSs, and 2 (out of 5) SIMs that identifying PSs use the form of a service model to describe the service landscape. In our opinion, a service model should be used more often as long as CSs and PSs are concerned.

Some other formats of output produced by the SIMs are implementation-driven. One of such formats is *formal service specification*, often used to describe services identified under more formal techniques (e.g. algorithms used by S15; another format is *service implementation*, often used when services as executable programs are created by wrapping source codes of legacy systems (e.g. S30).

2.4   R2.c What Types of Strategies and Techniques?

The previous two research questions (RQ2.a and b) mainly focus on *what* is involved in the SIMs. In this section we shall focus on *how* to carry out the SIMs. In this paper, we define *strategy* as the style, approach or plan for identifying services; we define *technique* as the technical procedures or actions taken to accomplish certain tasks defined in a SIM.

Strategies. Hubbers et. al [8] suggested ten common ways (or strategies) for identifying services. To find out if these ten ways are indeed used by the SIMs, we analyzed the data elicited from the primary studies and mapped all of the SIMs on at least one of these ways. We also identified one way (*W11*) that has not been discussed in [8]. All these ways and their use by SIMs are given in Table 4 (note that a SIM may use multiple strategies).

Table 4. Strategies used by the SIMs

Strategy	Description	SIM	Total
W1 (Business Process Decomposition)	Decompose business process models that depict how the work is done within an organization	S3,S7,S10,S12,,S15,S16, S17,S21,S23,S24,S25, S26,S30	13
W2 (Business Functions)	Decompose business function models that depict what an organization does	S1,S2,S8,S9,S11,S18, S19,S22,S28	9
W3 (Business Entity Objects)	Model services according to business object models	S6,S29,S21,S16	4
W4 (Ownership and Responsibility)	Take the ownership of processes into consideration when identifying services	S7,S11,S28	3
W5 (Goal driven)	Decompose a company's goals down to the level of services	S8,S14,S13,S22	4
W6 (Component-Based)	Identifies services based components	-	0
W7 (Existing Supply)	Identify services from the functionality provided by existing legacy applications	S2,S4,S5,S13,S20,S27, S30	7
W8 (Front-Office Application Usage Analysis)	Select a set of applications that support business processes and extracts comparable functions into a single service	-	0
W9 (Infrastructure)	keep the technical infrastructure into consideration when identifying services	-	0
W10 (NFRs)	Use non-functional requirements as the primary input to identify services	-	0
W11 (User interface)	**Identify services based on the design of user interface**	S15	1

Four strategies (*W6, 8, 9, 10*) are discussed in [8] but have not been used by any of the SIMs that we studied. As explained in [8], W6 has practical difficulties due to the different nature of component and services; W8 might be risky if existing application design is of low quality; and W9 results in services heavily coupled with infrastructure. Due to these issues, it is understandable that the SIMs avoid using these strategies. W10 points out the importance of non-functional requirements (NFRs) in SI as conflicting NRFs might cause redesign. As no SIM relies on W10, further research is required in supporting NFRs.

Interestingly, we also identified a new strategy, *W11 user interface* (not discussed in [8]). User interface (UI) design, an integral part of the software design process, is often considered out of scope of SOA design [9]. However, a UI design helps one to distinguish the purely presentation aspects from data and process aspects and hence aids the identification of services. The use of UI design in SI is regarded as an innovative approach.

Some SIMs use only one strategy (*W1, 2, 3 or 7*) and we call these strategies *primary strategies*; while the others are always used in combination with the primary strategies and we call them *complementary strategies*. The most popular primary strategies are *W1, 2 and 7*, used by 13, 9 and 7 SIMs respectively. The first two are top-down approaches by examining the business requirements while the last one represents a bottom-up approach by extracting valuable and/or reusable functions from existing applications. In most of the cases, the strategies used by a SIM are directly related to its input. E.g., all the SIMs that use *business process* as their input use *W1* (decompose business process) as its strategy, only S15 exceptionally uses a combination of *W4* and *W11*.

The complementary strategies are *W4, 5* and *W11* which are specifically aided by the information about goals, stakeholders and user interfaces. However, this information alone is often not sufficient for identifying services. For instance, in S15 user interfaces are first designed based on business process decomposition and then services are identified by extracting abstract WSDL specifications from user interface specifications. Obviously using *W11* (user interface) only is not sufficient in this example. The use of these complementary strategies often results in services more business-driven as explained in e.g. [10].

Techniques. After studying the data about the techniques used in the SIMs, we have identified six different types of techniques, summarized in Table 5.

Table 5. Techniques used by the SIMs

Technique	Description	SIM	Total
Algorithm	A formal approach to problem solving, such as heuristic or formalized rules	S1,S2,S3,S5,S8,S11, S15,S16,S17,S25,S26	11
Guidelines	A set of pre-defined regulations, such as criteria or policies; suggested but not codified	S7,S9,S10,S14, S28,S29,S30	7
Analysis	A process of studying, interpreting, reasoning and synthesizing data	S4,S12,S13,S18, S21,S22	6
Ontology	A technique to conceptually represent (domain) knowledge	S24,S23,S19,S27	4
Pattern	Defined as recurring solution to recurring problems	S6	1
Information manipulation	A text process techniques for identifying or eliciting useful information, such as information retrieval or textural similarity analysis	S20	1

Some of them are more formal, in the sense that they formally codify formulas or rules to specify the way that services are identified, such as *algorithm, ontology, pattern* and *information manipulation*. Nearly half of the SIMs use these formal techniques and thanks to the advantage of codification, some SIMs partially automate the SI process. For instance, in S17 a tool called SQUID was developed to automate the process of SI and in S2 executable algorithms are used to analyze the legacy code.

A less formal technique is *guidelines*, which is used by 7 SIMs as shown in Table 5. These SIMs provide advices like how to identify the right-grained services from goal-scenario models (S14) and how to map tasks in business process models to services (S30).

Different from these relatively formal techniques, *analysis* is a technique that is more abstract and requires its users to deeply understand the problem they face and make motivated decisions. Accordingly, the subjectivity of using the technique is relatively high and different actors may achieve different results by applying the same SIM.

3   An Input-Output Matrix for the Selection of SIMs

The variety in the types of inputs, outputs and processes discussed in Sec. 2 explains why practitioners often face difficulties to select a SIM that both fits their needs and copes with the available resources. To help compare and select among the SIMs, we use these results (summarized in Table 7) to created an input-output matrix. The matrix is presented in Table 6, where rows represent the types of outputs produced by the SIMs and columns represent the types of inputs being used. Each cell of the matrix describes a specific SIM (in terms of its output format, strategy and technique) if it uses the input and produces the output represented by the column and row respectively. For instance, a SIM that uses *Application domain* as its input (column 1) and produces *Business services as well as composite service (BS+CS)* (row 2) is S14, whose output is described in terms of a service model *(SM)*, uses *goal driven (W5)* as its strategy and *guidelines* as technique. In the following, we shall explain how this matrix aids the selection of SIMs in three different ways.

Selection driven by the targeted output. Sometimes, before performing the task of SI, it is expected that certain types of services are identified. For instance, an enterprise that focuses on improving the efficiency and maintainability of its business processes may be interested in business services; while an enterprise that intends to expose its business functions to other partners for business collaboration might be also interested in partner services. In our input-output matrix, the SIMs are classified horizontally, according to the types of services they produce. When the target types of services to be identified are decided, one can use the matrix to eliminate those SIMs that are irrelevant to the needs. Suppose partner services *(PS)* are of great importance, one can see from our matrix that five SIMs (row 8 to 12) could be selected. By determining more types of services to be identified (e.g. *DS*), one can further narrow down the number of candidate SIMs (e.g. S17 and S16 at row 10 and 12). Further, the matrix also provides a straightforward view on what types of inputs are needed if certain SIMs are selected. For example, we can see from the matrix that to identify partner services, either business processes or business centric entities *(data)* should be known. This helps one to judge the feasibility of the SIMs.

Selection driven by the available resources. Knowing what kinds of resources are available for SI, one can also choose a SIM based on its starting point. In the input-output matrix, the SIMs are classified vertically, according to the types of inputs they start with. Using the matrix, one can have an overview of what types of services can be produced given the available resources and at the same time find out the SIMs that support these resources. For instance, if the only available resource is a set of *use cases* (see Table 6 column 7) describing some business functions, one can find from our matrix that two SIMs, S11 and S28 (column 7, row 2) start SI from this resource. Accordingly, one can also expect that business services and their compositions *(BS+CS)* can be identified using either of these two SIMs.

Table 6. Input-output matrix of the SIMs

Out. \ In	1.Application domain	2.Business process	3.Legacy system	4.Mix	5.Data	6.Feature	7.Use case
1.BS		S23(List, W1, Onto)				S18(ISP, W2, Anal) / S19(ISP, W2, Onto)	
2.BS+CS	S14(SM, W5, Gline)	S12(SM, W1, Anal)					S11(ISP, W2-&4, Algo) / S28(ISP, W2-&4, Gline)
3.BS+DS+CS		S15(FSP, W1&11,Algo) / S25(ISP, W1, Algo)		S21(ISP, W1&3, Anal)			
4.BS+DS+IS	S9(ISP, W2, Gline) / S22(ISP, W2&5, Anal)	S24(SM, W1, Onto)					
5.BS+DS+IS+CS	S7(ISP, W1&4, Gline) / S8(SM, W2&5, Algo)			S13(SM, W5&7, Anal)			
6.BS+IS		S10(SM, W1, Gline)					
7.DS					S6(ISP, W3, Patt)		
8.PS+BS		S26(FSP, W1, Algo)					
9.PS+BS+CS					S29(ISP, W3, Gline)		
10.PS+BS+DS+IS+CS		S17(List, W1, Algo)					
11.PS+BS+IS		S3(SM, W1, Algo)					
12.PS+DS		S16(SM, W1&3, Algo)					
13.WS	S1(List, W2, Algo)		S4(SI, W7, Anal) / S5(SI, W7, Algo) / S20(FSP, W7, Infor) / S27(SI, W7, Onto)	S30(SI, W1&7, Gline) / S2(FSP, W2&7, Algo)			

Legenda: **Output format**: List - A list of services, ISP: Informal service specification, FSP - Formal service specification, SM - Service model, SI - Service implementation; **Technique**: Algo - Algorithm, Gline - Guideline, Onto - Ontology, Anal - Analysis, Patt - Pattern, Info - Information manipulation

Selection by comparison of alternative SIMs. Some SIMs can be seen as alternative methods when they share the same type of inputs and outputs. Despite of these commonalities, these methods often differ in the way that the outputs are described, and/or the strategy and technique they use. Using the input-output matrix, one can easily pinpoint and compare these alternative methods since they are grouped and located in the same cell of the matrix. For instance, given *legacy system* (column 3) as starting point and *web services* (row 13) as output, the matrix shows four SIMs: S4, S5, S20 and S27. Comparing these four SIMs in terms of their output formats, strategies and techniques, we can see that the main difference lies in the techniques they use. Therefore, one can choose among these four SIMs based on their preference of one technique over another, depending available technologies, competencies in place, etc. To give another example, given *application domain* (column 1) as starting point and *BS+DS+IS* (row 4) as output, our matrix shows two SIMs: S9 and S22. By comparing these two SIMs, it is also easy to see that S22 uses *W5* (*goal driven*) complementary to *W2* (*business functions*) as its strategy; and thereby an enterprise that have clearly defined business goals might opt to select S22 over S9. However, if the enterprise prefers to follow guidelines to provide relatively objective results than to perform analysis to produce relatively subjective results, it might select S9 over S22. As such, our matrix provides a way to preliminarily select alternative SIMs before more comprehensive comparison (if needed).

4   Conclusion

In this paper, we report the classification and comparison of 30 SIMs identified from a systematic literature review. The many different types of inputs, outputs and processes of the SIMs show a significant heterogeneity. Our results provide a holistic overview of the SIMs and highlight their differences. To help practitioners compare and select from these SIMs, we created an input-output matrix that aids the selection of SIMs in three different but complementary ways.

Further, the findings of this review outlines future research directions to further improve the existing SIMs and to guide the design of new SIMs. Our main observations are 1) *IT services* that leverage business processes and underlying IT infrastructure require more attention (Sec. 2.3); 2) Services for internal use and external consumption should be differentiated due to their different characteristics (Sec. 2.3); and 3) NFRs should be explicitly considered due to their importance through the entire service life cycle (Sec. 2.4).

References

1. Bieberstein, N., Bose, S., Fiammante, M., Jones, K., Shah, R.: Service-Oriented Architecture Compass: Business Value, Planning, and Enterprise Roadmap. Prentice-Hall, Englewood Cliffs (2005)
2. Erl, T.: Service-Oriented Architecture: Concepts, Technology, and Design. Prentice-Hall, Englewood Cliffs (2005)
3. Kohlborn, T., Korthaus, A., Chan, T., Rosemann, M.: Identification and analysis of business and software services—a consolidated approach. IEEE Transactions on Services Computing 2(1), 50–64 (2009)
4. Boerner, R., Goeken, M.: Service identification in SOA governance literature review and implications for a new method. In: Int. Conference on Digital Ecosystems and Technologies, pp. 588–593 (2009)
5. Kitchenham, B.: Guidelines for performing systematic literature reviews in software engineering (2007)
6. Gu, Q., Lago, P.: Exploring service-oriented system engineering challenges: A systematic literature review. SOCA 3(3), 171–188 (2009)
7. Gu, Q., Lago, P.: A service aspects driven evaluation framework for service-oriented development methodologies (under submission, 2010)
8. Hubbers, J., Ligthart, A., Terlouw, L.: Ten ways to identify services. The SOA Magazine (2007)

9. Mani, S., Sinha, V.S., Sukaviriya, N., Ramachandra, T.: Using user interface design to enhance service identification. In: Int. Conference on Web Services. IEEE, Los Alamitos (2008)
10. Klose, K., Knackstedt, R., Beverungen, D.: Identification of services - a stakeholder-based approach to SOA development and its application in the area of production planning. In: ECIS, pp. 1802–1814. University of St. Gallen (2007)
11. Jain, H.K., Zhao, H., Chinta, N.R.: A spanning tree based approach to identifying web services. Int. J. Web Service Res. 1(1), 1–20 (2004)
12. Zhang, Z., Yang, H.: Incubating services in legacy systems for architectural migration. In: Asia-Pacific Soft. Eng. Conf., pp. 196–203. IEEE CS, Los Alamitos (2004)
13. Wang, Z., Xu, X., Zhan, D.: Normal forms and normalized design method for business service. In: Int. Conference on e-Business Eng, pp. 79–86. IEEE CS, Los Alamitos (2005)
14. Chen, F., Li, S., Chu, W.C.C.: Feature analysis for service-oriented reengineering. In: Asia-Pacific Soft, pp. 201–208. IEEE Computer Society, Los Alamitos (2005)
15. Zhang, Z., Liu, R., Yang, H.: Service identification and packaging in service oriented reengineering. In: Int. Conference on Software Engineering and Knowledge Engineering, pp. 241–249 (2005)
16. Baghdadi, Y.: Reverse engineering relational databases to identify and specify basic web services with respect to service oriented computing. Information Systems Frontiers 8(5), 395–410 (2006)
17. Chaari, S., Biennier, F., Favrel, J., Benamar, C.: Towards a service-oriented enterprise based on business components identification. In: Enterprise Interoperability II, pp. 495–506 (2007)
18. Kohlmann, F., Alt, R.: Business-driven service modeling - a methodological approach from the finance industry. In: Int. Working Conference on Business Process and Services Computing (2007)
19. Inaganti, S., Behara, G.K.: Service identification: BPM and SOA handshake (2007)
20. Kim, Y., Doh, K.G.: The service modeling process based on use case refactoring. In: Abramowicz, W. (ed.) BIS 2007. LNCS, vol. 4439, pp. 108–120. Springer, Heidelberg (2007)
21. Amsden, J.: Modeling SOA: Part 1. service specification. IBM Dev. Works (2007)
22. Fareghzadeh, N.: Service identification approach to SOA development. World Academy of Science Engineering and Technology 35 (2008)
23. Kim, S., Kim, M., Park, S.: Service identification using goal and scenario in service oriented architecture. In: APSEC, pp. 419–426. IEEE, Los Alamitos (2008)
24. Jamshidi, P., Sharifi, M., Mansour, S.: To establish enterprise service model from enterprise business model. In: Int. Conf on Services Computing. IEEE, Los Alamitos (2008)
25. Dwivedi, V., Kulkarni, N.: A model driven service identification approach for process centric systems. In: Congress on Services, pp. 65–72. IEEE CS, Los Alamitos (2008)
26. Lee, J., Muthig, D., Naab, M.: An approach for developing service oriented product lines. In: Int. Software Product Line Conf., pp. 275–284. IEEE, Los Alamitos (2008)
27. Kang, D., Song, C.Y., Baik, D.K.: A method of service identification for product line. In: ICCIT, pp. 1040–1045. IEEE, Los Alamitos (2008)
28. Aversano, L., Cerulo, L., Palumbo, C.: Mining candidate web services from legacy code. In: Int. Symposium on Web Site Evolution, pp. 37–40 (2008)

29. Cho, M.J., Choi, H.R., Kim, H.S., Hong, S.G., Keceli, Y., Park, J.Y.: Service identification and modeling for service oriented architecture applications. In: Int. Conference on Software Engineering, Parallel and Distributed Systems, pp. 193–199. World Scientific and Engineering Academy and Society (2008)
30. Bianchini, D., Cappiello, C., De Antonellis, V., Pernici, B.: P2S: A methodology to enable inter-organizational process design through web services. In: van Eck, P., Gordijn, J., Wieringa, R. (eds.) CAiSE 2009. LNCS, vol. 5565, pp. 334–348. Springer, Heidelberg (2009)
31. Yousef, R., Odeh, M., Coward, D., Sharieh, A.: BPAOntoSOA: A generic framework to derive software service oriented models from business process architectures. In: ICADIWT, pp. 50–55 (2009)
32. Azevedo, L.G., Santoro, F., Baiao, F., Souza, J., Revoredo, K., Pereira, V., Herlain, I.: A Method for Service Identification from Business Process Models in a SOA Approach. In: Enterprise, Business-Process and Information Systems Modeling, pp. 99–112 (2009)
33. Kim, Y., Doh, K.G.: Formal identification of right-grained services for service-oriented modeling. In: Vossen, G., Long, D.D.E., Yu, J.X. (eds.) WISE 2009. LNCS, vol. 5802, pp. 261–273. Springer, Heidelberg (2009)
34. Chen, F., Zhang, Z., Li, J., Kang, J., Yang, H.: Service identification via ontology mapping. In: Int. Computer Software and Applications Conference. IEEE, Los Alamitos (2009)
35. Huayou, S., Yulin, N., Lian, Y., Zhong, C.: A service-oriented analysis and modeling using use case approach. In: Int. Conference on Computational Intelligence and Software Engineering, pp. 1–6 (2009)
36. Yun, Z., Huayou, S., Yulin, N., Hengnian, Q.: A service-oriented analysis and design approach based on data flow diagram. In: Int. Conference on Computational Intelligence and Software Engineering, pp. 1–5 (2009)
37. Ricca, F., Marchetto, A.: A "quick and dirty" meet-in-the-middle approach for migrating to SOA. In: ACM IWPSE-Evol. (2009)

Table 7. An overview of the existing SIMs (Appendix)

SIM	Year	Type of input	Strategy	Output format	Type of output	Technique	Validation
S1 [11]	2004	Application domain	W2	WS	A list of services	Algorithm	Evaluated
S2 [12]	2004	Mix	W2&7	WS	Formal service specification	Algorithm	Evaluated
S3 [13]	2005	Business process	W1	PS+BS+IS	Service model	Algorithm	No
S4 [14]	2005	Legacy system	W7	WS	Service implementation	Analysis	Case study
S5 [15]	2005	Legacy system	W7	WS	Service implementation	Algorithm	Case study
S6 [16]	2006	Data	W3	DS	Informal service specification	Pattern	No
S7 [10]	2007	Application domain	W1&4	BS+DS+IS-+CS	Informal service specification	Guidelines	Case study
S8 [17]	2007	Application domain	W2&5	BS+DS+IS-+CS	Service model	Algorithm	No
S9 [18]	2007	Application domain	W2	BS+DS+IS	Informal service specification	Guidelines	Project
S10 [19]	2007	Business process	W1	BS+IS	Service model	Guidelines	No
S11 [20]	2007	Use case	W2&4	BS+CS	Informal service specification	Algorithm	Example
S12 [21]	2007	Business process	W1	BS+CS	Service model	Analysis	Example
S13 [22]	2008	Mix	W5&7	BS+DS+IS-+CS	Service model	Analysis	Case study
S14 [23]	2008	Application domain	W5	BS+CS	Service model	guidelines	Case study
S15 [9]	2008	Business process	W1&11	BS+DS+CS	Service implementation	Algorithm	Case study
S16 [24]	2008	Business process	W1&3	PS+DS	Service model	Algorithm	Evaluated
S17 [25]	2008	Business process	W1	PS+BS+DS+-IS+CS	A list of services	Algorithm	Example
S18 [26]	2008	Feature	W2	BS	Informal service specification	Analysis	Case study
S19 [27]	2008	Feature	W2	BS	Informal service specification	Ontology	Case study
S20 [28]	2008	Legacy system	W7	WS	Service implementation	Information manipulation	Project
S21 [29]	2008	Mix	W1&3	BS+DS+CS	Informal service specification	Analysis	Example
S22 [3]	2009	Application domain	W2&5	BS+DS+IS	Informal service specification	Analysis	No
S23 [30]	2009	Business process	W1	BS	A list of services	Ontology	Case study
S24 [31]	2009	Business process	W1	BS+DS+IS	Service model	Ontology	Case study
S25 [32]	2009	Business process	W1	BS+DS+CS	Informal service specification	Algorithm	Case study
S26 [33]	2009	Business process	W1	PS+BS	Service implementation	Algorithm	Evaluated
S27 [34]	2009	Legacy system	W7	WS	Service implementation	Ontology	Case study
S28 [35]	2009	Use case	W2&4	BS+CS	Informal service specification	Guidelines	Example
S29 [36]	2009	Data	W3	PS+BS+CS	Informal service specification	Guidelines	Example
S30 [37]	2009	Mix	W1&7	WS	Service implementation	Guidelines	Case study

Self-adapting Applications Based on QA Requirements in the Cloud Using Market-Based Heuristics

Vivek Nallur and Rami Bahsoon

University of Birmingham,
Birmingham, B15 2TT, United Kingdom
{v.nallur,r.bahsoon}@cs.bham.ac.uk

Abstract. There are several situations where applications in the cloud need to self-manage their quality attributes (QA). We posit that self-adaptation can be achieved through a market-based approach and describe a marketplace for web-services. We simulate agents trading web-services on behalf of self-managing applications and demonstrate that such a mechanism leads to a good allocation of web-services to applications, even when applications dynamically change their QA requirements. We conclude with a discussion on evaluating this mechanism of self-adaptation, with regards to scalability in the cloud.

Keywords: self-adaptation, web-services, quality attributes, cloud.

1 Introduction

Many users experience a need to change the *quality attributes*(QA) exhibited by their application. By QA, we mean non-functional aspects of an application like performance, security etc. The need for change can occur due to dynamic changes in the users' requirements and the environment in which the system operates. An unexpected time constraint, for instance, can require an organization to increase the performance of its service provision. Governmental regulation can require an organization to want to increase the audit trail or the security level, whilst not changing the functionality of its application. Spikes and troughs in business demand can spur a change in storage and performance requirements. These examples (and requirements) are fairly commonplace, and yet mechanisms to achieve them are not very clear. It seems obvious (and desirable) that applications should adapt themselves to these changing requirements, specially QA requirements. Users find it difficult to understand, why a change that does not affect the functionality of an application, but merely its security requirements is difficult to achieve. However, in an arbitrary case, making an application adapt is a difficult process. It has to be architected in such a manner that adaptation is possible. This means that it should be able to:

1. Dynamically identify changed requirements, which will necessitate runtime adaptation;

E. Di Nitto and R. Yahyapour (Eds.): ServiceWave 2010, LNCS 6481, pp. 51–62, 2010.

2. Initiate the search for new services, which better address the changed requirements
3. Substitute old web-services for new web-services

In this paper, we look at the second of those three steps. Web-Service composition allows an application to switch one web-service for another, at runtime. However, searching for new services, even ones that are functionally the same but exhibit different QA levels, is a difficult process. This is exacerbated when the application is resident on a cloud and has a plethora of web-services to choose from. Applications can typically find web-services, based on their functionality, using WSDL and UDDI registries. However, the number of available web-services to chose from, is typically large, and the number of parameters on which to match, adds to the complexity of choosing. Most of the current research on dynamic web-service composition focuses on ascertaining the best match between the QA demanded by the application and the QA advertised by the services. The best match, however, is difficult if not impossible to find in a reasonable time, given the dynamic nature and scalability of the cloud. Given time constraints, our approach advocates getting a *good match*, as fast as possible. A good match is one where the chosen service meets the application's minimum QA requirements, but is not necessarily the best possible choice.

The problem can be illustrated in more detail by an example from the domain of rendering 3D graphics(section 3). In [9], we proposed using a self-adapting mechanism, viz *Market-Based Control* for finding a fast, valid solution. We propose that principles and tools of economics be used as a heuristic to explore the search space. This paper is structured as follows: we first review other approaches in self-adaptation (section 2), present a motivating example for our approach (section 3), propose the design of a market (section 4), and report on the scalability of the approach. We conclude by highlighting the strengths and weaknesses of our approach (section 5) and discuss mechanisms that could improve it further.

2   Related Work

There have been a plethora of attempts at creating self-managing architectures. These attempts can be classified as approaching the problem from the following perspectives:

- Map system to ADL, dynamically change ADL, check for constraints, transform ADL to executable code [6].
- Create a framework for specifying types of adaptation possible using constraints and tactics thus ensuring 'good adaptation' [4].
- Using formalized methods like SAM [12], middleware optimizations [11] and control theory [8]

However, all of these approaches envision a closed-loop system. That is, all of them assume that

1. The entire state of the application and the resources available for adaptation are known/visible to the management component.
2. The adaptation ordered by the management component is carried out in full, never pre-empted or disobeyed.
3. The management component gets full feedback on the entire system.

However, in the context of the cloud, with applications being composed of services resident on several (possibly different) clouds, the assumptions above do not hold true. It is unreasonable to expect that third-party services would obey adaption commands, given by an application's self-management component. Therefore, instead of making third-party services adapt, self-adaptive applications simply choose services, that meet their changed requirements. That is, they substitute old services providing a given QA, with new ones providing better-matched QA. *Zeng et al.* [14] were amongst the first to look at non-functional attributes while composing web-services. They proposed a middleware-based approach where candidate execution plans of a service-based application are evaluated and the optimal one is chosen. The number of execution plans increase exponentially with the number of candidate services and linear programming is used to select an optimal plan. *Anselmi et al.* [1] use a mixed integer programming approach to look at varying QA profiles and long-lived processes. Increasing the number of candidate services however means an exponential increase in search time, due to the inherent nature of linear programming. *Canfora et al.* [3] have used genetic algorithms to replan composite services dynamically and also introduce the idea of a separate triggering algorithm to detect the need for re-planning. While much better than the time taken for an exact solution, GAs are still not scalable enough to deal with hundreds or thousands of services in real-time. *Yu et al.* [13] propose heuristics to come up with inexact, yet good, solutions. They propose two approaches to service composition, a combinatorial model and a graph model. The heuristic for the graph model (MSCP-K) is exponential in its complexity, while the one for the combinatorial model (WS_HEU) is polynomial.

The main difference between our approach and these algorithms, lies in the context of the problem that is being solved. We are looking at the **simultaneous adaptation** of hundreds of applications in the cloud, whereas the research above looks at optimal selection of web-services for a single application. The cloud, by definition, offers elasticity of resources and immense scale. Any solution for the cloud therefore, needs to dynamic and fast, and not necessarily optimal. Adaptation also emphasizes timeliness and constraint satisfaction, which is easier to achieve using decentralized approaches. Most middleware type approaches (as outlined above) are centralized in nature. A marketplace, on the other hand, is a decentralized solution, which adapts quickly to changes in conditions. A double auction is known to be highly allocation-efficent [7], thus meeting the criteria of timeliness and goodness of adaptation within constraints. Also, the market-based approach is resilient to failures of individual traders or even marketplaces. In the event of one marketplace failing, the buyers and sellers simply move to another market.

3   Rendering 3D Graphics

Consider a company that specializes in providing 3D rendering services. To save on capital expenditure, it creates an application that lives on the cloud and uses web-services to do the actual computation. This allows it to scale up and scale down the number of computational nodes, depending on the size of the job. However as business improves, the company implements a mechanism for automated submission of jobs, with differentiated rates for jobs with different priorities, requirements and even algorithms. For instance, a particular job may require texture and fluid modelling with a deadline of 30 hours, while another might require hair modelling with a tighter deadline of 6 hours. Yet another job might require ray-tracing with a deadline of 20 hours. Also, any of these jobs might have dynamically changing deadlines. This means that the application would need to change its *performance QA* dynamically. Depending on the kind of data and algorithm being used, the application's storage requirements would change as well. For certain tasks, the application might require large amounts of slow but reliable storage, while others might require smaller amounts of higher-speed storage. This company would like to create an application, that self-managed its QA, depending on the business input that was provided, on a per-task basis. Each of these self-management decisions are constrained by the cost of change. Now consider a multiplicity of such companies, each with several such applications, present on a cloud that provides web-services for computation, storage as well as implementations of sophisticated graphics algorithms. Each of the providing web-services have differing levels of QA as well as differing prices. Matching a dynamically changing list of buyers and sellers, each with their own QA levels and prices, is an important and difficult task for a cloud provider. It is important because, if a large number of buyers do not get the QA levels they desire, within their budget, they will leave for other clouds that **do** provide a better matching mechanism. It is also difficult because the optimal assignment at one time instance could be different from the optimal assignment at the next time instance. *Aradgna et al.* have shown in [2] that assignment of web-services when QA levels are static is equivalent to a Multiple-Choice Multi-Dimensional Knapsack Problem, which is NP-hard. Thus, the problem of assignment, when QA levels change dynamically, is also NP-hard. We contend therefore, that cloud implementations should provide a mechanism that solves this problem. Ideally it should be a self-managing approach that accounts for changes in operating environment and user preferences.

4   Description of Market

We describe a marketplace where multiple applications try to self-manage, in order to dynamically achieve their targetted QA. Each application has a private utility function with regard to certain fixed QAs. From utility theory, we use a von Neumann-Morgenstern utility function [10], that maps a QA(ω) to a real number, $u_\omega : X_\omega \longrightarrow \mathbb{R}$, which is normalized to $[0, 1]$. Each application is composed of several services that contribute to the QA of the application. In the marketplace, each of these services is bought and sold by a trading agent. The agents trading on behalf of the application (the buyers) do not know the application's private utility function and attempt to approximate it. The only information that flows from the application to the agents, upon the completion of a trade, is a penalty or a reward. This enables the agent to work out two pieces of information: the direction it should go and the magnitude of that change. Although this meagre information flow makes the task of approximation harder, we think that it is more realistic since application architects would concentrate on creating the right composition of web-service functionality while third-party trading agents would concentrate on buying in the marketplace. There is no overriding need for trust amongst these two entities. In the motivating example above, the application for rendering graphics would be buying services that provide CPU, storage and algorithmic functionality. Each of these three services would be managed by a buying agent, that monitors the required QA, assesses the available resources and trades in the market. Enterprises that sell CPU time, storage space and implementations of graphics algorithms would be the selling agents in their respective markets. The market is a virtual auction house, created in a cloud, to whom the buyers and sellers would submit their trading requests.

We populate several markets with buying agents and selling agents. Each market describes a certain service class (s_x). A service class (s_x) contains services that are fundamentally identical in terms of functionality. The only differentiating factor, amongst the various services in a class, are the QA that each one exhibits. Thus, storage services belong to one service class, while services offering CPU time would belong to another service class, and so on. All the buying and selling agents in this market, trade services that deliver s_x, where $s_x \in S_x$. The number of markets is at least equal to $\mid S \mid$, with each market selling a distinct s_x. In other words, we assume that there exists a market for every s_x, that is needed by an application.

Buyer. The Buyer is a trading agent that buys a service for an Application, *i.e.*, it trades in a market for a specific service class s_x. Each service, available in s_x, exhibits the same QAs ($\omega \in QA$). Hence, if an application has K QAs that it is concerned about, then the QAs that it gets for each of the S_x that it buys is:

$$\Omega^{S_x} = \langle \omega_1^{s_x}, \omega_2^{s_x}, \omega_3^{s_x}, \ldots, \omega_K^{s_x} \rangle \tag{1}$$

The amount that the buyer is prepared to pay is called the *bid price* and this is necessarily *less than or equal to* the B_{s_x}, where B_{s_x} is the budget available with the buyer. The combination of Ω demanded and the *bid price* is called a *Bid*.

In its attempt to reach the Application's QA requirement, the Buyer uses a combination of *explore* and *exploit* strategies. When trading begins, the Buyer randomly chooses an Ω (explore) and *bid price*. Based on whether it trades successfully and how close its guess was to the private QA, the Application provides with feedback in the form of how close the buyer is, to the private QA. Based on this feedback, the Buyer either continues with the previously used

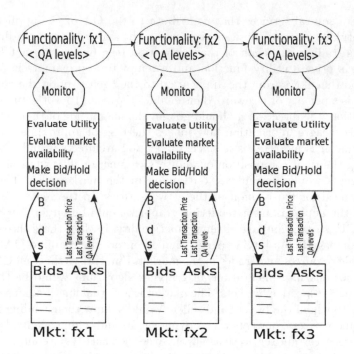

Fig. 1. Decentralized MAPE Loop; each service, in the application, self-adapts

strategy (exploit) with slight changes in price or changes strategies (explore). The trading strategy is essentially a combination of reinforcement learning and ZIP [5]. We expect the simultaneous use of this, by large number of traders, to result in an efficient search for a good assignment.

Seller. Each seller is a trading agent, selling a web-service that exhibits the QA required in (1). The degree to which each $QA(\omega)$ is exhibited in each s_x being sold, is dependent on the technological and economic cost of providing it. Hence, if the cost of providing s_x with $\Omega = \langle 0.5, 0.6 \rangle$ is low, then there will be many sellers providing s_x with a low *ask price*. Conversely, if the cost of providing s_x with $\Omega = \langle 0.8, 0.9 \rangle$ is high, then the *ask price* will be high. An individual seller's *ask price* can be higher or lower based on other factors like number of sellers in the market, the selling strategy etc., but we mandate that the *ask price* is always *greater than or equal to* the cost. The combination of Ω and *ask price* is called the *Ask*. The obvious question that arises, is that of truth-telling by Seller. That is, how does the buyer know that the Seller is not mis-representing the Ω of her web-service? We currently assume that a Seller does tell the truth about Ω of her web-service and that a Market has mechanisms to penalize Sellers that do not.

Market. A market is a set of buyers and sellers, all interested in the same service class s_x. The factor differentiating the traders are:

- Ω: The combination of $\langle \omega_1, \omega_2, \ldots \omega k \rangle$
- **Price:** Refers to the *bid price* and *ask price*. The buyers will not pay more than their respective *bid price* and the sellers will not accept a transaction lower than their respective *ask price*.

The mechanism of finding a matching buyer-and-seller is the *continuous double auction*(CDA). A CDA works by accepting offers from both buyers and sellers. It maintains an orderbook containing both, the *bids* from the buyers and the *asks* from the sellers. The bids are held in descending order of price, while the asks are held in ascending order, *i.e.*, buyers willing to pay a high price and sellers willing to accept a lower price are more likely to trade. When a new *bid* comes in, the offer is evaluated against all the existing *asks* in the book and a transaction is conducted when the price demanded by the *ask* is lower than the price the *bid* is willing to pay **and** all the QA attributes in Ω of the ask are *greater than or equal to* all the QA attributes in the Ω of the *bid*. Thus, a transaction always meets a buyer's minimum QA constraints. Each transaction generates a corresponding *Service Level Agreement*(SLA), which sets out the QA levels that will be available for x invocations of a particular web-service. After a transaction, the corresponding *bid* and *ask* are cleared from the orderbook. Since this procedure is carried out for every offer (*bid/ask*) that enters the market, the only bids and asks that remain on the orderbook are those that haven't been matched. It has been shown that even when buyers and sellers have Zero-Intelligence, the structure of the market allows for a high degree of allocative efficiency [7]. A market is said to be allocatively efficient, if it produces an optimal allocation of resources. That is, in our case, the optimum assignment of sellers to buyers, based on multiple criteria of QA and price. Obviously, the market is not guaranteed to produce a completely efficient allocation, but even a high degree of efficiency is acceptable to us.

Applications. The Application is a composition of buyers from different markets. In our example, it would be the agent performing the orchestration of the CPU service, the storage service and the graphics service. An application is composed of at most $| (S_x) |$ buyers with a privately known Ω_{s_x} for each buyer. The buyer gets a certain budget (B_{s_x}) from the Application for each round of trading. The total amount of budget B represents the application's global constraint on resources available for adaptation. After each round of trading, depending on the Ω obtained by the buyer, the Application has procured a total QA that is given by:

$$\forall s_x \in S_x, \sum \Omega^{s_x} \tag{2}$$

Buying and using a web-service involves many costs, and these must be compared against the projected utility gain to decide whether it is worthwhile to switch. These may be enumerated as:

- *Buying Cost:* The price of purchasing the web-service for n calls (p_{s_x})
- *Transaction Cost:* The amount to be paid to the market, for making the transaction (t_{s_x})

– *Switching Cost:* The amount of penalty to be paid, for breaking the contract with the current web-service (sw_{s_x})

Thus, the total cost that the application must consider is:

$$TC_{s_x} = p_{s_x} + t_{s_x} + s_{s_x} \tag{3}$$

We assume that, for every application there exists a function that maps TC_{s_x} to an equivalent Ω^{s_x}. The application could easily buy the best possible web-service(s) available, if it was prepared to spend an infinite amount of money. However, in reality, every application is constrained by a budget(B) that it is willing to spend. Allocating M amongst the functionalities that it is buying ($s_x \in F_x$) is a matter of strategy and/or the relative importance of each s_x.

$$\forall s_x \in S_x, \sum B_{s_x} = M \tag{4}$$

After every round, the application compares the privately known Ω_{s_x} with the $\Omega^b_{s_x}$ and determines whether to punish/reward the buyer. From this piece of information, the buyer can only guess whether it needs to improve the $\Omega^b_{s_x}$ that it obtained or the price that it paid. Once the $\Omega^b_{s_x}$ is close enough to the private Ω_{s_x}, then the application refrains from trading any further, until it changes the privately known Ω_{s_x}. Changing of the private Ω_{s_x} simulates the change in the environment, which has prompted adaptation by the application. The buyers have to now re-approximate the private Ω_{s_x}.

Trigger for Adaptation. There are two possible scenarios for adaptation, continuous and criteria-based. In *continuous* adaptation, the application never really leaves the market, even after the Buyer agents have successfully fulfilled its QA requirement. It continues to employ Buyer agents in the hope that the buyer agent might procure a web-service with comparable QA, but at a lower cost. In *criteria-based* adaptation, a separate monitoring agent watches the Application's utility function as well as its budget. Any change in these, beyond a threshold, would trigger the monitoring agent to re-employ Buyer agents. This scenario also allows a human to enter the adaptation loop, by manually triggering the Buyer agents. We opted to simulate the continuous adaptation scenario, since we're interested in observing a long-lived, large system where human intervention might not be possible.

5   Evaluation

We intend to find out whether an application, following rules outlined above, could achieve the overall QA that it expects from its constituent web-services, keeping in mind the fact that the buying agents responsible for the individual services, are not aware of the QA levels expected by the application. They merely attempt to approximate it, based on the feedback given by the application. The evaluation of the market-based approach is particularly hard, since it is a probabilistic approach. After every trading round, the *bid price* and *ask price* of every buyer and seller changes. This changes the optimal assignment, for every trading round. Hence, we do not consider whether the mechanism achieves optimal assignment, rather only whether it results in achievement of the Application's QA levels. In our simulation, each application composes 5 web-services to function. For each of these web-services, it has a private, different QA expectation. At the end of each trading round, the application examines the QA achieved by each buying agent. For each agent, it compares the private QA level with the achieved QA level, using a cosine similarity function. The cosine similarity compares two vectors for similarity and returns a result between 0 and 1(1 denoting an exact match). The combined similarity score is reflective of the degree to which the application's QA needs were satisfied. The theoretical maximum score, it could ever achieve with 5 web-services, is therefore 5.0.

5.1   Adaptation Level

The following graphs show simulations under three different market conditions. All values are the mean value of 30 simulations, each simulation consisting of 300 rounds of trading. The band (shaded area) around the line are the standard deviations. The line marked as 'ideal score'represents the theoretical maximum level of QA that the Application privately wants to have. The QA values for various services in the market were generated from a gaussian distribution. All simulations were done a dual-core P4 class machine with 2GB of RAM.

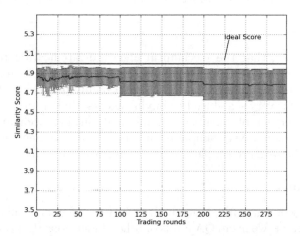

Fig. 2. Self-adaptation in the presence of equal demand and supply

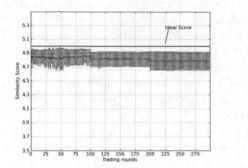 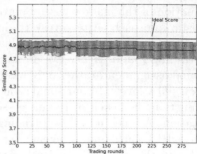

The figure above shows markets with excess supply (left) and excess demand (right). Notice that in the figure with extra demand (right), the line showing the self-adaptation squiggles around for slightly longer than the other two figures (left and above). But, this is in line with intuition, where, the application finds it more difficult to get the QA that it demands, since there are a lot of buyers in the market demanding the same QA. It is interesting to note that even with simple agents, the application, as a whole, is able to reach very close to its ideal level of QA.

5.2   Scaling

One of the central themes of this paper has been scaling to the level of the cloud, which might contain hundreds or even thousands of services. We ran our simulations with increasing number of service candidates (in each market), and we found that the auction mechanism scales gracefully(Fig.3). As the number of service candidates (the number of buyers and sellers) increases from 100 to 1600, the time taken to reach an assignment rises in a near-linear fashion.

5.3   Strengths

We see in all cases, that the mechanism allows an application to reach very close to its desired level of QA. The nature of the mechanism is that it is highly distributed and asynchronous. This allows for a highly parallelizable implementation, and hence is very scalable. The buying agents, that trade on behalf of the application, are very simple agents with a minimal learning mechanism. Also, the concept of an auction is very simple to understand and implement. All the entities in the mechanism are simple and it is their interaction that makes it richer.

5.4   Limitation

Our implementation currently does not allow for more than one global constraint. By global constraint, we mean QA levels or other dimensions that the application has to meet, as a whole. Since, each market addresses one service class only, the QA constraints for each individual service are met. However, the collective QA generated by the composition of services is not subjected to any constraint, other than price. This, however, is a limitation of our current implementation, and not

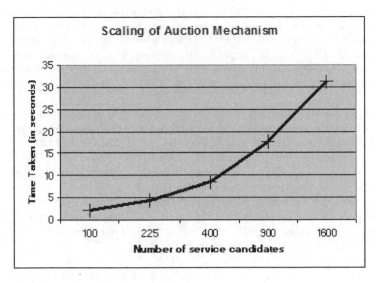

Fig. 3. Time taken by auction mechanism to perform matching

of the approach. It is easy to envision a more complex Application entity that tests web-services, for their contribution to the total utility, before accepting it for a longer term contract.

The market-based approach does not currently reason about the time taken for adaptation. In cases where the timeliness of adaptation is more important than the optimality of adaptation, this could be an issue.

6   Conclusion and Future Work

We consider that the Market-based approach to self-adaptation is a promising one. Since the entities in the market are inherently distributed and asynchronous, the market-based approach lends itself to highly parallelizable implementations. However more formal work needs to be done to prove its scalability. There is little literature on assessing the quality of a self-managing architecture. As future work, we will be looking at measures to assess the quality of the solution found by the Market-based approach as compared to other search based approaches. We aim to complement our approach with sensitivity analysis, where we analyze the impact of changing individual QA of a given service, on the entire application's utility.

References

1. Anselmi, J., Ardagna, D., Cremonesi, P.: A qos-based selection approach of autonomic grid services. In: Proceedings of the 2007 Workshop on Service-Oriented Computing Performance: Aspects, Issues, and Approaches, SOCP 2007, pp. 1–8. ACM, New York (2007), http://doi.acm.org/10.1145/1272457.1272458

2. Ardagna, D., Pernici, B.: Global and local qos constraints guarantee in web service selection. In: ICWS 2005: Proceedings of the IEEE International Conference on Web Services, pp. 805–806. IEEE Computer Society, Washington (2005)
3. Canfora, G., Di Penta, M., Esposito, R., Villani, M.L.: Qos-aware replanning of composite web services. In: ICWS 2005: Proceedings of the IEEE International Conference on Web Services, pp. 121–129. IEEE Computer Society, Washington (2005)
4. Cheng, S., Garlan, D., Schmerl, B.: Architecture-based self-adaptation in the presence of multiple objectives. In: Proceedings of the 2006 International Workshop on Self-Adaptation and Self-Managing Systems. ACM, Shanghai (2006), http://dx.doi.org/10.1145/1137677.1137679
5. Cliff, D., Bruten, J.: Less than human: Simple adaptive trading agents for cda markets. Tech. rep., Hewlett-Packard (1997), http://www.hpl.hp.com/agents/papers/less_than_human.pdf
6. Dashofy, E.M., van der Hoek, A., Taylor, R.N.: Towards architecture-based self-healing systems. In: WOSS 2002: Proceedings of the First Workshop on Self-Healing Systems, pp. 21–26. ACM Press, New York (2002), http://dx.doi.org/10.1145/582128.582133
7. Gode, D.K., Sunder, S.: Allocative efficiency of markets with zero-intelligence traders: Market as a partial substitute for individual rationality. The Journal of Political Economy 101(1), 119–137 (1993), http://www.jstor.org/stable/2138676
8. Hellerstein, J.: Engineering Self-Organizing Systems, p. 1 (2007), http://dx.doi.org/10.1007/978-3-540-74917-2_1
9. Nallur, V., Bahsoon, R., Yao, X.: Self-optimizing architecture for ensuring quality attributes in the cloud. In: Proceedings of the 7th Working IEEE/IFIP Conference on Software Architecture (WICSA 2009), Cambridge, UK, September 14-17 (2009)
10. von Neumann, J., Morgenstern, O.: Theory of Games and Economic Behavior, 3rd edn. Princeton University Press, Princeton (January 1953)
11. Trofin, M., Murphy, J.: A Self-Optimizing container design for enterprise java beans applications. In: Proceedings of the Second International Workshop on Dynamic Analysis, WODA 2004 (2003), http://citeseerx.ist.psu.edu/viewdoc/summary, doi=10.1.1.59.2979
12. Wang, J., Guo, C., Liu, F.: Self-healing based software architecture modeling and analysis through a case study. In: Proceedings of IEEE on Networking, Sensing and Control, pp. 873–877 (2005), http://dx.doi.org/10.1109/ICNSC.2005.1461307
13. Yu, T., Zhang, Y., Lin, K.J.: Efficient algorithms for web services selection with end-to-end qos constraints. ACM Trans. Web. 1(1), 6 (2007)
14. Zeng, L., Benatallah, B., Ngu, A.H.H., Dumas, M., Kalagnanam, J., Chang, H.: Qos-aware middleware for web services composition. IEEE Trans. Softw. Eng. 30(5), 311–327 (2004)

Enabling Proactive Adaptation through Just-in-Time Testing of Conversational Services

Dimitris Dranidis[1], Andreas Metzger[2], and Dimitrios Kourtesis[1]

[1] South East European Research Centre (SEERC)
Research Centre of the University of Sheffield and CITY College
Thessaloniki, Greece
dranidis@city.academic.gr, dkourtesis@seerc.org
[2] Paluno (The Ruhr Institute for Software Technology)
University of Duisburg-Essen, Essen, Germany
andreas.metzger@sse.uni-due.de

Abstract. Service-based applications (SBAs) will increasingly be composed of third-party services available over the Internet. Reacting to failures of those third-party services by dynamically adapting the SBAs will become a key enabler for ensuring reliability. Determining when to adapt an SBA is especially challenging in the presence of conversational (aka. stateful) services. A conversational service might fail in the middle of an invocation sequence, in which case adapting the SBA might be costly; e.g., due to the necessary state transfer to an alternative service. In this paper we propose just-in-time testing of conversational services as a novel approach to detect potential problems and to proactively trigger adaptations, thereby preventing costly compensation activities. The approach is based on a framework for online testing and a formal test-generation method which guarantees functional correctness for conversational services. The applicability of the approach is discussed with respect to its underlying assumptions and its performance. The benefits of the approach are demonstrated using a realistic example.

Keywords: service testing, online testing, stateful services, test generation, proactive adaptation.

1 Introduction

Service-based applications (SBAs) are increasingly composed of third party services available over the Internet [22]. Third party services are owned and controlled by organizations different from the service consumers and thus can change or evolve in ways not anticipated by the service consumer. This means that even if third-party services have shown to work during design-time, they need to be (re-)checked during the operation of the SBA to detect failures. Such failures then should trigger the adaptation of an SBA to ensure that it maintains its expected functionality and quality.

E. Di Nitto and R. Yahyapour (Eds.): ServiceWave 2010, LNCS 6481, pp. 63–75, 2010.
© Springer-Verlag Berlin Heidelberg 2010

1.1   Problem Statement

Determining when to trigger an adaptation is especially challenging if conversational services are employed in a service composition. A conversational service is one that only accepts specific sequences of operation invocations. This is because some operations may have preconditions which depend on the state of the service. The set of all acceptable invocation sequences is called the *protocol* (or choreography) [10] of the service. An example is the shopping basket of an online store. The shopping basket is initialized first. Then, some items are added to the basket, some might be removed, until a checkout is performed.

The first invocation of a conversational service can work as expected. However, the invocation of that service at a later stage of the interaction sequence could fail due to the service not conforming to the expected protocol. Adapting the SBA to react to such a failure could be very costly: First, the state of the conversational service (e.g., the items in the shopping basket) might need to be transferred to an alternative service. Second, compensation actions might need to be initiated (e.g., if the items have been marked as reserved in a warehouse service, those reservations need to be revoked).

1.2   Contributions of the Paper

This paper introduces an automated technique to determine when to proactively trigger adaptations in the presence of conversational services, thus avoiding costly compensation actions. The proposed technique builds on previous work on testing and monitoring of conversational services [9,10] and on online testing for proactive adaptation [13,19].

We advocate performing *just-in-time* online tests of the relevant operation sequences of the constituent services of the SBA. Here, just-in-time means that "shortly" before a conversational service is invoked for the first time within the service composition, the service is tested to detect potential deviations from the specified protocol.

The generation of the test cases is grounded in the formal theory of Stream X-machines (SXMs). SXMs have been utilised [9] for the automated generation of test cases, which, under well defined conditions, guarantee to reveal all inconsistencies among the implementation of a service and its expected behaviour.

To ensure that just-in-time testing can be done with feasible cost and effort, as well as in reasonable time, we propose a new way of reducing the number of test cases, such that we can still guarantee that the conversational service behaves as expected in the context of the concrete SBA. In addition, we propose executing most of the "costly" test preparation activities during deployment time.

The remainder of the paper is structured as follows. In Sect. 2, we discuss related work. Sect. 3 introduces a running example to illustrate our technique for just-in-time online testing. Sect. 4 provides an introduction to the formal underpinnings as well as the available tool support. Based on these foundations, Sect. 5 describes our technique, which is then critically discussed in Sect. 6, focusing on its applicability in realistic settings.

2   Related Work

Various approaches have been introduced in the literature to determine when to trigger the adaptation of SBAs. Typically, in such a setting, monitoring is used to identify failures of the constituent services (see [2] for a comprehensive survey) by observing SBAs during their actual use and operation [5]. However, monitoring only allows for a reactive approach to adaptation (cf. [13]), i.e., the application is modified *after* a failure has been monitored. To support pro-active adaptation, prediction of the future functionality and quality of the SBA is needed. Initial solutions are available for predicting the violation of SLAs (e.g., [18]). However, the focus of that work is on quality attributes and not on protocol conformance.

In our previous work, we have introduced online testing as an approach to predict the future quality of the SBA and thus to trigger pro-active adaptation [13,19]. Online testing means that the constituent services of an SBA are systematically fed with test inputs in parallel to the normal use and operation of the SBA. Although our approach [19]—different from other uses of online testing (cf. [23,6,3,1])—has shown how to employ online testing for triggering pro-active adaptation, it has only focused on stateless services and violations of quality contracts (such as performance). Thus, those techniques, are not yet capable of addressing the challenges introduced by predicting whether conversational services will violate their functional contracts in the context of an SBA.

Our proposed online testing approach also differs from existing testing and monitoring techniques for services (see [20] for a comprehensive survey). Those techniques only perform tests before or during deployment, whereas after deployment, they resort to monitoring to assess the quality (e.g., see [12] where an approach for protocol testing and monitoring of services is introduced).

3   The e-Shop Example

The example presented in this paper concerns an e-Shop SBA which is composed of three services: CartService, ShipmentService and PaymentService. Clients select the items they wish to purchase, then provide the shipment details, and finally pay. The composition has the following workflow (i.e., main flow of service invocations):

- An order is created by adding items to the order via the CartService.
- Using the ShipmentService, a shipment is created given the origin, destination, date and weight of the order; the shipment rate is calculated based on delivery type.
- The customer is charged the total cost by the PaymentService.

There are many alternative third-party services which could provide the ShipmentService, such as UPS, FedEx, and DHL. There are also alternative third-party services which could provide the PaymentService, such as Paypal, and VISA payment. Therefore, we consider this composition as a realistic example for demonstrating our approach for just-in-time testing for proactive adaptation.

Table 1. The interface of the ShipmentService

Operations	Inputs	Outputs
create	origin, destination, shipmentDate, weight	-
getShipmentRate	shipmentType	rate
oneStepShipment	shipmentType	-
cancel	-	-
confirm	-	-
getConfirmedRate	-	rate

Since we will use the ShipmentService as an example for how to perform just-in-time online testing, we describe that service and its operations in more detail. Table 1 lists the complete interface of the service.

The ShipmentService is initiated by calling the `create` operation with the origin and the destination of the delivery, the date of the shipment and the total weight of the package as arguments. The shipment cost is calculated for different types of delivery (e.g. normal or express) via the `getShipmentRate` operation. The `confirm` operation finalizes the shipment. Once confirmed, the operation `getConfirmedRate` is used instead of the `getShipmentRate` operation for getting informed about the cost of the shipment. The shipment can be canceled with the `cancel` operation, unless it has been confirmed. The ShipmentService provides also the `oneStepShipment` operation, which does not expect a confirmation from the client.

The ShipmentService is a typical example of a conversational service in which only specific sequences of operation invocations (protocol) are allowed. The following restrictions specify the protocol:

- initially no operation can be called except the `create` operation;
- `confirm` can only be called after at least one `getShipmentRate` call;
- `getShipmentRate` can be called many times to get different rates for different types of delivery but not after `confirm` or `oneStepShipment`;
- `getConfirmedRate` can only be called after `confirm` or `oneStepShipment`;
- `cancel` cannot be called after `confirm`, nor after `oneStepShipment`;
- no operation can be called after `cancel`.

4   Fundamentals

4.1   Stream X-Machines

A Stream X-Machine (SXM) [17,14] is a computational model capable of modeling both the data and the control of a system. An SXM is like a finite state machines but with two important differences: (a) the machine has some internal store, called *memory*; and (b) the transition labels are not simple symbols, but *processing functions* that represent elementary operations that the machine can perform. A processing function reads inputs and produces outputs while it may also change the value of the memory.

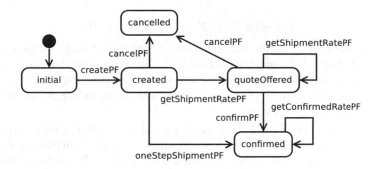

Fig. 1. State transition diagram of the conversational interface of ShipmentService

An *SXM* [14] is defined as the tuple $(\Sigma, \Gamma, Q, M, \Phi, F, q_0, m_0)$ where:

- Σ is the finite *input alphabet* and Γ is the finite *output alphabet*;
- Q is the finite set of *states*;
- M is a (possibly) infinite set called *memory*;
- Φ is a finite set of partial functions ϕ (called *processing functions*) that map input-memory pairs to output-memory pairs, $\phi : \Sigma \times M \to \Gamma \times M$;
- F is the next state partial function that given a state and a processing function it provides the next state, $F : Q \times \Phi \to Q$;
- q_0 and m_0 are the *initial state* and *initial memory* respectively.

Parallels can be drawn between an SXM and a stateful Web service: SXM inputs correspond to SOAP request messages, outputs correspond to SOAP response messages, and processing functions correspond to Web service operation invocations [10,9].

Example. The conversational behavior of the ShipmentService (see Sect. 3) can be modelled with an SXM. The diagram in Fig. 1 shows the state transition diagram of the SXM (i.e., the next state function F). Each processing function (e.g., cancelPF) is triggered by the corresponding operation (e.g., `cancel`). The memory of the SXM consists of a single numeric variable: the cost of the shipment.

4.2 Test Case Generation

SXMs have the significant advantage of offering a testing method [16,15,14] that ensures the conformance of an implementation under test (IUT) to a specification. The production of a finite test set is based on a generalization of the W-method [4]. It is proved that only if the specification and the IUT are behaviorally equivalent, the test set produces identical results when applied to both of them. The testing method rests on certain assumptions and conditions which will be explained and discussed in Sect. 6.

The first step of the method consists of applying the W-method on the associated finite automaton $A = (\Phi, Q, F, q_0)$ of the SXM and produces a set $X \subseteq \Phi^*$ of sequences of processing functions:

$$X = S\left(\Phi^{k+1} \cup \Phi^k \cup \ldots \cup \Phi \cup \{\epsilon\}\right) W$$

where W is a *characterization set* and S a *state cover* of A and k is the estimated difference of states between the IUT and the specification. A characterization set is a set of sequences for which any two distinct states of the automaton are distinguishable and a state cover is a set of sequences such that all states are reachable from the initial state.

Finally, the test set $T \subseteq \Sigma^*$ is constructed by converting each sequence of processing functions in X to a sequence of inputs. For this purpose, appropriate input data sequences need to be generated, that trigger the corresponding processing function sequences. The input sequences and the corresponding output sequences produced by the model animation (the model acts as an oracle) provide the test cases that guarantee the equivalence of the IUT to the specification.

Due to space limitations, more information about the test generation method, its application on the specific example, and the generated test cases can be found online at [11].

4.3   Tool Support

A tool suite for the specification of SXMs and automated test case generation [8] is available in Java (JSXM). The JSXM language for modeling SXMs is based on XML and Java inline code. The XML-based specifications in JSXM facilitate easier integration with Web technologies and related XML-based Web service standards. JSXM supports animation of SXM models, model-based test case generation and test transformation. The test case generation implements the testing method introduced in Sect. 4.2 and generates a set of test cases in XML. As such, the test cases are independent of the programming language of the IUT. Test transformation is then used for transforming the XML test cases to concrete test cases in the underlying technology of the IUT. Currently, both a Java test transformer and a Web Service test transformer are available, which automatically generate JUnit and XMLUnit test cases respectively.

Example. Due to space limitations, the corresponding code for representing the SXM of the example in JSXM can be found online at [11].

5   Just-in-Time Online Testing

As motivated in Sect. 1.2, we want to check that all constituent services will behave according to their contract before they are invoked in the context of the SBA, thus increasing confidence that the execution will not be aborted due to a failure at a later point. We achieve this by means of just-in-time online testing, which means that the protocol of the service is tested "shortly" before the service is actually invoked from the service composition (the SBA).

Example. In our running example, the execution of the composition begins with invoking the CartService. This leaves some time[1] for on-line testing of the

---

[1] This is especially feasible when a user takes some time to enter the items via a GUI.

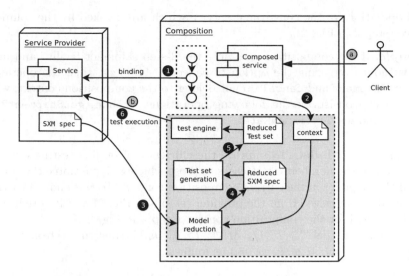

Fig. 2. Just-in-time online testing during composition deployment and execution

ShipmentService and the PaymentService. In the case, for example, that the ShipmentSevice is not functionally correct, an adaptation will be triggered. A possible adaptation might suggest to choose a ShipmentService from an alternative provider.

5.1 Test Generation during Composition Deployment

Test generation is a time-consuming process which could slow down the execution of the service composition if tests were generated during the operation of the SBA. Therefore, we propose performing the test case generation during the design or deployment of the service composition.

During the definition of the business process (or workflow) and the deployment of the service composition, specific service providers for each constituent service are chosen and bound to the composition (step 1 in Fig. 2).

The provider provides both the service implementation (possibly as a Web service) and the service specification (as an SXM model) and claims that the implementation conforms to the specification.[2] Applying the test generation method to the SXM model generates a complete test set for the whole protocol. This test set will thus also include invocations of services not used by the current composition. Testing these operations is unnecessary and increases the testing time during test execution.

Determining the Composition Context. The *context of the service w.r.t the composition* (shortly called the *composition context*) is defined as the subset

---

[2] A method to derive an SXM specification from a semantically annotated Web service utilizing ontology-based and rule-based descriptions is proposed in [21].

of all operations of the constituent service which are invoked by the composed service (step 2 in Fig. 2).

Example. If the composition uses only the 2-step shipment facility and more-over without ever using the option to cancel a shipment, then the operations oneStepShipment and cancel do not belong to the composition context, which in that case consists of the following operations: create, getShipmentRate, confirm, and getConfirmedRate.

Reducing the Model. To improve the efficiency of on-line testing our technique reduces the number of test-cases to those which will guarantee the correctness of the behavior in the current composition context. To this end, the original SXM model is retrieved from the provider (step 3 in Fig. 2) and it is reduced to an SXM model for the composition context (step 4 in Fig. 2).[3]

The reduced model $(\Sigma_r, \Gamma_r, Q_r, M, \Phi_r, F_r, q_0, m_0)$ is constructed from the original model $(\Sigma, \Gamma, Q, M, \Phi, F, q_0, m_0)$ as follows:

1. Σ_r : Inputs from the input alphabet Σ which correspond to service operations not in the composition context are removed;
2. Φ'_r : Processing functions triggered by removed inputs are removed from Φ;
3. F'_r : Transitions labeled with removed functions are removed from F;
4. Q_r : States which are not reachable from the initial state via the transitions in F'_r are removed from Q;
5. F_r : Transitions starting from a removed state or ending to a removed state are removed from F'_r;
6. Φ_r : Processing functions which do not label any remaining transitions in F_r are removed from Φ'_r;
7. Γ_r : Outputs which are not the result of any remaining processing functions in Φ_r are removed from Γ.

M, q_0, and m_0 remain the same.

Example. Fig. 3 illustrates the state transition diagram of the reduced SXM. Removed states, transitions, and processing functions are shown in gray.

Generating the Test Cases. The test generation method (Sect. 4.2) is applied to the reduced SXM resulting to a reduced test set (step 5 in Fig. 2). For the test generation, both the state cover and the characterization sets need to be calculated for the reduced SXM, as, in the general case, they will be different from the respective sets of the original model.

Example. Test sets for the complete and the reduced SXMs for the ShipmentService example can be found online at [11].

---

[3] Although filtering the set of test cases (generated from the original SXM model) would be possible in theory, this leads to practical problems if the state cover and characterization sets contain operations which are not part of the operational context (as in such a situation, relevant test cases might be filtered out).

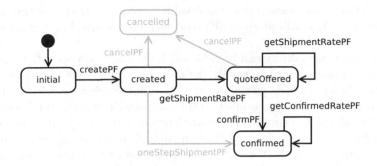

Fig. 3. State transition diagram of the reduced SXM for the composition context

Testing during Deployment. The final step during deployment involves testing the service (step 6 in Fig. 2). This ensures that the service behaves according to its specification, at least concerning the part of its interface which belongs to the composition context and thus ensures that a "correct" SBA is being deployed. However, as motivated in Sect. 1, even if a service was shown to work during design-time, it needs to be (re-)checked during the operation of the SBA to detect deviations (especially if such a service is provided by a third party).

5.2 Just-in-Time Testing after Deployment

After deployment, when the client starts executing the composition (step a in Fig. 2), the testing engine is invoked to perform online tests.

To this end, the testing engine will read the stored, reduced test set and execute the test cases (step b in Fig. 2) until all the tests have passed or one of them has failed. In the latter case an adaptation is triggered.

6 Critical Discussion

This section reflects on the applicability of our proposed technique in realistic settings by discussing its underlying assumptions, as well as scalability and efficiency.

6.1 Assumptions of the Testing Approach

As mentioned in Sect. 4.2, the SXM test case generation relies on certain assumptions to guarantee its results. Specifically, the testing method assumes that the implementation of the individual processing functions is correct, and, based on this assumption, ensures that the system correctly implements their integration. As suggested in [16] this assumption could be checked in practice through a separate quality assurance process (e.g., using traditional black-box testing techniques or formal verification).

Additionally, the testing method relies on the following "design for test" conditions [16]: *controllability* and *observability*. Controllability (also called input-completeness) requires that any processing function can be exercised from any memory value using some input. Observability requires that any two different processing functions will produce different outputs if applied on the same memory/input pair.

In our case observability can be achieved by having each operation providing a distinct response (which is usually the case with SOAP Web services).

Controllability depends on the model. The ShipmentService used as an example in this paper is an input-complete (thus controllable) model. Furthermore, the proposed model reduction preserves completeness, since processing functions are not modified but merely removed from the model. If the initial processing functions were input-complete, then the remaining functions are also input-complete.

Moreover, a fundamental premise for the just-in-time online testing approach presented here—as well as for service testing in general— is that service providers offer some practical way for their services to be tested without triggering real world side effects, such as shipping items or charging credit cards.

There are several ways that this can be realised from a technical point of view. In general, it is accomplished by allowing services to be executed in a special testing environment or configuration mode, often called a "sandbox", which allows the functionality of services to be fully exercised in isolation from the real production environment and databases. The sandbox environments of Paypal and Amazon Web Services are typical examples.

A requirement that logically follows, if we are to increase our confidence for some service which is tested under such a "non-production" mode, is that the special test-mode instance of the service which is actually executed during testing is identical to the actual production instance that will be invoked shortly after.

6.2   Scalability and Efficiency

Table 2 shows the sizes and the lengths of the test set for different values of k, both for the complete and the reduced model. The actual numbers are much smaller than the (theoretically estimated) maximums.[4]

The complete SXM models a service with an interface of 6 operations whereas the reduced SXM models an interface of 4 operations. The time savings from the reduction range between 55–60%.

As it has been discussed above, even if only the reduced set of test cases is executed, testing still takes some time to complete and thus might take longer than the time that is available before the conversational service is invoked for the first time.[5]

---

[4] Based on [16], the maximum number of test sequences, i.e., $card(X)$, is less than $n^2 \cdot r^{k+2}/(r-1)$, where $n = card(Q)$, $r = card(\Phi)$, and (continued on next page) (continued from previous page) k the estimated number of extra states in the implementation. The total length l of the test set is less than $card(X) \cdot n'$, where $n' = k + n$. Actual numbers are much lower than these maximums, mainly due to the fact that JSXM removes all those sequences which are prefixes of other sequences in the test set.

[5] Indicatively, it took about 0.5 seconds to execute the test set of length 98 to a Web service implementation of the ShipmentShervice in a LAN.

Table 2. The sizes and the lengths of the test set for the complete and reduced model for different k values

card(X), l	k									
	0		**1**		**2**		**3**		**4**	
complete SXM	38	122	61	234	89	398	122	624	160	922
reduced SXM	17	54	25	98	36	168	50	270	67	410
savings %	55	56	59	58	60	58	59	57	58	56

A possible solution to this problem is to perform some kind of gradual testing: Online testing can begin with the execution of test cases for $k = 0$. If there is still time available execution of test cases for $k = 1$ can begin, and so on. This gradually increases the confidence that the implementation is correct.

In the worst case scenario there might be not enough time even for the execution of the $k = 0$ test set. In that case there are two possibilities: (1) delay the service execution in order to complete testing, or (2) stop the testing and start service execution. Those choices could be offered in a framework configuration and left to the designer of the composition to take the decision.

To take a more informed decision, the framework could provide some measurements from previous test executions. During test at deployment, gradual testing may be performed and the required times for the test execution for different values of k could be measured and stored. These values could be used for deciding how the framework should behave in cases there is not sufficient time to test. For example, the designer of the composition could decide that even when there is not enough time, tests for $k = 0$ should always be executed first before service execution.

In addition to time, testing costs can become a critical factor for the applicability of our technique, as the invocation of third-party services can be costly. Furthermore, intense online testing can have an adverse effect on the provisioning of the services, as testing might reduce the resources available on the provider's side and thus could, for instance, impact on performance (cf. [7]). This means that the number of online test cases that can be executed is limited by economic and technical considerations. Especially if more than one SBA instance is running, applying our technique to each of those SBA instances individually can lead to redundant online tests, which should be avoided. One solution would be to use a "central" component in our framework that governs the online testing activities and, for instance, does not execute a test if an identical test has already been performed (provided that it can be assumed that its outcomes are still representative of the current situation).

7   Conclusions

This paper introduced a novel technique for just-in-time online testing of conversational services, which enables proactively triggering adaptations of service-based applications. Such a technique is especially relevant in the setting of the

"Internet of Services", where applications will increasingly be composed from third party services, which are not under the control of the service consumer and thus require that they are (re-)checked during the operation of the SBA to detect failures.

We are currently integrating the presented technique into the PROSA framework (PRO-active Self-Adaptation [13]) in the context of the S-Cube project. Although, possible adaptation strategies have not been in the focus of this paper, they can be considered to further extend our proposed techniques. For example, if an alternative service is chosen to replace a faulty one, the alternative service may be (pre-)tested to ensure it provides the same functionality before the actual adaptation will be performed.

Acknowledgments. We cordially thank the anonymous reviewers for their constructive and detailed comments on improving the paper.

The research leading to these results has received funding from the European Community's Seventh Framework Programme FP7/2007-2013 under grant agreement 215483 (S-Cube). For further information please visit http://www.s-cube-network.eu/.

References

1. Bai, X., Chen, Y., Shao, Z.: Adaptive web services testing. In: 31st Annual Int'l Comp. Software and Applications Conf. (COMPSAC), pp. 233–236 (2007)
2. Benbernou, S.: State of the art report, gap analysis of knowledge on principles, techniques and methodologies for monitoring and adaptation of SBAs. Deliverable PO-JRA-1.2.1, S-Cube Consortium (July 2008), http://www.s-cube-network.eu/results/
3. Chan, W., Cheung, S., Leung, K.: A metamorphic testing approach for online testing of service-oriented software applications. International Journal of Web Services Research 4(2), 61–81 (2007)
4. Chow, T.S.: Testing software design modelled by finite state machines. IEEE Transactions on Software Engineering 4, 178–187 (1978)
5. Delgado, N., Gates, A.Q., Roach, S.: A taxonomy and catalog of runtime software-fault monitoring tools. IEEE Trans. Softw. Eng. 30(12), 859–872 (2004)
6. Deussen, P., Din, G., Schieferdecker, I.: A TTCN-3 based online test and validation platform for Internet services. In: Proceedings of the 6th International Symposium on Autonomous Decentralized Systems (ISADS), pp. 177–184 (2003)
7. Di Penta, M., Bruno, M., Esposito, G.: et al.: Web Services Regression Testing. In: Baresi, L., Di Nitto, E. (eds.) Test and Analysis of Web Services, pp. 205–234. Springer, Heidelberg (2007)
8. Dranidis, D.: JSXM: A suite of tools for model-based automated test generation: User manual. Tech. Rep. WPCS01-2009, CITY College (2009)
9. Dranidis, D., Kourtesis, D., Ramollari, E.: Formal verification of web service behavioural conformance through testing. Annals of Mathematics, Computing & Teleinformatics 1(5), 36–43 (2007)
10. Dranidis, D., Ramollari, E., Kourtesis, D.: Run-time verification of behavioural conformance for conversational web services. In: Seventh IEEE European Conference on Web Services, pp. 139–147. IEEE, Los Alamitos (2009)

11. Dranidis, D., Metzger, A., Kourtesis, D.: Enabling proactive adaptation through just-in-time testing of conversational services (supplementary material). Tech. rep., S-Cube (2010), http://www.s-cube-network.eu/results/techreport/sw2010

12. Hallé, S., Bultan, T., Hughes, G., Alkhalaf, M., Villemaire, R.: Runtime verification of web service interface contracts. IEEE Computer 43(3), 59–66 (2010)

13. Hielscher, J., Kazhamiakin, R., Metzger, A., Pistore, M.: A framework for proactive self-adaptation of service-based applications based on online testing. In: Mähönen, P., Pohl, K., Priol, T. (eds.) ServiceWave 2008. LNCS, vol. 5377, pp. 122–133. Springer, Heidelberg (2008)

14. Holcombe, M., Ipate, F.: Correct Systems: Building Business Process Solutions. Springer, Berlin (1998)

15. Ipate, F.: Theory of X-machines with Applications in Specification and Testing. Ph.D. thesis, University of Sheffield (1995)

16. Ipate, F., Holcombe, M.: An integration testing method that is proven to find all faults. International Journal of Computer Mathematics 63, 159–178 (1997)

17. Laycock, G.: The Theory and Practice of Specification Based Testing. Ph.D. thesis, University of Sheffield (1992)

18. Leitner, P., Michlmayr, A., Rosenberg, F., Dustdar, S.: Monitoring, prediction and prevention of SLA violations in composite services. In: IEEE International Conference on Web Services (ICWS) Industry and Applications Track (2010)

19. Metzger, A., Sammodi, O., Pohl, K., Rzepka, M.: Towards pro-active adaptation with confidence augmenting service monitoring with online testing. In: Proceedings of the ICSE 2010 Workshop on Software Engineering for Adaptive and Self-managing Systems (SEAMS 2010), Cape Town, South Africa, May 2-8 (2010)

20. Pernici, B., Metzger, A.: Survey of quality related aspects relevant for service-based applications. Deliverable PO-JRA-1.3.1, S-Cube Consortium (July 2008), http://www.s-cube-network.eu/results/

21. Ramollari, E., Kourtesis, D., Dranidis, D., Simons, A.J.H.: Leveraging semantic web service descriptions for validation by automated functional testing. In: Aroyo, L., Traverso, P., Ciravegna, F., Cimiano, P., Heath, T., Hyvönen, E., Mizoguchi, R., Oren, E., Sabou, M., Simperl, E. (eds.) ESWC 2009. LNCS, vol. 5554, pp. 593–607. Springer, Heidelberg (2009)

22. Tselentis, G., Domingue, J., Galis, A., Gavras, A., Hausheer, D.: Towards the Future Internet: A European Research Perspective. IOS Press, Amsterdam (2009)

23. Wang, Q., Quan, L., Ying, F.: Online testing of Web-based applications. In: Proceedings of the 28th Annual Int'l Comp. Software and Applications Conference (COMPSAC), pp. 166–169 (2004)

PROVIDENCE: A Framework for Private Data Propagation Control in Service-Oriented Systems*

Systems[*]

Roman Khazankin and Schahram Dustdar

Distributed Systems Group, Vienna University of Technology
Argentinierstr. 8/184-1, A-1040 Vienna, Austria
lastname@infosys.tuwien.ac.at

Abstract. As data integration proliferates, private information can be spread across the system extensively. Striving for protection of possessed sensitive information, enterprises thus need comprehensive means to control such propagation. As shown in the paper, approaches to date do not address this need sufficiently. We, therefore, propose a private data propagation control framework (Providence), which aims to give a comprehensive view on private data usage throughout the system and to facilitate privacy-related decision making.

1 Introduction

The proliferation of data integration intensifies the propagation of data throughout the enterprise, since the result of one activity can serve as a source for another. The more sources are involved, the easier it is to overlook the inappropriate use of data, as it comes to be maintained in various locations by different parties. Indeed, proliferation of resource virtualization and cloud computing requires even more delicate consideration of privacy concerns [11,18]. Thus, striving for protection of possessed sensitive information, enterprises need comprehensive means of control over the propagation of private data.

We address the problem in the general case of Service Oriented Architectures (SOAs) where actual implementation of services is inaccessible and their functionality is unrestricted. This implies, for example, that data might be stored by one service and retrieved or transferred later by another service, so this fact can't be established by workflow analysis. To our best knowledge, there are no solutions to date that address this problem.

In this paper we present the *Private Data Propagation Control* Framework (Providence). Monitoring the message exchange, it employs content inspection that is successfully applied in Data Loss Prevention (DLP) solutions[1]. The framework detects and logs private data disclosures that happen in the SOA environment. The log is then used to give a comprehensive view on private data usage

---

* This work was supported by the Vienna Science and Technology Fund (WWTF), project ICT08-032.
[1] http://www.cio.com/article/498166/Best_Data_Loss_Prevention_Tools

E. Di Nitto and R. Yahyapour (Eds.): ServiceWave 2010, LNCS 6481, pp. 76–87, 2010.

throughout the SOA and to facilitate privacy-related decision making. The rationale behind the framework is to have a practically-applicable solution that requires as few integration efforts as possible.

The paper is organized as follows: Section 2 outlines the motivating scenario for our work, Section 3 discusses the Providence framework; related work is discussed in Section 4, evaluation of the approach and the framework is given in Section 5. Section 6 concludes the paper.

2   Motivating Scenario

[16] outlines the scenario with harmful inappropriate use of private data, where Alice, who has a child with a severe chronic illness, buys a book about the disease from online book store. Later she applies for a job and gets rejected because the employer somehow received the information about her purchase and flagged her as high risk for expensive family health costs.

Below we show how the aforementioned scenario can take place due to inappropriate control over the private data in manifold data integration activities in SOAs.

Consider an enterprise Things'n'Books, which runs several businesses including online book trading. It has complex infrastructure with various departments, each responsible for a particular business. Things'n'Books also has a delivery department handling all delivery needs of a company and a joint human resources department. To achieve interoperability between departments, Things'n'Books employs SOA based on Web services.

When the client orders books on-line, the order details are put into orders database exposed as a data service (OrderService). Once the payment is received, a delivery workflow, implemented in BPEL, is initiated. It takes care of order preparation and eventually calls the Web service exposed by the delivery department (DeliveryService) which takes delivery items and the recipient contact data on input.

The delivery department, in time, besides using the received data to perform delivery, stores this data for both accounting reasons and further usage in delivery routes analysis and optimization through the instrumentality of an enterprise mashup M. The human resources department also uses an enterprise mashup platform and benefits from partial re-use of mashup M. Also, it outsources some duties to an independent HR company, and a representative of that company, *Eve*, works in Things'n'Books's office.

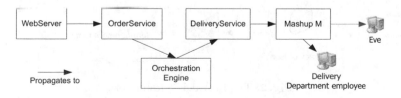

Fig. 1. Private data propagation scenario

Thus, if Alice purchases a book from Things'n'Books's, Eve has an opportunity to access this information via the mashup M having no access to its origin source, the online orders database. The propagation chain is illustrated on Fig. 1.

3   Providence Framework

In this section we introduce the Providence framework. We show the architecture of the framework, give formal specifications for control paradigms and replaceable components, specify implementation remarks, and outline limitations of the framework.

3.1   Architecture

We start from specifying required adoptions in SOA, then we describe each component of the framework. The design of the framework is illustrated in Fig.2. The framework demands two adoptions to be performed in SOA infrastructure, requiring it to:

1. Submit private data entries to the registrator service of the framework, whenever such entries appear in the system (e.g., when private data is entered manually, received from a partner organization, or submitted to a service in SOA).
2. Intercept messages exchanged in the integration and submit them together with the context information to the monitor service of the framework for inspection (e.g., SOAP messages that travel on Enterprise Service Bus). Context information enables the framework to distinguish between different integration activities. Examples of context elements are shown in Table 1.

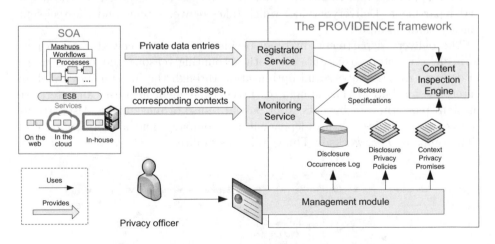

Fig. 2. The Providence framework

Table 1. Examples of context elements

Level	Context element
Network	Requestor host
	Responding endpoint
Application	Consuming application's identifier
	Requestor's credentials from responder's perspective
	Requestor's credentials in requestor application, e.g. in mashup platform
Process	Corresponding process identifier, e.g. in business process engine

Registrator Service. Private data entries are submitted to the Registrator Service in form of *disclosures*. Each disclosure contains typified pieces of private data, *primitives*, and a logical rule, whose variables correspond to those primitives. Also, each disclosure has a type. For example, a disclosure of private information about a 50000$ bank loan issued to John Johnson who lives at 1040 Paulanergasse 2 can be specified as primitives p_1 of type *Name* which has value *"John Johnson"*, p_2 of type *Address* which has value *"1040 Paulanergasse 2"*, and p_3 of type *Amount* which has value *50000*, with rule "$(p_1$ or $p_2)$ and p_3" and type *"PersonalLoan"*. It means that if the message exchange contains the amount together with either address or name, possibly in the different form (e.g., J. Johnson), then the disclosure occurs. The type of primitive indicates how its form can vary. When a disclosure is submitted, primitives are separated from rule and group identifier, so only the mapping is kept. The rule and group identifier are stored to Disclosure Specification Repository, the primitives are registered at the Content Inspection Engine.

Table 2. Examples of primitive types

Type	Value	Possible detectable forms
Name	John Johnson	John Johnson, J. Johnson, JOHNSON J
Date	02.01.2010	02/01/10, 1 Feb 10
Amount	50000	50 000, 50.000

Monitoring Service. The monitoring service receives messages exchanged in data integration processes and corresponding context information. The messages are forwarded to the Content Inspection Engine that detects previously registered primitives in messages' content. If any primitives are detected, the corresponding disclosures are retrieved from Disclosure Specifications Repository and their rules are checked against detected primitives. Occurred disclosures are logged together with the context.

Content Inspection Engine. The Content Inspection Engine is responsible for detecting primitives in the messages content. It receives primitives from

Registration Service and content for inspection from the Monitoring Service. The type of a primitive defines the possible transformations of its data value. Examples of such types are shown in Table 2. There are various content inspection techniques and algorithms [15,8] whose explanation and evaluation is beyond the scope of this paper.

Management Module. This is the core component of the framework. Using the information from disclosure occurrences log, this module provides means to control private data propagation to the privacy officer. She can (i) assign privacy promises to contexts according to real data usage practices in those contexts, (ii) assign privacy policies to disclosure types, and, based on actual disclosure occurrences log and assigned policies, (iii) get answers to following types of questions:

1. Which privacy policy violations happened?
2. Which disclosures happen in specified context?
3. In which contexts disclosure of specified type happens?
4. What promise is enough for specified context to keep compliant with current private data usage practices?
5. How is the private data of specified type actually used?
6. How was the particular piece of private information used?
7. What if we want to set another policy for private data or context, what violations will it produce for the current environment?

The explanation of corresponding answers is given in the next section.

3.2   Formal Specifications

The framework is not coupled to a particular policy and context specification. Nevertheless, the framework's logic heavily relies on these components. Therefore, we specify formal requirements for these components and formally explain the logic of the management module as follows:

Policy. We assume that both private data policies and context promises are expressed in the same form. The policy specification should reflect both requirements (policies) and promises for data usage. It can encapsulate allowed usage purposes, receiving parties, and required obligations[2]. The implementation must provide a means to check whether data treatment under one policy satisfies another policy (promise) and to calculate the intersection and union of policies.

Formally, let P - set of all possible policies. There must be defined relation *satisfies* on P which we mark as $\leftarrow$, so that $p_1 \leftarrow p_2; p_1, p_2 \in P$ indicates that data treatment under policy p_1 satisfies policy p_2.

Further, there must be defined union operator $\cup : P \times P \rightarrow P$ that associates two policies with a policy that is satisfied by either of them: $\forall p_1, p_2 \in P \ p_1 \leftarrow (p_1 \cup p_2), p_2 \leftarrow (p_1 \cup p_2)$.

---

[2] Currently the framework does not support temporal policy elements such as Retention.

Finally, there must be defined intersection operator $\cap : P \times P \rightarrow P$ that associates two policies with a policy that satisfies both of them: $\forall p_1, p_2 \in P$ $(p_1 \cap p_2) \hookleftarrow p_1, (p_1 \cap p_2) \hookleftarrow p_2$.

Context. Context specification should distinguish activities that happen in SOAs in a way that it is possible to assign feasible privacy promises to those activities. The implementation must provide a means to check whether one context is a subcontext of another. Occurrence of a disclosure in some context implies its occurrence in all contexts, of which the given context is a subcontext.

Formally, let C - set of all possible contexts. There must be defined relation $\subseteq$ on C, so that $c_1 \subseteq c_2; c_1, c_2 \in C$ indicates that c_1 is a subcontext of c_2.

Configuration. The privacy officer manages context promises and private data policies. Formally, we can consider that for a given point in time there is *configuration*, which contains these mappings. As policy or promise might be unassigned, we introduce unassigned policy Ω, and extend P to $P' = P \cup \{\Omega\}$. The rationale of unassigned policy is passivity in computations, thus we refine $\hookleftarrow, \cap, \cup$ for P' as follows: $\Omega \hookleftarrow \Omega, \Omega \cap \Omega = \Omega, \Omega \cup \Omega = \Omega$; $\forall p \in P \Rightarrow \Omega \hookleftarrow p, p \hookleftarrow \Omega$; $\forall p \in P \Rightarrow \Omega \cap p = p, p \cap \Omega = p$; $\forall p \in P \Rightarrow \Omega \cup p = p, p \cup \Omega = p$.

Configuration is a tuple $(Promise, Policy)$, where $Promise : C \rightarrow P'$, $Policy : T \rightarrow P'$, where T is a set of all disclosure types. $Promise$ maps contexts to privacy promises assigned, $Policy$ maps disclosure types to privacy polices assigned. For any context, its promise must always satisfy a promise of any its subcontext: $\forall c, c' \in C : c' \subseteq c \Rightarrow Promise(c) \hookleftarrow Promise(c')$.

Management Actions Logic. Based on the current configuration and a part of the log (e.g., log for last month), management module enables the privacy officer to get answers on question templates.

Formally, let $L = \{\langle c_i, d_i \rangle\} : c_i \in C, d_i \in D, 1 \le i \le N$ - disclosure occurrences log, where D is a set of all registered disclosures, N is number of log records, d_i is a disclosure and c_i is a context that corresponds to log entry i. Let $Type(d), d \in D$ indicate the type of disclosure d. Now, given current configuration $\Lambda = (Promise, Policy)$, for any part of log $L' \subset L$ answers can be given as specified in Table 3:

3.3   Implementation

The prototype of Providence framework was designed and implemented considering separation of concerns. The core components implement the principal logic using unified interfaces to replaceable components that are responsible for content inspection and privacy policies storing. Replaceable components were implemented in an elementary way to demonstrate functionality of the framework. The prototype's work is demonstrated in the screencast[3]. The evaluation of results is given in Section 5.

---

[3] http://www.infosys.tuwien.ac.at/prototype/Providence/

Table 3. Privacy-related questions and answers

Question	Answer
1. Which privacy policy violations happened?	$\langle c, d \rangle \in L'$: $Promise(c) \not\vdash Policy(Type(d))$
2. Which disclosures happen in context c	$d : c' \subseteq c, \langle c', d \rangle \in L'$
3. In which contexts disclosure of type T happens?	$c : Type(d) = T, \langle c, d \rangle \in L'$
4. What promise p is enough for context c to keep compliant with current private data uses?	$p = \displaystyle\bigcap_{c' \subseteq c, \langle c', d \rangle \in L'} Policy(Type(d))$
5. What policy p reflects the actual usage of private data in disclosures of type T?	$p = \displaystyle\bigcup_{Type(d)=T, \langle c, d \rangle \in L'} Promise(c)$
6. What policy p reflects the actual usage of private data in disclosure d?	$p = \displaystyle\bigcup_{\langle c, d \rangle \in L'} Promise(c)$
7. If we want to change the configuration, what violations will the new configuration Λ' produce?	(1.) for configuration Λ'.

The success of the framework will depend on the selection of particular adoption points and replaceable components. The context elements should be chosen in a way that (i) disclosures that occur during the same data integration activity share as much contexts as possible, and (ii) disclosures that occur during different activities share as few contexts as possible.

3.4 Limitations

Our framework has several limitations:

- Context elements must be accessible by message submitting adoption point. However, it is a technical matter.
- Content inspection might give false negatives for complex data integration patterns. False positives might occur as well. The balance between false positives, false negatives, and the detection rate in general will always depend on particular information systems, business specifics, IT architecture and inspection engine settings. Therefore, to estimate these rates, it is necessary to test the approach in real business environments. However, fine-tuned DLP tools provide 80-90% accuracy and almost no false positives in commercial product tests[4].
- It is impossible to obtain the data for inspection from encrypted messages. However, the adoption points can be selected in such a way, that data will be sent to inspection before encoding. As the monitoring service does not forward the data any further and is supposed to be deployed in-house, this should not raise any security issues.
- Content inspection of internally exchanged messages brings computational overhead in the system. However, submitted messages can be analyzed asynchronously on the dedicated resource, neither interrupting nor slowing down

---

[4] http://www.cio.com/article/498166/Best_Data_Loss_Prevention_Tools

business processes. Thus, we regard the framework's performance as a secondary concern.
- The privacy officer will need to obtain actual context privacy promises. However, it is inevitable due to assumption of inaccessibility of service implementations. Moreover, given the solution that is able to conclude about actual treatment of data by a service (e.g., using source code analysis), it can be coupled with the framework, thus automating context promises assignment.

4   Related Work

To the best of our knowledge, none of current research fully addresses the issue of private data propagation control within the organization SOAs.

Works like [6,9,1] eventually come to rule-based access restriction to private data. However, none of these solutions can control the usage of private data *after* it gets released from the guarded resource.

Approaches like [7,4,3] address the issue only within bounds of processes or workflows, whereas integration techniques go beyond this paradigm. For instance, services can call each other independently of the workflow engine, or they can store private data, so it can be later picked up by other processes.

[17] proposes a framework for building privacy-conscious composite Web services which confronts service consumer's privacy preferences with component services' policies. This framework does not address scenarios where private data is firstly stored by a component service and then retrieved outside of the composite service's scope, whereas such scenarios are inevitable for data integration.

[14] proposes to record and store logs of private data usage together with this data throughout its lifespan. It requires services, which consume private data, to record all actions performed with this data to the log, and return this log together with the response. Such logs can then be analyzed to conclude about appropriate use of data. Unlike our framework, this approach interferes with the business logic of services, requiring them to report performed actions. Therewith, it does not consider cases, when private data is stored by one service and then retrieved and used by another.

[10] proposes to encrypt the messages that are exchanged between enterprises, so that a request to the trusted authority must be performed to decrypt them. Using this technique, trusted authority can check privacy promises of enterprises and control the access to the private data. This technique neither applies to private data control within the enterprise, nor addresses the usage of data once access to it was granted.

[13] provides tool support for solving a number of problems in data usage control. However, the authors rely on their own model of a distributed system [12] which assumes that each concerned peer has a secure data store that possesses all the private data available to this peer, and that the peer routes this data through the usage control mechanisms whenever the data leaves this store. Such assumption makes the work inapplicable for SOAs in the general case.

[2] addresses similar problems of private data misuses. The authors build their work upon the Private Data Use Flow expressed as a state machine. However,

they give neither instructions nor any explanations of how to build this state machine in an automated fashion having a live system. Unlike it, our approach was designed to work in real SOAs.

Data Loss Prevention solutions are different to our approach in a way that they protect the system from casual leakages of private data from end users, whereas our approach aimed to detect systematic inappropriate uses of data which ensue from SOA complexity.

5   Evaluation

To evaluate our work, we emulated (created and deployed) the environment and business logic of scenario from Sec. 2 using the Genesis 2 testbed [5] and adopted the implemented Providence prototype using service interceptors for monitoring. Besides elements and logic outlined in Sec. 2, the testing environment included printery department which executes private orders and employs the delivery department for shipping. After performing the business logics simulation, we tested the management module's functionality to proof the concept. The screencast of the performed emulation is available online[5].

The business logic was executed as enumerated below. Figure 3 depicts the testing environment and log records inserted during the emulation.

1. Two online book orders are made, thus two *BooksPurchase* disclosures are registered in the framework.
2. *PlaceOrder* operation of *OrderService* is called for each purchase, disclosures are detected, and log records 0,1 are generated.
3. For each purchase orchestration engine retrieves details via *GetOrder* operation of *OrderService* (log records 2,4) and later submits it to *Deliver* operation of *DeliveryService* (log records 3,5).
4. Delivery department uses *MashupService* to run the mashup, which features *BooksPurchase* disclosures (log records 6,7).
5. HR department accesses private information via *OrderService* (log record 8), *DeliveryService* (log records 9,10), and *MashupService* (log records 11,12)
6. Printery department composes private printery order, thus a *PrinteryOrder* disclosure is registered in the framework.
7. The order details are submitted to the *Deliver* operation of *DeliveryService* thus generating log record 13.
8. Delivery department runs the mashup which now involves printery order (log record 14).

Disclosure type policies and context promises of the testing environment are shown in Fig. 4. Data from *BooksPurchase* disclosures is allowed to be used for system administration and research and development; *PrinteryOrder*'s policy is not assigned. Data submitted to *OrchestrationHost* within bounds of *OrderProcess* is known to be used for system administration and individual analysis. Data

---

[5] http://www.infosys.tuwien.ac.at/prototype/Providence/

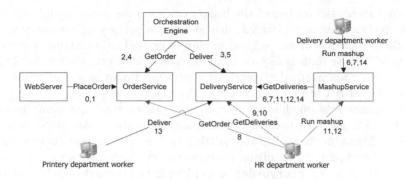

Fig. 3. Testing environment

Disclosure type	Policy
BooksPurchase	Self=[admin, develop]
PrinteryOrder	Unassigned

Context		Promise
process	= OrderProcess	Self=[admin, individual-decision]
destinationHost	= OrchestrationHost	
destinationHost	= DeliveryServiceHost	Self=[historical]
destinationLogin	= DeliveryWorker	Self=[develop]
destinationHost	= MashupHost	
destinationHost	= HRDepartmentHost	ThirdParty=[other]
destinationLogin	= HRWorker	ThirdParty=[other]
destinationHost	= MashupHost	

Fig. 4. Privacy policies and promises in testing environment

Table 4. Detected violations

Record N	Context		Policies
2,4	process	= OrderProcess	Private data policy:{Self=[admin, develop]}
	host	= OrderServiceHost	Context promise:{Self=[admin, individual-decision]}
	destinationHost	= OrchestrationHost	
3,5	process	= OrderProcess	Private data policy:{Self=[admin, develop]}
	host	= OrchestrationHost	Context promise:{Self=[historical]}
	destinationHost	= DeliveryServiceHost	
8	host	= OrderServiceHost	Private data policy:{Self=[admin, develop]}
	destinationHost	= HRDepartmentHost	Context promise:{ThirdParty=[other]}
9,10	host	= DeliveryServiceHost	Private data policy:{Self=[admin, develop]}
	destinationHost	= HRDepartmentHost	Context promise:{ThirdParty=[other]}
11,12	hostLogin	= MashupService	Private data policy:{Self=[admin, develop]}
	destinationLogin	= HRWorker	Context promise:{ThirdParty=[other]}
	host	= DeliveryServiceHost	
	destinationHost	= MashupHost	

propagated to *DeliveryServiceHost* is known to be used for historical preservation. If data is sent to *MashupHost* and remote login is *DeliveryWorker*, then it is used for research and development. Data propagated to *HRDepartmentHost* or retrieved by *MashupHost* with remote login *HRWorker* is known to be exchanged with third party for undefined purposes.

Table 4 shows the output of the framework's management module for violation detection. Having discovered such violations, privacy officer can decide to strengthen context promise (e.g., as in case of orchestration engine, log records 2,4), loose private data policy (e.g., as in case of delivery service, log records 3,5) or assume administrative measures to prevent similar access to private data (e.g., in case of HR worker, log records 8,9,10,11,12).

The management module is able to give answers on question templates from Sec. 3.2, such as itemizing disclosure types that take place in a context (e.g., `BooksPurchase`, `PrinteryOrder` for the context `destinationHost = DeliveryServiceHost`), itemizing the contexts, in which disclosure of particular type happens (e.g., `PrinteryOrder` takes place in two contexts, see Fig. 5), or inferring the actual policy for particular disclosure type (e.g., `Self=[historical, develop]` for `PrinteryOrder`).

```
host            = PrinteryDepartmentHost
destinationHost = DeliveryServiceHost

hostLogin        = MashupService
destinationLogin = DeliveryWorker
host             = DeliveryServiceHost
destinationHost  = MashupHost
```

Fig. 5. Contexts where PrinteryOrder disclosure takes place

Thus, the framework explicitly detects any disclosures that happen during the data integration and helps to prevent the inappropriate access to the data even after it is propagated throughout the system.

6 Conclusion

In this paper we discussed the challenges of private data propagation control in SOAs. We introduced the Providence framework which is able to give a comprehensive view of private data usage throughout the enterprise and to facilitate privacy-related decision making. We demonstrated our framework's functions and discussed limitations regarding its adoption in real-world SOAs. Future investigations include (i) extension for temporal policy elements, (ii) framework integration with enterprise policy brokers, (iii) automation of decisions to prevent violations, (iv) coupling the framework with data integration tools to facilitate design-time privacy concerns consideration.

References

1. Ashley, P., Hada, S., Karjoth, G., Schunter, M.: E-p3p privacy policies and privacy authorization. In: Jajodia, S., Samarati, P. (eds.) WPES, pp. 103–109. ACM, New York (2002)
2. Benbernou, S., Meziane, H., Hacid, M.: Run-time monitoring for privacy-agreement compliance. In: Krämer, B.J., Lin, K.-J., Narasimhan, P. (eds.) ICSOC 2007. LNCS, vol. 4749, pp. 353–364. Springer, Heidelberg (2007)

3. Cheung, W., Gil, Y.: Towards privacy aware data analysis workflows for e-science. In: AAAI Workshop on Semantic e-Science 2007, pp. 22–26. AAAI Press, Menlo Park (2007)
4. Gil, Y., Fritz, C.: Reasoning about the appropriate use of private data through computational workflows. In: Spring Symposium on Intelligent Privacy Management. AAAI Press, Menlo Park (2010)
5. Juszczyk, L., Dustdar, S.: Script-based generation of dynamic testbeds for soa. In: ICWS, pp. 195–202. IEEE Computer Society, Los Alamitos (2010)
6. Karjoth, G., Schunter, M., Waidner, M.: Privacy-enabled services for enterprises. In: DEXA Workshops, pp. 483–487. IEEE Computer Society, Los Alamitos (2002)
7. Li, Y., Paik, H., Chen, J.: Privacy inspection and monitoring framework for automated business processes. In: Benatallah, B., Casati, F., Georgakopoulos, D., Bartolini, C., Sadiq, W., Godart, C. (eds.) WISE 2007. LNCS, vol. 4831, pp. 603–612. Springer, Heidelberg (2007)
8. Lin, P.C., Lin, Y.D., Lai, Y.C., Lee, T.H.: Using string matching for deep packet inspection. IEEE Computer 41(4), 23–28 (2008)
9. Casassa Mont, M., Pearson, S., Thyne, R.: A systematic approach to privacy enforcement and policy compliance checking in enterprises. In: Fischer-Hübner, S., Furnell, S., Lambrinoudakis, C. (eds.) TrustBus 2006. LNCS, vol. 4083, pp. 91–102. Springer, Heidelberg (2006)
10. Mont, M.C., Pearson, S., Bramhall, P.: Towards accountable management of identity and privacy: Sticky policies and enforceable tracing services. In: DEXA Workshops, pp. 377–382. IEEE Computer Society, Los Alamitos (2003)
11. Pearson, S.: Taking account of privacy when designing cloud computing services. In: Proceedings of the 2009 ICSE Workshop on Software Engineering Challenges of Cloud Computing, pp. 44–52. IEEE Computer Society, Los Alamitos (2009)
12. Pretschner, A., Hilty, M., Basin, D., Schaefer, C., Walter, T.: Mechanisms for usage control. In: Proceedings of the 2008 ACM Symposium on Information, Computer and Communications Security, pp. 240–244. ACM, New York (2008)
13. Pretschner, A., Ruesch, J., Schaefer, C., Walter, T.: Formal analyses of usage control policies. In: ARES, pp. 98–105. IEEE Computer Society, Los Alamitos (2009)
14. Ringelstein, C., Staab, S.: Dialog: A distributed model for capturing provenance and auditing information. International Journal of Web Services Research 7(2), 1–20 (2010)
15. Sourdis., I.: Designs & Algorithms for Packet and Content Inspection. Ph.D. thesis, Delft University of Technology (2007)
16. Weitzner, D.J., Abelson, H., Berners-Lee, T., Feigenbaum, J., Hendler, J., Sussman, G.J.: Information accountability. Commun. ACM 51(6), 82–87 (2008)
17. Xu, W., Venkatakrishnan, V.N., Sekar, R., Ramakrishnan, I.V.: A framework for building privacy-conscious composite web services. In: 4th IEEE International Conference on Web Services (Application Services and Industry Track) (ICWS) (2006)
18. Yuhanna, N., Gilpin, M., Hogan, L., Sahalie, A.: Information fabric: Enterprise data virtualization. White Paper. Forrester Research Inc. (2006)

Utility Driven Service Routing over Large Scale Infrastructures*

Pablo Chacin[1], Leando Navarro[1], and Pedro Garcia Lopez[2]

[1] Departament d'Arquitectura dels Computadors,
Universitat Politénica de Catalunya, Barcelona, Spain
pchacin@ac.upc.edu
[2] Department d'Enginyeria Informàtica i Matemàtiques,
Universitat Rovira i Virgili, Tarragona, Spain

Abstract. In this paper we present UDON, a novel Utility Driven Overlay Network framework for routing service requests in highly dynamic large scale shared infrastructures. UDON combines an application provided utility function to express the services's QoS in a compact way, with an epidemic protocol to disseminate this information in a scalable and robust way. Experimental analysis with a simulation model suggests that the proposed overlay allocates requests to service instances that match their QoS requirements with a high probability and low overhead, adapting well to a wide variety of conditions.

1 Introduction

Recent years have witnessed the emergence of service oriented applications deployed on large scale shared infrastructures such as computational clouds [15]. Under this paradigm, services are reused and combined, new services are introduced frequently, usage patterns varies continuously and diverse user populations may exist, with different QoS requirements in terms of attributes like response time, execution cost, security and others [11].

As service instances run on non dedicated servers, it results difficult to predict the QoS that they can provide due to the fluctuations on servers' workload. Additionally, the number of instances may vary over time in response to variations in the service demand.

In such infrastructures, the allocation (or routing) of service requests to instances that match their QoS requirements becomes a significant challenge in terms of how to: a) route requests accurately despite the dynamism of the environment; b) scale up to a very large number of service instances; c) handle the churn of instances as they are activated and deactivated or fail; d) accommodate different resource management policies, as nodes may belong to different administrative domains; and e) clearly separate the from application specific aspects from routing, to offer a generic infrastructure that supports multiple services.

---

* This work has been partly supported by Spanish MEC grant TIN2010-20140-C03-01.

E. Di Nitto and R. Yahyapour (Eds.): ServiceWave 2010, LNCS 6481, pp. 88–99, 2010.

The main contribution of this paper is the proposal of UDON, a novel Utility Driven Overlay Network framework for routing service requests to service instances in highly dynamic large scale environments. UDON combines an application provided utility function to express the service's QoS, with an epidemic protocol for information dissemination.

The utilization of utility functions allows a compact representation of the QoS requirements for services and facilitates the comparison of the QoS that different instances provide, even if they run on very heterogeneous nodes [9]. The utilization of an epidemic style dissemination algorithm (on which information is randomly propagated among nodes) makes UDON highly adaptable to changes in the infrastructure, scalable, and resilient to failures and churn, maintaining its routing capabilities with a modest maintenance cost.

In this paper we evaluate extensively the proposed overlay using simulation. Experiments show that UDON can route requests with a high probability of success and in a low number of hops under a wide variety of conditions. In particular, it adapts well to random fluctuations in the QoS provided by service instances, high churn rates due to instance activations/deactivations, and the scarcity of instances that provide an adequate QoS.

The rest of this paper is organized as follows. Section 2 introduces the system model and describes the algorithms used for overlay construction and routing. Section 3 presents an evaluation of UDON under diverse conditions and discusses the results. Section 4 reviews relevant related work. Finally, section 5 presents the conclusions, open issues and planned future work.

2 The Utility Driven Overlay

In UDON (see fig. 1) each service has an utility function that maps the attributes and execution state of a service instance (e.g response time, available resources, trustworthiness, reliability, execution cost) to a scalar value that represents the QoS it provides.

Requests coming from users are processed through a set of entry-points, which correspond to segments of users with similar QoS requirements, and must be routed to service instances that offer an adequate QoS. The QoS required by a request is defined as the minimum acceptable utility that must be provided by a service instance to process it.

Entry points and service instances are organized in a routing overlay on which each node maintains a local view with the utility of a subset of other nodes, and use this information to route the requests. The main objective of the overlay is to help each node to maintain fresh information about other nodes, while addressing the challenges of scalability, resilience and adaptability of the environment.

Service instances are continuously activated/deactivated from/to a pool of available servers in response to fluctuations in the service demand using one of different approaches proposed elsewhere [10] [13]. The scope of the present work concentrates on how requests are routed to the active service instances.

The next sections describe in detail how the overlay is constructed and how requests are routed.

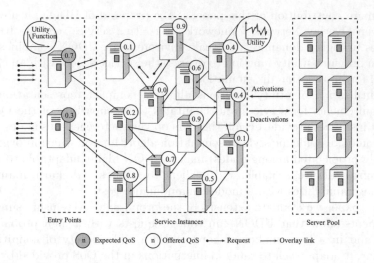

Fig. 1. Usage scenario and its mapping to the UDON's overlay model

2.1 Overlay Construction

UDON uses a push style epidemic algorithm to construct the overlay and disseminate information about the nodes. Epidemic algorithms in general are inherently scalable, robust, and resilient [5]. Push style algorithms in particular have a fast initial propagation rate [8], a desirable property in UDON because the information is used only locally and system wide propagation is not needed. Additionally, they are simple to implement using a lightweight communication protocol like UDP, not requiring synchronization between nodes.

A generic push algorithm works as follows. Periodically each node selects a subset of its neighbors (the exchange set) and sends a message with its local view (the neighbor set) and its own current state. When a node receives this message, merges it with its current neighbor set and selects a subset as the new neighbor set.

The different epidemic algorithms proposed in the literature differ basically in how they select the neighbors to be contacted, and how they merge the information received (see [7] for a study of different alternatives). In UDON, a node selects a random subset of neighbors to exchange its local view, and merges the received information selecting those entries with the more up to date information.

The two key parameters for this generic algorithm are the exchange size, which impacts the network traffic, and the neighbor set size, which impacts the memory and bandwidth requirements.

2.2 Request Routing

We propose the utilization of a simple greedy unicast routing algorithm. On the reception of a request, the routing uses an *admission* function to determine if the node can accept the request for processing. This function can be service dependent and may also be different for each node, to accommodate different allocation policies. In this work we use a simple admission function for evaluation purposes, as described in the experimental evaluation section.

If the request is not accepted, then a *ranking* function is used to rank the neighbors and select the most promising one as the next hop in the routing process. This function accommodates the heuristic for selecting the next hop. In the present work we use a simple heuristic which selects the neighbor whose utility more closely matches the QoS demanded by the request. The exploration of other heuristics adapted to specific scenarios is a subject of further research.

The process described above continues until either the request is accepted by a node or the TTL limit is reached, in which case the request is dropped.

3   Experimental Evaluation

In this section we analyze the performance of the UDON overlay and its sensitivity to different operational conditions. We first describe the simulation model and metrics used in this evaluation, then summarize the results of multiple experiments, and finally discuss those results from the perspective of the objectives of UDON.

To put the evaluation in perspective, we compare UDON with two other alternative overlays that use variations of the generic epidemic algorithm discussed in sec. 2: a gradient overlay as proposed in [14] and a random overlay. Both overlays select a random subset of peers to disseminate the information, but differ in how a node merges the information received from other peers with its own local information and in how requests are routed.

In the gradient overlay, each node merges the received information selecting those nodes that have an utility similar to its own current utility. Requests are routed using a simple greedy routing that exploits the resulting utility gradient. This overlay was selected to evaluate if, under the changing conditions of the scenarios of interest, organizing nodes according to their utility offered any advantage.

In the random overlay, each node merges the received information by selecting a random sample of nodes. The routing is done by means of a random walk. This overlay was selected as a base line to evaluate if UDON offers any systematic advantage over a random search.

It is important to notice that the exchange set and the neighbors set were the same for the three overlays so the memory and communication cost are similar.

3.1   Simulation Model

For our experiments, we have simulated an idealized network that mimics a large cluster, on which nodes can communicate with a uniform delay. The base experimental setup has 1024 nodes, with a 5% of entry points and the rest of service instances. Other proportions of entry points in the range 1% to 10% show similar results to this base setup.

Each node maintains a neighbor set of 16 nodes and contacts 2 of them periodically (the exchange set). These values correspond, as discussed later, to the optimal trade off between information freshness and communication costs found in our experiments.

On each simulation cycle a percentage (the *Churn* rate) of service instances are replaced to simulate the activation/deactivation process, but maintaining the size of the overlay to facilitate the comparison or results.

To make this evaluation as general as possible, instead of using a concrete utility function which will be necessarily relevant only to an specific service and usage scenario, the utility of each service instance is simulate as a random variable, capturing the fact that the utility is affected by factors not controlled by UDON, like background workload in the servers.

This variable is modeled as a random walk which starts from an initial random value (uniformly distributed in the [0.0,1.0] range) and has a certain *Variability* on each simulation cycle and a *Drift* or tendency to follow a trend upwards or downwards. Figure 2 shows the effect of these parameters in the behavior of one node's utility over time. This model is consistent with the observed behavior of the load on shared servers [12] [16].

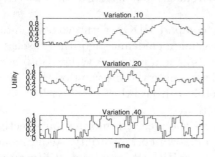
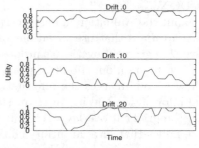
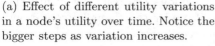

(a) Effect of different utility variations in a node's utility over time. Notice the bigger steps as variation increases.

(b) Effect of different utility drifts in a node's utility over time, with a fixed variation of ±020. Notice the larger trends as drift increases.

Fig. 2. Effect of utility simulation parameters on a node's utility over time

Each entry point is given a QoS *Preference* (minimum acceptable utility) following an uniform distribution in the range [0.0,1.0], to evaluate the ability of UDON to find nodes which any arbitrary utility. Additionally, we evaluate the accuracy of UDON to find nodes with a given QoS by using a *Tolerance* parameter in the admission function that indicates the maximum acceptable difference (from above) between the QoS required by a request and the QoS offered by an instance to admit it.

In our simulations the utility of instances is not affected by the number of requests processed, as we are more interested in evaluating the capacity of UDON for matching requests and instances. Therefore, the arrival rate of requests is not relevant to our experiments.

Metrics

We evaluate the performance of UDON using the following metrics related to its various objectives.

Age. Measures how up to date is the information at each node. It is calculated at each node by averaging, over all the entries in its neighbor set, the time this information has been circulating on the overlay. Age is measured in terms of update cycles, being a cycle the frequency of the epidemic propagation process in the overlay.

Staleness. Measures how accurate is the information in the neighbor set of a node and affects the reliability of the decisions made using this information. The Staleness is measured as the average of the (absolute) difference between the utility of a node's entry in the neighbor set the current (real) utility of that node. It depends on both the Age of the information and the variability of the utility.

Satisfied demand. Is the fraction of requests that are assigned to a node with an adequate utility before being dropped due to the routing TTL. In our simulations we have set this TTL to a sufficiently large number (12).

Number of hops. Measures the cost of routing a request towards a node that satisfies its requirements in terms of the number of hops starting from the entry point.

3.2   Results

Information dissemination. In UDON the Age of the information is significantly lower and has less variation than in the other two overlays (fig. 3a), and the information is much more accurate (fig. 3b). More importantly, those attributes converge very quickly and remains very stable along its execution.

Routing. UDON exhibits a significantly better performance than the gradient or random overlays with respect of both the satisfied demand and the number of hops (see fig. 4), allocating requests to a matching instance efficiently even when a high precision (i.e. a low tolerance) is required. This can be explained by the higher accuracy in the information maintained by UDON (see fig. 3b), which enables it to make better routing decisions.

Load Balancing. Another important consideration for a routing algorithm is its capacity of balancing the requests over all the service instances. Figure 5 shows that the number of requests processed by service instance has a low variability, in terms of the interquartile range. This balancing is achieved by the continuous renewal of the neighbor set of each node with a random selection of new, more updated, peers.

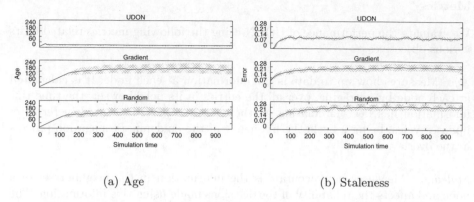

(a) Age   (b) Staleness

Fig. 3. Evolution of metrics for a run with the base experimental setup

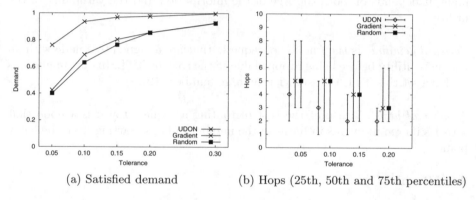

(a) Satisfied demand   (b) Hops (25th, 50th and 75th percentiles)

Fig. 4. Efficiency of the UDON overlay for different request tolerances. For each tolerance, the percentiles 25, 50 and 75 of the number of routing hops are shown.

Utility distribution. The base setup assumes that the utility of the nodes follows an uniform distribution and nodes with any utility are equally probable to be found. We also studied the case when the requests demand a QoS offered only by a few nodes. To simulate this scenario, all the service requests are generated with an expected QoS uniformly distributed in the range $[0.4, 0.6]$. The utility of nodes initially has an normal distribution with mean 0.5, and each node has a sustained trend to lower its utility. As a result, the number of nodes with utility in the range needed by requests decreases over time.

Figure 6 shows the evolution of the utility distributions, the percentage of nodes with utility in the range $[0.4, 0.6]$, and the percentage of satisfied demand. As can be seen, UDON works reasonably well in system with highly skewed distributions, satisfying over 85% of demand when the target number of nodes is just above 5%. From this point on, performance degrades significantly.

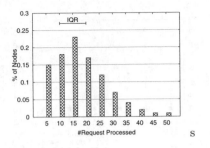
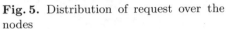

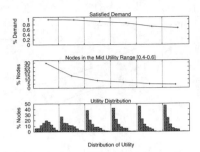

Fig. 5. Distribution of request over the nodes

Fig. 6. Evolution of satisfied demand with respect of the distribution of utility

3.3 Sensitivity Analysis

In this section we evaluate the impact of different parameters that affect the topology construction as well as parameters of the utility function to explore the applicability of the proposed approach to different usage conditions.

Network size. Our experimental results show that UDON scales well, maintaining its performance as the network size increases from 1024 up to 32768 nodes[1]. The most relevant metrics like age, satisfied demand and average routing hops maintain the same value. Corresponding graphics are omitted for brevity as they are identical to those shown in figures 3 and 4. This result can be easily explained by the fact that UDON nodes work only on local information.

Exchange and neighbor sets size. Our experiments (not shown here for brevity) indicate that further increments of those parameters above the values of the base setup have no noticeable effect on UDON's performance, suggesting that contacting more neighbors or exchanging more information do not improve the information dissemination because it generates mostly redundant messages. These results hold even for larger network sizes.

Churn rate. Is the percentage of nodes that are replaced in the overlay on each simulation cycle. The principal effect of churn is that the effective in and out degrees (that is the references from and to active nodes) of each node fall as the rate increases, and references to failed nodes are more common (see fig. 7a). However, fig. 7b shows UDON is still fairly robust with respect of the churn rate, as its performance degrades smoothly when the rate increases.

Utility variation and drift. Figure 8 shows that the performance of UDON degrades smoothly as the variability increase. It is also remarkable that even under a very high variation (0.40), UDON performs better than the other two studied

---

[1] Limitations in our simulator prevented the evaluation of larger overlays. Future work includes the study of the overlay with well over 128K nodes.

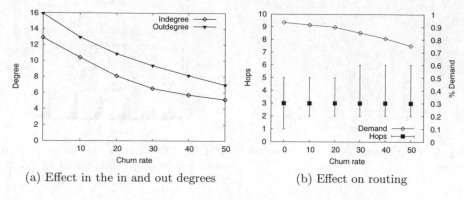

(a) Effect in the in and out degrees   (b) Effect on routing

Fig. 7. Effect of churn in the routing metrics

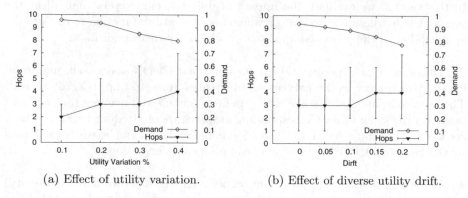

(a) Effect of utility variation.   (b) Effect of diverse utility drift.

Fig. 8. Effect of utility variation in overlay performance

overlays under a much lower variation of 0.20 (see fig. 4). However, fig. 8b shows that UDON is very sensitive to large drifts, when the utility of the node have a sustained trend over time (see fig 2b).

3.4   Discussion

Experimental results suggest that the proposed overlay works well within a wide variety of conditions with respect of the utility distribution and variability. It also scales well not requiring to increase the network traffic generated by each node to maintain its performance. More over, UDON achieves its best performance with low values of both the exchange and neighbor set, and therefore, with low overhead in memory and communications. The utilization of local information and the random nature of the epidemic protocol account largely for these properties.

UDON seams to fit better in scenarios where the utility of nodes varies frequently and the request must be allocated considering a narrow range for the targeted utility. As the allocation becomes less restrictive, the Random overlay becomes more competitive.

When comparing the performance of the two alternative overlays it is interesting to notice how, under the scenarios we study, the performance of the gradient overlay is very close to that of the random overlay, implying that organizing nodes in a gradient offers no real advantage.

Additionally, UDON is clearly robust under churn. Two aspects of the overlay maintenance algorithm account for this robustness. Firstly, the continuous renewal of the neighbor set of each node with the more recently updated peers quickly removes the failed nodes. Secondly, entering nodes are initialized with a set of randomly chosen active nodes and therefore have a very up to date information, which they propagate to their neighbors.

Finally, results make clear that the principal limitation of UDON is when the utility of nodes exhibits a sustained trend over time, as the utilization of stale information is much less effective, lowering considerably the percentage of satisfied demand. We relativise this limitation as we consider that in a shared infrastructure, where the requests of multiple services are being randomly distributed over a large set of non-dedicated server, its difficult that many of them will exhibit a similar trend for sustained periods. Still, we consider this one of the more relevant areas for further exploration in UDON.

4   Related Work

There have been different efforts to incorporate both epidemic dissemination and the utility functions for routing requests over an overlay. However, they differ significantly in how they apply those concepts and the scenarios on which they are applicable.

In [14] authors use an epidemic algorithm to build a gradient topology on which each node maintains as peers those nodes with a similar utility. Over this topology, a greedy routing algorithm is guarantee to find a node to process requests, if it exists. As we show experimentally, it's much less effective when utility varies frequently.

A middleware for large scale clusters is proposed in in [1] on which nodes self-organize in a per-service overlay using an epidemic algorithm to create a random topology and flood periodically all their neighbors with an load status.Request are routed randomly to any non overloaded neighbor. If none is found, a random walk is employed to find one. In UDON requests are routed also considering the utility of the nodes and therefore finer allocation policies are possible.

In [3] authors use a push style gossiping algorithm to maintain a distributed bulletin board with a complete view on each node of the performance information of all other nodes, with is guaranteed to have a bounded average age for all the entries as a function of the size of the exchange window. Comparing experimental results, UDON shows a significantly lower average and maximum age, scales better and is more resilient to churn (which has a significant effect in the proposed bulletin board).

Using a completely different approach to the epidemic nature of UDON, different structured overlays for resource allocation has also been explored [4,6]. However they require the attributes (and in some cases the range of values for each attribute) to be fixed and known in advance, and the maintenance cost makes them unsuitable for frequently changing attributes.

5   Conclusions

The main contribution of this work is the proposal of UDON a simple, efficient and low overhead overlay framework that combines and epidemic style dissemination and utility functions to route service requests over a large scale and highly dynamic infrastructures. UDON clearly separates the application specific aspects and offers a generic routing substrate for services, while allowing service specific optimizations when needed.

The work presented here is an initial step and much work is still needed. However, the results obtained are encouraging and have helped us to identify a variety of promising alternatives for future development.

We plan to explore the inclusion of locality information, such as the IP address or latency metrics, as part of the selection of peers and the propagation of information and evaluate its effect in the performance of UDON.

Equally, UDON currently does not exploit the fact that all the requests coming from an entry point may have similar QoS requirements because correspond to the same user segment. We plan to explore the effect of propagating with a higher probability the information about nodes that could handle the QoS of the requests that a node have recently routed, which should improve the probability of allocating requests and lower the average number of routing hops.

Finally, we plan to evaluate UDON in an scenario of service composition, following the model proposed in [2] on which the utility function that defines the QoS of a composite service is decomposed into a series of utility functions which can be evaluated independently for each basic service, making it amenable to be integrated with UDON for request routing.

References

1. Adam, C., Stadler, R.: Service middleware for self-managing large-scale systems. IEEE Transactions on Network and Service Management 4(3), 50–64 (2007)
2. Alrifai, M., Risse, T., Dolog, P., Nejdl, W.: A scalable approach for qos-based web service selection. In: 1st International Workshop on Quality-of-Service Concerns in Service Oriented Architectures (QoSCSOA 2008), vol. 5472, pp. 190–199 (2008)
3. Amar, L., Barak, A., Drezner, Z., Okun, M.: Randomized gossip algorithms for maintaining a distributed bulletin board with guaranteed age properties. Concurrency and Computation: Practice and Experience 21(15), 1907–1927 (2009)
4. Basu, S., Banerjee, S., Sharma, P., Lee, S.J.: Nodewiz: peer-to-peer resource discovery for grids. In: IEEE International Symposium on Cluster Computing and the Grid (CCGrid) (2005)

5. Eugster, P., Guerraoui, R., Kermarrec, A.M., Massoulie, L.: Epidemic information dissemination in distributed systems. Computer 37(5), 60–67 (2004)
6. Hauswirth, M., Schmidt, R.: An overlay network for resource discovery in grids. In: Proceedings of Sixteenth International Workshop on Database and Expert Systems Applications, pp. 343–348 (2005)
7. Jelasity, M., Voulgaris, S., Guerraoui, R., Kermarrec, A.M., van Steen, M.: Gossip-based peer sampling. ACM Transactions on Computer Systems 25(3) (2007)
8. Karp, R., Schindelhauer, C., Shenker, S., Vocking, B.: Randomized rumor spreading. In: Proceedings. 41st Annual Symposium on Foundations of Computer Science, pp. 565–574 (2000)
9. Kephart, J.O., Das, R.: Achieving self-management via utility functions. IEEE Internet Computing 11(1), 40–48 (2007)
10. Karve, A., Kimbrel, T., Pacifici, G., Spreitzer, M., Steinder, M., Sviridenko, M., Tantawi, A.: Dynamic placement for clustered web applications. In: Proceedings of the 15th International Conference on World Wide Web, pp. 595–604 (2006)
11. Menasce, D.A.: Qos issues in web services. IEEE Internet Computing 6(6), 72–75 (2002)
12. Oppenheimer, D., Chun, B., Patterson, D., Snoeren, A.C., Vahdat, A.: Service placement in a shared widearea platform. In: USENIX Annual Technical Conference, pp. 273–288 (2006)
13. Ruth, P., McGachey, P., Xu, D.: Viocluster: Virtualization for dynamic computational domains. In: IEEE International Conference on Cluster Computing (2005)
14. Sacha, J., Dowling, J., Cunningham, R., Meier, R.: Using aggregation for adaptive super-peer discovery on the gradient topology. In: Keller, A., Martin-Flatin, J.-P. (eds.) SelfMan 2006. LNCS, vol. 3996, pp. 73–86. Springer, Heidelberg (2006)
15. Vaquero, L.M., Rodero-Merino, L., Caceres, J., Lindner, M.: A break in the clouds: towards a cloud definition. ACM SIGCOMM Computer Communication Review 39(1), 50–55 (2009)
16. Yang, L., Foster, I., Schopf, J.: Homeostatic and tendency-based cpu load predictions. In: Proceedings of International Parallel and Distributed Processing Symposium, p. 9 (2003)

A Chemical Based Middleware for Workflow Instantiation and Execution*

Claudia Di Napoli[2], Maurizio Giordano[2], Jean-Louis Pazat[1], and Chen Wang[1]

[1] Université Européenne de Bretagne, INSA/INRIA/IRISA, F-35708 Rennes, France
{chen.wang,jean-louis.pazat}@irisa.fr
[2] Istituto di Cibernetica CNR, Via Campi Flegrei 34, 80078 Pozzuoli, Naples, Italy
{c.dinapoli,m.giordano}@cib.na.cnr.it

Abstract. Service-Oriented Architecture (SOA) is widely adopted today for building loosely coupled distributed applications. With this approach, new applications can be built by creating a business process that defines a concrete workflow composed of different partner services available via the network. In this scenario, the bindings between the business process and partner services are predefined by statically referencing the corresponding endpoints. This paper proposes a middleware architecture for dynamical workflow instantiation and execution. Using this middleware, partner services are selected and bound in the run-time and the aggregated QoS values are ensured to satisfy the requester's end-to-end QoS requirement. The selection is based on both non-functional requirement (such as price and response time) of the global composition, and Quality of Service (QoS) performance of each candidate service. The implementation is based on chemical computing, a parallel and autonomic computing paradigm that allows to model workflow instantiation and execution as an evolving and adaptable process.

1 Introduction

Today, the need for designing loosely-coupled distributed applications requires service collaboration across enterprise boundaries. Service-Oriented Architecture (SOA) brings us standards-based, robust and interoperable solutions [1]. From the viewpoint of SOA, new applications can be built by composing a set of independent software modules called *services*. Within the scope of this paper, a *service* is a software system designed to support interoperable machine-to-machine interaction over computer networks. It can be seen as a black box providing certain functionality to its clients through a set of interfaces.

The traditional approach to build a composite application is to use an executable language (such as WS-BPEL [2]) to create a business process by defining a workflow that specifies business logic and execution order. In this context, the bindings between the business process and all its partner services are statically

---

* The research leading to these results has received funding from the European Community's Seventh Framework Programme [FP7/2007-2013] under grant agreement 215483 (S-CUBE).

E. Di Nitto and R. Yahyapour (Eds.): ServiceWave 2010, LNCS 6481, pp. 100–111, 2010.

predefined. However, it is very likely that different service providers can provide a given functionality under different quality levels related to some non-functional characteristics. These characteristics may change in time depending on both provider policies and consumer requirements. For example, the cost associated to a service can be different according to market conditions (driven by demand-supply mechanisms), or the response time may vary according to the workload of the provider. Given the dynamic nature of service non-functional characteristics, the possibility of configuring service composition dynamically becomes a crucial requirement when taking into account the dynamic execution environment.

This paper addresses the problem of on-demand selecting and binding partner services in response to dynamic requirements and circumstances. A middleware architecture is proposed for dynamic workflow instantiation and execution. In our approach, a workflow is described in an abstract manner by specifying the functional requirement of each workflow activity and the dependencies among them. Each execution request is associated with a global QoS requirement (such as total price and overall response time) specified by the client. Then, the instantiation process is carried out to construct an instantiated workflow by mapping each workflow activity to a candidate service provider. The instantiated workflow ensures that the aggregated QoS value of all the selected service providers can match the client's end-to-end requirement. The implementation is based on chemical programming [3]. It is a parallel and autonomic programming paradigm that models computation as chemical reactions controlled by a set of rules and all molecules involved represent computing resources.

This paper is organized as follows: in Section 2, some of the main existing approaches for dynamic service selection are introduced. In Section 3, we propose a middleware architecture for workflow instantiation and execution. Section 4 presents the implementation of this middleware based on chemical computing. Finally, conclusions and future works are addressed in Section 5.

2   Related Work and Motivations

Recently, the problem of dynamically selecting partner services that meet user's requirements in terms of both functional and non-functional characteristics has gained wide attention. Some research works have concentrated on the design of languages and ontologies to represent these characteristics. In this case, automatic mechanisms are implemented to select the appropriate services to build service composition. Mukhija et al. [4] present an approach for QoS specification and service provider selection. The selection algorithm takes into account both the trustworthiness of the provider and the relative benefit offered by a provider with respect to the requester-specified QoS criteria. In [5] the authors propose an extension to the ontology framework based on OWL-S, which enables defining the composite services at the abstract level and then at runtime filtering and plugging in the candidate services that are chosen from a service instance pool.

Other research works have studied the development of frameworks to dynamically select service implementations. The Sword project [6] explores techniques for composing services using logical rules to express the inputs and outputs associated with services. A rule-based expert system is used to automatically determine whether a process could be implemented with the given services. It also returns a process plan that implements the composition. Maximilien et al. [7] propose a framework and ontology for dynamic Web Service selection based on software agents coupled with a QoS ontology. With this approach, participants can collaborate to determine each other's service quality and trustworthiness. Keidl et al. [8] propose the serviceGlobe environment that implements dynamic service selection using UDDI's notion of a tModel.

Other solutions aim at integrating service selection and execution. In [9] the authors present an architecture for dynamic Web service selection within a workflow enactment process. The dynamic selection of services is performed through a Proxy Service interacting with a Discovery Service and an Optimization Service. In [10] the eFlow system is proposed that allows nodes (activities) to have service selection rules. When the eFlow engine tries to execute an activity it calls a service broker which executes the service selection rules and returns a list of services (with ranking information).

Within this context, the present work proposes a middleware architecture that integrates late binding service selection mechanisms with a workflow execution module. The selection mechanisms are carried out at two levels. The first occurs at the composition request level and it allows selecting *abstract services* by taking into account global QoS requirements on the composition of services, such as the overall delivery time and the total price. Then, the second selection mechanism takes place at the concrete binding level. It allows further selecting suitable service implementation to forward the invocation request. The selection is based on some local QoS dimension (such as performance, reliability) so that each abstract service still meets the constraints derived by the global requirements. Using this middleware, dynamical selection of service implementations is an autonomous process that can react to environmental changes.

3   Middleware for Workflow Instantiation and Execution

As shown in Figure 1, the middleware is built upon the Web service implementation layer. All components in the proposed middleware are organized in two levels: the *Service Representation* level and the *Workflow Execution* level. The former resolves the abstract representation of concrete services in the middleware layer while the latter takes charge of workflow instantiation and execution.

3.1   Middleware Architecture

In this middleware, we assume that all the available functionalities are provided by a set of *Abstract Service* (AS). An *AS* is a description of functional interfaces related to a certain Web service rather than the relative implementation. Thus, in order to perform the real calculation, it groups a set of *Concrete Services* (CS) in order to forward the invocation requests (see AS_1 in Figure 1). An AS can deliver a given functionality with different quality levels by publishing various

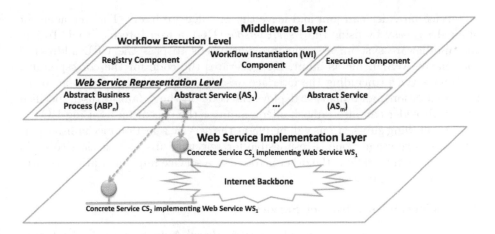

Fig. 1. Middleware Architecture

offers in the *Registry* component. The *Registry* acts as a directory maintaining the information of all currently available offers. An *offer* specifies both functional and non-functional characteristics of a service delivery.

A group of *Abstract Business Processes* (ABP) act as service consumers. An *ABP*, similar to a WS-BPEL business process, is a collection of interrelated tasks and activities that function in a logical sequence to achieve the ultimate business goal. The business logic and execution sequence are defined by an Abstract Workflow (*AW*). It is described by an directed acyclic graph whose nodes represent the functional requirements of the workflow activities and edges specify the dependency among those activities.

Each request to an ABP is associated with a global QoS constraint specified by the requester (such as how much he can offer to purchase a service delivery with the response time less than 10s). Before the execution, the abstract workflow is forwarded to the *Workflow Instantiation* (WI) component. This component is responsible for building a possible *Instantiated Workflow* (IWF) by assigning each workflow activity to a suitable *AS*. The selection of adequate *AS* is based on all currently available offers in the Registry and the global QoS constraints specified by the client. Our system aims at searching a feasible IWF that can satisfy the client's requirement rather than the optimal one.

Once a feasible IWF is found, it is passed to the *Execution Component* which then takes charge of workflow execution. As proposed in [11], the execution of a workflow can be decentralized. IWF information is separated into several blocks and then forwarded to the relative abstract services. A partial IWF block for a partner service includes the information about its predecessor(s), successors(s) as well as the QoS value to be delivered. An abstract service works as an autonomic system: it receives the request from the predecessor service(s), calculates and then forwards the results to the successor service(s). The calculation recurs to the selection of a concrete service to forward the service invocation request. This selection is based on the historical invocation information.

Service provider can join and leave the middleware freely. The management of an *AS* is easy by using the *User Console* (UC), a user interface tool. To join the middleware system, a service provider needs to pass the URL address of the relative WSDL file as input, UC generates the code for the corresponding abstract service (including the interface descriptions and the connection to the implementation), and finally it deploys the code on the default or user specified server. Provider can also publish offers, monitor the execution by using UC.

The following sub-sections will highlight the service selection mechanisms performed in two stages: one is responsible for selecting abstract services to build an instantiated workflow, the other is to select a service implementation to carry out the real computation.

3.2   Selection of Abstract Service

A client requests the execution of a Service-Based Application (SBA) by specifying an abstract workflow. A request is composed of: 1) the functionality of each execution activity, 2) the dependence constraints among those activities and 3) user QoS requirements for the entire application. It is assumed that the global QoS can be computed by combining the non-functional parameters associated to each abstract service of the workflow. To instantiate a workflow, a WI component requires the information of all currently available offers from the *registry*. For each workflow activity, multiple *offers* may be available since the same service can be provided by different providers or under different QoS levels.

The WI component maps the currently available offers to each activity and then it checks the possibility to construct a fully instantiated workflow. Initially, each offer mapped to an activity represents a *chain*. The instantiation is a recursive process: smaller chains mapped to the abstract workflow are concatenated to form larger ones, or assembled around the split and merge nodes (representing workflow branches). The workflow instantiation process is driven by the objective of fulfilling the client's global QoS request on the entire workflow. This is possible only when a QoS of an entire workflow can be expressed by combining the QoS of the single service offers. The instantiation process is not a sequential one that begins from the start node of the abstract workflow. Instead, workflow chains are aggregated and instantiated in a parallel and concurrent way.

The execution state of the Workflow Instantiation component at a given time is represented by the set of available service offers together with the partial results of the workflow instantiation process. The set of offers may change when new offers become available or others disappear from the system. With this design, the result of the instantiation process is not determined only by the initial state of the component, but also by its state evolution in time since the availability of new offers during the process may produce alternative instantiations of the abstract workflow.

3.3   Selection of Concrete Service

Similar to a letting agent, through which a tenancy agreement is made between a landlord and a tenant for the rental of a residential property, an abstract service takes charge of making agreement between requester and a service implementation, either short-term or long-term. Thus, it has to connect to a number of concrete services in the similar way as a letting agent manages various residential properties. The concrete service can join and leave freely. To achieve this, it composes several *invokers*, each *invoker* takes the responsibility of communicating with a certain concrete service, such as forwarding the invocation request and retrieving the result. As a rule, only one invoker can be active and capable of forwarding the request message to the relative concrete service at a time. As a result, a concrete service is selected by activating the corresponding invoker.

Besides the invokers, an abstract service also defines three functional modules. If an invocation demand arrives to the abstract service, the *Evaluation Module* checks whether the concrete service connected by the currently active invoker can satisfy the user's requirement. If not, it deactivates this invoker and informs the *Selection Module* to select another concrete service to avoid the penalty. The selection criteria is based on the historical invocation information. Some non-functional characteristics are monitored by the *Monitoring Module* for each service invocation. After the invocation, monitored results are stored as a record in the relative *invoker*. The *Selection Module* evaluates a concrete service according to these records information (i.e. the response time can reflect the workload of a concrete service as well as network condition). If a qualified concrete service is found, the relative invoker is activated so that the invocation demand can be forwarded to it.

4   Implementation

The implementation of this middleware architecture is based on the chemical programming paradigm inspired by the chemical metaphor. All the computing resources are represented by molecules and the computation can be seen as a series of chemical reactions controlled by a set of rules. Analogous to a chemical equation which reflects nature laws by specifying the reactants and resultants of a chemical reaction, a *rule* defines the law of calculation by specifying the input, output as well as the condition.

Each component in the middleware architecture in Figure 1 is implemented by an HOCL program, defined later on. An HOCL program defines a *multi-set* acting as a chemical reaction container where objects inside represent molecules. Multi-set extends the concept of "set" with "multiplicity": an element can be present only once in a set whereas many times in a multi-set. A multi-set contains elements and rules to perform the computation. As an example, an abstract service defines a multi-set containing some invokers as molecules along with a set of rules to perform the functionalities of three functional modules. This implementation is highly distributed. All the multi-sets are implemented in a decentralized way and they have the ability to talk with each other by writing elements into remote multi-sets.

The chemical-based implementation enables the middleware to adapt to the dynamic environment. A multi-set is implemented as an autonomic system and it works independently and concurrently to the others. Computation in a multi-set can be seen as a perpetual motion that never needs to stop or intervene. If some unexpected incident happens, due to the dynamic and unpredictable characteristic of distributed computing, certain rules are activated to take actions.

4.1 Higher Order Chemical Language

HOCL stands for Higher Order Chemical Language which implements chemical programming model. It is based on the γ-calculus [12] which extends the Gamma [13] language with higher-order property [14]. In Figure 2, an HOCL program is defined to calculate the maximum number of a set of given integers.

```
1    let max =
2        replace x::int,y::int
3        by x
4        if x>y
5    in
6    < Max, 13, 45, 65, 54, 25, 2, 5, 4, 36 >
```

Fig. 2. HOCL program: calculate the maximum integer

An HOCL program is composed of two parts: *Rule Definition* (*Line 1-5*) and *Multi-set Organization* (*Line 6*). In HOCL, a multi-set is defined by a pair of operators "<" and ">", you can define all kinds of elements inside a multi-set such as data, rules as well as other multi-sets. From the chemical perspective, a multi-set is also called a *solution* that can be seen as a membrane so that all the molecules inside it cannot react with the ones outside it.

All the rules appearing in the multi-set have to be defined before. A rule defines how to rewrite a multi-set: it replaces a part of elements by new ones. As a result, rules are defined in the form of `replace P by M if V`. From the perspective of computer science, a rule plays the same role as a function. The `let` keyword gives the name of the function, `replace` lists all the input parameters while `by` keyword indicates the output. More information about how to write HOCL program can be found in [15].

The execution of an HOCL program has the following characteristics: firstly, it is non-deterministic. A rule reacts with the molecules that are chosen non-deterministically. Furthermore, it is parallel in nature. Thus, different reactions can be carried out simultaneously. Thirdly, it is automated and self-coordinated. The results of a certain reaction can activate other rules to perform further calculation. These characteristics make HOCL suitable for distributed applications programming.

4.2 Abstract Service Selection Using Chemical Rules

The chemical implementation of the *workflow instantiation* (WI) component uses the following chemical representations for input and output data:

- **Abstract Workflow** (input): it is defined in a "NODES" chemical solution that contains the abstract descriptions of workflow tasks and their dependences:

  `"NODES":<"Node":<"ID":Si, "TO":<T1,...>,"FROM":<F1,...>>,other nodes>`

  It contains a number of "Node" sub-solutions. Each "Node" sub-solution defines a certain task by specifying its functional requirement (Si) as well as its predecessor nodes ("FROM" sub-solution) and successor nodes ("TO" sub-solution).

- **Offer** (input): a chemical sub-solution representing the abstract service ei that offers the service interface Sm with a QoS ci:

  `"Offer":<ei:Sm,"QOS":ci>.`

- **Instantiated Workflow** (output): a chemical sub-solution representing a composition of service offers:

  `<"FIRST":<ei:Sm>,"LAST":<ej:Sn>,"SPLIT":<ek:Sp>,"MERGE":<el:Sq>,`
  `<first-branch sub-solution>,<second-branch sub-solution>,"QOS":c,...>`

  $ei:Sm$ and $ej:Sn$ are abstract services selected for the first and last activity of the workflow subgraph, and $ek:Sp$ and $el:Sq$ are those associated to split and merge nodes. c is the QoS value computed by combining the QoS partial values of the abstract service offers selected by the instantiation process when building the composition. In the chemical notation the branched paths of the split are represented by nested sub-solutions.

In Figure 3, a workflow with associated abstract service offers is drawn on the top side, while the result of a full instantiated workflow is on the bottom of the figure. In Figure 4, the chemical notations of the abstract workflow, the offers and the result of the mapping between offers and tasks with reference to the example of Figure 3 are reported. Please note that the task-to-offer mapping is one-to-one. The WI component selects an offer for each task of the workflow as well as combining offers according to QoS constraints.

The chemical rules that implement the workflow instantiation process act recursively by concatenating simpler components, named *Partial Instantiated Workflows* (PIWFs), defined as follows: a PIWF is a set of abstract service offers that maps a subgraph of the workflow whose nodes have sources and sinks belonging to the same subgraph, except the first and last nodes which may have respectively sources and sinks outside the subgraph. According to this definition, a single node is a PIWF. Every service offer when put in the notation: `<"FIRST":<ei:Sm>,"LAST":<el:Sm>,...>` represents a PIWF by definition.

Abstract service compositions are built by means of two chemical rules. The first one, named **chainrule** concatenates two PIWFs linked by only one edge. The second rule, named **splitrule** assembles four PIWFs: the first one contains the split node as LAST node, the second one contains the merge node as FIRST node. The other two PIWFs represent the workflow paths from a split node to the associated merge node. A more detailed description of the chemical rules can be found in [16].

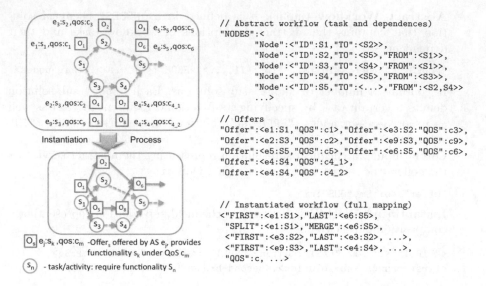

```
// Abstract workflow (task and dependences)
"NODES":<
        "Node":<"ID":S1,"TO":<S2>>,
        "Node":<"ID":S2,"TO":<S5>,"FROM":<S1>>,
        "Node":<"ID":S3,"TO":<S4>,"FROM":<S1>>,
        "Node":<"ID":S4,"TO":<S5>,"FROM":<S3>>,
        "Node":<"ID":S5,"TO":<...>,"FROM":<S2,S4>>
        ...>

// Offers
"Offer":<e1:S1,"QOS":c1>,"Offer":<e3:S2:"QOS":c3>,
"Offer":<e2:S3,"QOS":c2>,"Offer":<e9:S3,"QOS":c9>,
"Offer":<e5:S5,"QOS":c5>,"Offer":<e6:S5,"QOS":c6>,
"Offer":<e4:S4,"QOS":c4_1>,
"Offer":<e4:S4,"QOS":c4_2>

// Instantiated workflow (full mapping)
<"FIRST":<e1:S1>,"LAST":<e6:S5>,
 "SPLIT":<e1:S1>,"MERGE":<e6:S5>,
 <"FIRST":<e3:S2>,"LAST":<e3:S2>, ...>,
 <"FIRST":<e9:S3>,"LAST":<e4:S4>, ...>,
 "QOS":c, ...>
```

Fig. 3. Workflow instantiation   **Fig. 4.** HOCL workflow representation

4.3 Concrete Service Selection Using Chemical Programming Model

A service implementation is selected by activating the corresponding invoker. An invoker can be seen as chemical-level reflection of a service implementation. It is implemented by an object which provides a group of functionalities through a set of interfaces. From the chemical level, this object can be regarded as a molecule which can participate in the chemical reactions. Chemical rules use its interfaces to operate on the invokers, such as activating or selecting an invoker. Here some of the principal interfaces are reported:

- **isValid/setValid/setInvalid.** To select an invoker, some interfaces are exposed to operate on its status. An invoker has two states: valid and invalid. *isValid* operation returns a boolean value indicating whether this invoker is active. *setValid* activates this invoker while *setInvalid* deactivates it.

- **getQoS/addQoS.** An invocation can be associated with multiple QoS requirements. To simplify the description, it is assumed that only one generic QoS parameter (you can regard it as price or response time) is monitored by the monitoring module for each invocation. The monitored data is stored in the relative invoker and can be accessed by a pair of interfaces. *addQoS* records the monitored data from the *monitoring module* into its built-in memory and *getQoS* returns the QoS value calculated based on the historical information. The calculation is based on a certain algorithm.

- **invoke.** This operation forwards the invocation request to the corresponding service implementation. It requires two parameters: one is the operation name and the other is a set of parameters. These parameters are encapsulated into a SOAP message to invoke the corresponding operation.

An *abstract service* is implemented by a multi-set which contains multiple invoker objects. The functionality provided by different modules is performed by a set of rules. Figure 5 lists some of the major rules.

```
let evaluation =
    replace "QoS_Client_Req":qos, invoker
    by invoker.setInvalid(), "QoS_Client_Req":qos, "COMMAND":"SELECT"
    if invoker.isValid()==true && qos < invoker.getQoS()
in
let select  =
    replace "QoS_Client_Req":qos, invoker, "COMMAND":"SELECT"
    by invoker.setValid(), "QoS_Client_Req":qos, "COMMAND":"INVOKE"
    if invoker.isValid()==false && invoker.getQoS()<qos
in
let invoke =
    replace invoker,"INVOKE":operation:<?p>,"COMMAND":"INVOKE"
    by invoker, "RESULT":<invoker.invoke(operation,p)>
    if invoker.isValid()==true
in ...
```

Fig. 5. The Implementation of Concrete Services Selection

The rule `evaluation` implements the evaluation module. The expecting QoS delivery is expressed by `"QoS_Client_Req":qos` tuple. The value of `qos` is determined by the offer that is formerly published by this abstract service. The `evaluation` rule reacts with the current invoker (`invoker.isValid()==true`). If the current invoker can not deliver the service to meet the expecting QoS requirement (`qos<invoker.getQoS()`), it will be deactivated (`invoker.setInvalid()`) and a `COMMAND":"SELECT"` tuple is generated. This tuple informs the system to carry out the selection process by activating the `select` rule which triggers a series of reactions in succession.

The rule `select` and `invoke` are defined in a similar way. Rule `select` gets an invoker, calculates its QoS performance and compare it with the expecting QoS requirement. If this invoker can meet the needs, it is set to `"VALID"` and a `"COMMAND":"INVOKE"` tuple is thrown, indicating the invocation can be performed. This tuple is caught by the rule `invoke` which will then forward the invocation request to the corresponding implementation through *invoke* interface of the active invoker.

5   Conclusion

In this paper, we presented a middleware architecture for dynamic workflow instantiation and execution. The run-time service selecting and binding mechanisms are implemented at two levels: the first occurs at the composition level and it allows to build a full instantiated workflow in consideration of the global QoS requirement. The second is to select a qualified concrete service for each execution activity to guarantee the global QoS compliance. This middleware has implemented the following desirable properties: 1) all partner services are selected and bound dynamically for each execution; 2) client's QoS requirements are taken into account in the selection of services, and 3) the execution of a workflow is decentralized.

The implementation of this middleware is based on chemical programming model. Each middleware component is implemented by a multi-set as an autonomic system adaptive to the fast changing execution environment. The execution can be viewed as perpetual motion that never need to stop. New elements and rules can be added on-demand to meet the new requirements. All components are implemented in a decentralized way and run independently and concurrently to each other. The interaction among them is performed by writing elements to remote multi-sets.

In the future, our work will concentrate on defining a SLA level in this chemical based middleware dealing with SLA negotiation and management. This level will provide the middleware with additional run-time service adaptation ability. We believe that chemical programming model is suitable for implementing service adaptation because of its dynamic, autonomic, independent execution process and distributed implementation.

References

1. Vasiliev, Y.: SOA and WS-BPEL: Composing Service-Oriented Solutions with PHP and ActiveBPEL. Packt Publishing (2007)
2. OASIS Standard: Web Services Business Process Execution Language (2007)
3. Banâtre, J.P., Fradet, P., Radenac, Y.: Principles of Chemical Programming. Electronic Notes in Theoretical Computer Science 124, 133–147 (2005)
4. Mukhija, A., Dingwall-Smith, A., Rosenblum, D.S.: QoS-Aware Service Composition in Dino. In: Proc. of the Fifth European Conference on Web Services, pp. 3–12. IEEE Computer Society, Los Alamitos (2007)
5. Dong, J., Sun, Y., Yang, S.: OWL-S Ontology Framework Extension for Dynamic Web Service Composition. In: Proc. of the Eighteenth International Conference on Software Engineering & Knowledge Engineering, pp. 544–549 (2006)
6. Ponnekanti, S.R., Fox, A.: SWORD: A Developer Toolkit for Web Service Composition. In: Proc. of the 11th World Wide Web Conference (2002)
7. Maximilien, E.M., Singh, M.P.: A Framework and Ontology for Dynamic Web Services Selection. IEEE Internet Computing 8(5), 84–93 (2004)
8. Keidl, M., Seltzsam, S., Stocker, K., Kemper, A.: ServiceGlobe: Distributing E-services Across the Internet. In: Bressan, S., Chaudhri, A.B., Li Lee, M., Yu, J.X., Lacroix, Z. (eds.) CAiSE 2002 and VLDB 2002. LNCS, vol. 2590, pp. 1047–1050. Springer, Heidelberg (2003)
9. Huang, L., Walker, D.W., Huang, Y., Rana, O.F.: Dynamic Web Service Selection for Workflow Optimisation. In: Proc. of the UK e-Science All Hands Meeting (2005)
10. Casati, F., Ilnicki, S., Jin, L., Krishnamoorthy, V., Shan, M.: Adaptive and Dynamic Service Composition in eFlow. In: Proc. of the International Conference on Advanced Information Systems Engineering, pp. 13–21 (2000)

11. Fernandez, H., Priol, T., Tedeschi, C.: Decentralized Approach for Execution of Composite Web Services Using the Chemical Paradigm. In: IEEE International Conference on Web Services (2010)
12. Banâtre, J.-P., Fradet, P., Radenac, Y.: Higher-order chemical programming style. In: Banâtre, J.-P., Fradet, P., Giavitto, J.-L., Michel, O. (eds.) UPP 2004. LNCS, vol. 3566, pp. 84–95. Springer, Heidelberg (2005)
13. Banâtre, J.P., Fradet, P., Le Métayer, D.: Gamma and the Chemical Reaction Model: Fifteen Years After. Multiset Processing, 17–44 (2001)
14. Banâtre, J.-P., Fradet, P., Radenac, Y.: Higher-Order Chemical Programming Style. In: Banâtre, J.-P., Fradet, P., Giavitto, J.-L., Michel, O. (eds.) UPP 2004. LNCS, vol. 3566, pp. 84–95. Springer, Heidelberg (2005)
15. Wang, C., Priol, T.: HOCL Programming Guide. INRIA Rennes (2009)
16. Di Napoli, C., Giordano, M., Németh, Z., Tonellotto, N.: Using Chemical Reactions to Model Service Composition. In: Proc. of the Second International Workshop on Self-Organizing Architectures, pp. 43–50 (2010)
17. Wang, C., Pazat, J.L.: Using Chemical Metaphor to Express Workflow and Orchestration. In: The 10th IEEE International Conference on Computer and Information Technology (2010)
18. Alonso, G., et al.: Web Services - Concepts, Architectures and Applications. Springer, Heidelberg (2004)
19. Banâtre, J.P., Le Métayer, D.: Programming by Multiset Transformation. Commun. ACM 36(1), 98–111 (1993)
20. Banâtre, J.P., Fradet, P., Radenac, Y.: The chemical reaction model recent developments and prospects. In: Wirsing, M., Banâtre, J.-P., Hölzl, M., Rauschmayer, A. (eds.) Soft-Ware Intensive Systems. LNCS, vol. 5380, pp. 209–234. Springer, Heidelberg (2008)
21. Banatre, J.P., et al.: Towards "Chemical" Desktop Grids. e-Science and Grid Computing, 135–142 (2007)
22. Németh, Z., Perez, C., Priol, T.: Workflow Enactment Based on a Chemical Metaphor. In: Software Engineering and Formal Methods, pp. 127–136 (2005)
23. Banâtre, J.-P., Priol, T., Radenac, Y.: Service Orchestration Using the Chemical Metaphor. In: Brinkschulte, U., Givargis, T., Russo, S. (eds.) SEUS 2008. LNCS, vol. 5287, pp. 79–89. Springer, Heidelberg (2008)
24. Banâtre, J.P., Fradet, P., Radenac, Y.: Generalized Multisets for Chemical Programming. Mathematical Structures in Computer Science 16, 557–580 (2006)
25. Li, Y., Yu, X., Geng, L., Wang, L.: Research on Reasoning of the Dynamic Semantic Web Services Composition. In: Proc. of the IEEE/WIC/ACM International Conference on Web Intelligence, pp. 435–441 (2006)

Consumer Mashups with Mashlight*

Luciano Baresi and Sam Guinea

Politecnico di Milano
Dipartimento di Elettronica e Informazione
Via Golgi 42, 20133 Milano, Italy
{baresi,guinea}@elet.polimi.it

Abstract. Mashlight is a lightweight service composition framework for creating process mashups out of Web 2.0 widgets. Widgets represent a simple means to access heterogenous services on the web that non-technical users can easily comprehend. The framework provides a well-defined conceptual model that defines both the notion of composable widget, and how to aggregate them through appropriate control and data flows. It also provides a set of design-time tools for creating widgets and process mashups, a desktop browser-based execution environment, and mobile environments for iOS and Android smartphones.

In this paper we illustrate Mashlight's core concepts, and place emphasis on the use of already existing mashups to dynamically configure and create new ones. This way users can exploit applications that fully meet their needs without programming them directly. The paper presents a detailed example in the tourism space. Consumers first use a process to search for touristic venues in a city they want to visit; then they use a personalized and automatically generated process to manage bookings for those venues.

1 Introduction

Web 2.0 technologies and the *Software as a Service* paradigm [14] are the underpinnings of *widgets*: special-purpose applications for retrieving data from heterogenous services on the Web and for rendering them. As an example, *iGoogle*, which is one of the most famous and well-known platform for widgets, allows users to display information taken from the web in a coherent and consistent way. With iGoogle users select the widgets they want to see in the context of a personalized home page. The actual integration however is very limited: there is no way to define data or control flows among the displayed entities, and thus *compose* them to provide a single service.

A second generation of widgets is trying to address this limitation. Solutions like Yahoo Pipes [4] and mashArt [11] do not consider single widgets in isolation, but provide users with means to compose them. Given the example of BPEL (Business Process Execution Language, [6]) and of workflow languages in general

---

* This research has been partially funded by the European Commission, Programme IDEAS-ERC, Project 227977-SMScom.

E. Di Nitto and R. Yahyapour (Eds.): ServiceWave 2010, LNCS 6481, pp. 112–123, 2010.

(e.g., XPDL [15]), researchers are starting to consider these widgets as the basic activities —building blocks— of light-weight *process mashups*. The idea is to empower the users and let them create their own composite services through an extensible library of components and some simple constructs to relate them.

The paper presents Mashlight, our proposal for process mashups that addresses all these limitations and provides a simple, but powerful, framework. There is no need for heavy Web servers and container technologies since the whole proposal is based on common client-side Web technologies. Conceptually, Mashlight provides a complete model to compose widgets. More pragmatically, it provides two sets of tools. At design time, Mashlight provides tools for both defining new widgets and for aggregating them. At runtime, it offers execution environments for conventional browsers (like Firefox and Chrome), and for iOS and Android mobile phones.

The paper introduces the composition technique, with all the elements needed to define both the data and control flows among the widgets. It also stresses the additions with respect to the first version of the work [5] and the new tool support offered to the different classes of users. Finally, special emphasis is placed on the automatic generation of user-oriented compositions. We advocate that already existing mashups can be used to configure and create new added-value mashups for the users. For example, if we think of planning a holiday trip in Milan, we may want to select the elements of interests (museums, churches, restaurants. etc.) from a Google Maps-like interface, and then proceed with the actual reservations. The first step can be a mashup that is shared among all the tourists in Milan, but the actual sites of interest may vary from person to person, and thus the second step needs to be a customized mashup that is built using the user's actual selections. This is where Mashlight hides the actual effort and automatically provides each visitor with a personalized application to complete the reservations and create a complete schedule.

The rest of the paper is organized as follows. Section 2 presents the abstractions that are at the core of the Mashlight model, and highlights some of the main novelties introduced in this paper. Section 3 gives a brief overview of the design-time tools provided for creating Mashlight compatible widgets and for composing them into mashups, and of the three execution environments that have been implemented. Section 4 introduces the notion of template-based process creation, and provides a detailed example in the tourism space. Section 5 surveys related work, and Section 6 concludes the paper.

2 Mashlight in a Nutshell

A consumer mashup solution needs to be simple. It needs to provide few key abstractions that the consumers can understand immediately. This is why Mashlight [5] applications are built defining a process-based composition of Web 2.0 widgets. Although widgets are typically designed as autonomous entities, in Mashlight they collaborate by exchanging data, and can be sequenced. A Mashlight process is modeled using a directed graph: nodes represent the widgets we

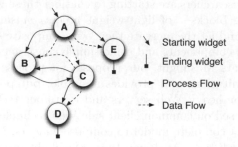

Fig. 1. Graph representation of a mashup

compose, while arcs represent the control flow (normal arcs) and the data flow (dotted arcs). When creating a Mashlight process a user simply defines "when" a widget has to be activated, and using "what" data.

Control flows connect widget *outlinks* to widget *inlinks* to determine the order in which the widgets are "activated" during the process' execution, i.e., the order in which they are shown to the user. Each widget can have only one inlink, but as many outlinks as desired. When a widget decides, either due to its internal logic or to a specific user action, that it is time to trigger the next widget in the process, it activates one, and only one, of its outlinks. For example, in Figure 1, widget A has two outlinks: one is connected to widget B and one is connected to widget E. Only one of them will be activated by A. By appropriately connecting outlinks and inlinks it is also possible to create loops in our processes. This is the case of widgets B and C in Figure 1.

Data flows connect widgets through their *input* and *output* parameters. Parameters can be defined as simple or complex XSD data types, can have multiple cardinality (i.e., arrays), and can be either mandatory or optional. Mashlight supports data exchanges with multiple destinations[1]. In Figure 1, when widget A terminates it passes its output data to B, C, and E. It also supports data exchanges with multiple sources. Indeed, B's input parameters can be set either by A or by C. The first time B is activated it gets its inputs from A. The second time, however, it has to solve an input conflict. Although A has not been re-executed, its outputs are still available to the process; C's outputs are also available. Mashlight solves conflicts by executing the assignment that involves the widget that was most recently executed (in this case C).

In this paper we present a new extension to this simple model: a new abstraction called the *super-widget*. It acts as a container for widgets that are "activated" in parallel. This allows more compelling mashups to be built. Instead of "showing" just one widget at a time, we can create iGoogle-like mashups with advanced data flows. Figure 2 shows a simple example of a super-widget containing widgets A and B.

---

[1] The security issues that can arise from exchanging data amongst widgets that have been designed by different parties, and that may have hidden dependencies, are currently beyond the scope of our work, but will be considered in the future.

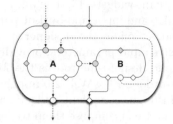

Fig. 2. The Mashlight super-widget

Externally a super-widget behaves the same way as any other widget, that is by participating in the overall process' control and data flows. Once it is activated, however, it shows the user multiple widgets that do not obey to any particular control flow. The user can interact with them in any order, and they all remain active until the super-widget, as a whole, indicates that the next widget in the overall process needs to be activated.

Inside a super-widget, the main form of collaboration becomes data exchanges. Data exchanges are triggered by outlink activations. Instead of causing an internal widget to be closed, the activation of an outlink causes it to notify the destinations of its output parameters that new data have become available. The notified widgets can then proceed to refresh all their input parameters, and their UI if deemed necessary. In our example, A has an outlink that causes it to pass its output parameters to B, and the same is true for B which can pass its parameters to A. The super-widget abstraction is completely transparent to the internal widgets; they do not know they are being used within a super-widget.

A super-widget's set of input paramaters is determined by the mandatory input parameters of its internal widgets, while its output parameters are a subset of the output parameters of its internal widgets. Internal output parameters that are not part of the super-widget's set of output parameters are lost once the super-widget is terminated. In our example, the super-widget's input and output parameters are determined by A, while B has no mandatory input parameters and its output parameters are lost when the super-widget is closed. Similarly, a super-widget's set of outlinks is a subset of the outlinks of its internal widgets; the subset excludes those that are already used internally to trigger data exchanges. When none of the outlinks can be used, the framework provides a special-purpose deactivation widget. Its sole goal is to present the user with a button he/she can use to close the super-widget and go to the next widget in the process. In our example, the super-widget's only outlink is determined by one of B's outlinks.

3   Tools

The Mashlight Suite provides two design-time tools, and three different execution environments. The first design-time tool is the *Mashlight Widget Builder*. It consists of an Eclipse-based programming environment in which designers can create new Mashlight compliant widgets. First of all, it helps the designer define the widget's inlinks, outlinks, and input and output parameters inside an XML-based manifest file. Second, it guides the designer in the use of the APIs the widget needs to use to receive input parameters, provide output parameters, and activate outlinks. The second design-time tool is the *Mashlight Process Builder* (see Figure 3 (a)). It is an Adobe Flex Web 2.0 application that keeps track of a searchable registry of Mashlight compliant widgets, and provides a drag-and-drop canvas in which designers can compose them to define processes. When the process design is completed, the designer can export the process to any of the three Mashlight execution environments.

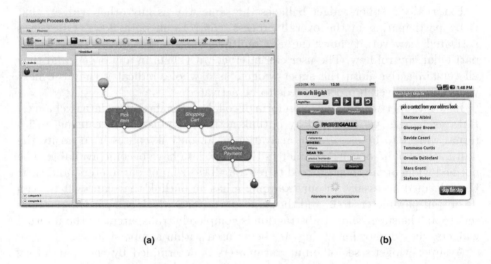

(a)   (b)

Fig. 3. (a) The Mashlight Process Builder development environment. (b) Mobile widgets.

The Mashlight suite provides three different execution environments. The first is a browser-based desktop environment implemented in JavaScript[2]. The other two environments are targeted towards mobile users (i.e. iOS and Android phones). With respect to their desktop counterpart, they do not support super-widgets. This is due to their limited screen sizes, which make it impossible to visualize more than one widget at a time. Besides standard widgets, each mobile platform has additional widgets that take advantage of its specific hardware and software features. Figure 3 (b) shows two examples of mobile widgets. The first is an iOS widget that implements a search on the italian equivalent of the yellow pages and takes advantage of the phone's geolocation capabilities. The second is an Android widget that allows the user to get a friend's details from the phone's contact list.

---

[2] The browser-based environment can be experienced online at http://home.dei. polimi.it/guinea/mashlight/index.html. A screen-cast showing how to use the tools is available at http://home.dei.polimi.it/guinea/mashlight/cast.mov.

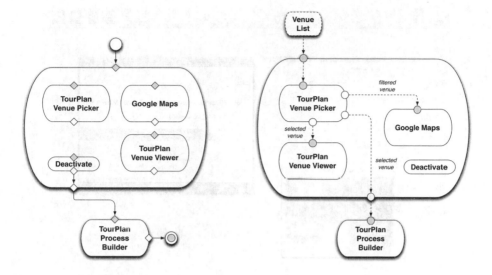

Fig. 4. TourPlan's first process control and data flows

4   Template-Based Generation of Compositions

The Mashlight Process Builder is a flexible design-time tool for defining a process' control and data flows. However, we advocate that the very notions of control and data flows are too complex for the average non-technical user. This is why we propose to use control flow templates to semi-automatically create processes based on the end-user's needs. A template does not define the process' data flows, which remains a domain-specific chore that must be performed manually. However, if sufficient domain-specific knowledge is available, the templates can be extended to provide the data flows as well, fully automatizing the composition of the process.

We currently provide implementations for three different general templates. Each template takes a set of widgets and composes them according to a specific topology. The *Sequential* template creates a sequence in which the widgets are activated one at a time. The *Container* template creates a single super-widget that contains all the widgets being composed. The *Star* template creates a star-like topology in which every widget can be accessed from a central core widget that acts as a dictionary. For lack of space we will concentrate on the star template and show how it is used in an example that takes place in the tourism space.

4.1   The TourPlan Application

TourPlan is an application that allows users to organize and manage visits to touristic cities. It takes place in two distinct steps. First, users search for venues of interest and add them to a "wish list". In the second step users plan the

Fig. 5. Searching for venues in the TourPlan mashup

visit. They are supported by their online Google calendar, and can create new
bookings for these venues or manage existing ones. Since the bookings are saved
as events in the online calendar, they remain available for offline viewing. The
TourPlan application is built as two different mashups, one for each of these
two steps. The first mashup is statically created by TourPlan, while the second
mashup is automatically generated using a customized and extended version of
the star template and info gathered during the execution of the first process.

The first mashup consists of a sequence of two widgets. The first is a super-
widget in which the user searches for venues of interest, while the second is
responsible for automatically generating the second mashup. The super-widget
contains four different widgets: a `TourPlan Venue Picker`, a `TourPlan Venue
Viewer`, `Google Maps`, and a deactivation widget. The `Venue Picker` initially
receives a list of all the TourPlan venues the user can choose from. Through
this widget the user can filter the venues by type (e.g., restaurant, theatre,
museum, etc.). The result is a set of venues that is passed to the `Google Maps`
widget so that they can be shown on the map. By clicking on a single venue,
either in the picker or on the map, the user gets a more detailed presentation
of the venue in the `Venue Viewer`. To add a venue to the "wish list", the user
must select a venue in the `Venue Picker` and click on the button "Add". The
final contents of the "wish list" constitute the output data that are sent from
the super-widget to the `TourPlan Process Builder` widget, i.e., the second
widget in the process. Figure 5 shows the super-widget being executed within
our browser-based desktop execution environment. In this case the user has
filtered the venues to show only those that are museums in the city of Milan,

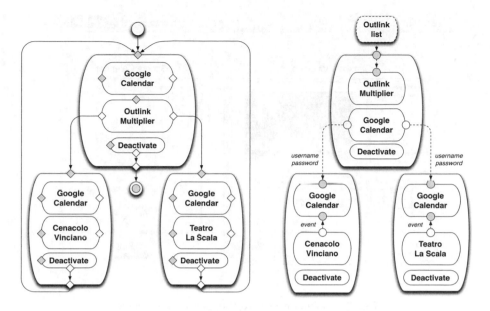

Fig. 6. TourPlan's second process control and data flows

and has selected the "Cenacolo Vinciano", which is where Leonardo Da Vinci's Last Supper is held.

The second mashup allows the user to plan a visit based on the venues selected in the first process. Figure 6 illustrates the mashup's control and data flows, which are derived from the star template. Since the TourPlan example consists of a "closed" scenario, i.e., one in which the venues are limited in number and well-known, we implemented an extended version of the template inside the `TourPlan Process Builder`. First of all, the topology is mainly the same as in the case of the standard star template, except that now a `Google Calendar` widget is made visible to the user at all times, to help him/her manage his/her bookings. Second, since the venues all support the same output parameters, we were able to automatically construct the process' data flows as well, making the process creation entirely automatic. In particular, we use the output parameters to store the user's bookings to the his/her online calendar using the `Google Calendar` widget. The extended template's structure presents a central super-widget in which the consumer can consult his/her online calendar, and the list of venues he/she wants to create/manage bookings for. From here the user can go back and forth between the central super-widget and the venue-specific super-widgets. The number of venue-specific super-widgets depends on the number of venues chosen in the first process.

In the example shown in Figure 6 the user has selected two venues: the "Cenacolo Vinciano" and the "Teatro La Scala". The control flow is made possible by the `Outlink Multiplier`, a widget implemented especially for the star template. The number of its outlinks is defined by the number of control flow arcs

Fig. 7. Booking a visit to the Cenacolo Vinciano

that are established while defining the process. The widget receives a list of out-link descriptions, and presents them to the user. When the user clicks on one of the descriptions, the widget is closed (together, in this case, with its surrounding super-widget), and the process proceeds. The process' control flow also allows the user to navigate back to the central super-widget once the user has finished creating or managing the booking for that venue.

The data flows in this process are also quite simple. First we have a dynamically determined number of data flows that connect the Google Calendar in the central super-widget to the `Google Calendar`s in the venue-specific super-widgets. These flows share the user's login username and password, so that the user does not need to re-insert them every time the `Google Calendar` widget is executed. Second, we have one additional data flow inside each venue-specific super-widget that connects the venue's widget to `Google Calendar`. This way, as soon as a management operation is performed, the activation of the venue's outlink will notify `Google Calendar` to update its online contents accordingly. Figure 7 illustrates the execution of the super-widget for managing bookings at the "Cenacolo Vinciano". On the left-hand side users can access the venue-specific widget where new bookings can be made, while on the right-hand side users can consult their online Google calendar.

5   Related Work

Research in the field of consumer-based mashups has followed an interesting trend in the last few years. After an initial surge in the number of competing approaches, mainly proposed by big industrial players, many apparently promising projects have been closed down. This is the case of Microsoft's Popfly project [8], a project in which users could aggregate predefined blocks to combine data web services with special visualization tools. One of the problems with Popfly was the limited number of predefined blocks that were made available. Another problem was the failure to provide a lightweight solution; mashups had to be uploaded to a web server and were only accessible through Microsoft Silverlight capable devices. Another project that was shutdown is Mozilla's Ubiquity [3] project; it provided a browser plugin for enriching the web browsing experience. The plugin consisted in a command line for inserting natural language commands, to manipulate the data present on the pages they were visiting. The project suffered from security issues since any JavaScript code could be triggered by these commands. Finally, another proposal that was shutdown was Google's own Mashup Editor [1].

The most prominent consumer mashup approach still provided by an industrial player is Intel's MashMaker [2] [9]. It consists of a browser plugin. When viewing a page users can enrich its content through special-purpose visualization widgets on top of the page's main content. The approach completely hides the composition chore from the end user. The plugin analyzes the page's data and suggests visualization widgets that may be of interest, based on previous use of the system. The approach is profoundly different from ours, since they do not support control flows, severely hampering the range of possible mashups.

Regarding academia there have been a number of interesting approaches. One of the most prominent is the mashArt project [11] [10]. mashArt provides a component model, an event-based composition model, and a development and execution platform. Components model and expose a state, events are used to communicate that there has been a change in a component's state, and operations are invoked as the result of these events. To support control flow, mashArt allows the designer to define conditions on operations, and split/join constructs. mashArt is similar to Mashlight in many ways. However, Mashlight provides a more sophisticated control flow model that does not focus on a single presentation canvas; mashArt is more focused on data flows. Another difference is that their component model is more taxing than our; designers require more effort to produce mashArt compliant components. In mashArt data are mainly name-value pairs that cover synchronization needs. Complex data exchanges need to be performed by the components' internal logic. A similar approach is followed by the ezWeb project [7]. They also concentrate on defining event-based data flows amongst widgets. A key difference is that they explicitly model the resources that lay behind the widgets using REST. This allows them to define data flows both at the resource level and at the GUI level. This gives them an extra degree of flexibility, at the cost of higher complexity: a trade-off we are approaching differently. Deri Pipes [12] is a data mashup technique that focuses on RDF data. It provides atomic operations that can be used in a pipe-and-filter fashion to combine data from different sources, to perform ontology alignments and mediations, and to query and filter data. The focus on semantic web technologies for RDF data manipulation, such as SPARQL, proves that there is a

market for such specific mashup solutions. We believe that the flexibility provided by Mashlight allows us to cover such needs through the implementation
of specific widget libraries. Finally, Kazhamiakin et al. [13] propose a radically
different approach. They advocate that mobile phones are offering more and
more services, yet there is no way to combine them to provide added value.
Their service composition is modeled around the mobile phone's calendar. The
calendar becomes the central point of access to the composition, and defines all
the data flows needed to effectively enact the mashup. The end-user is solely the
consumer of the mashup, while the application itself is built by an experienced
designer using the phone's software framework. It is possible to implement such
metaphors using Mashlight as a programming paradigm, given its high degree
of flexibility and the presence of special-purpose widgets that take advantage of
the hardware and services provided by the mobile devices.

6   Conclusions and Future Work

The paper has presented the latest version of Mashlight. It has introduced the
conceptual model and the tool support we offer to design widgets and assemble
them, but also to execute produced compositions on different devices.

State of the art shows us that there are a number of open issues that consumer
mashup approaches have not been able to solve, and that have become important
research challenges in themselves. The first is how to provide users with a critical
mass of composable entities. To this end we have begun the development of a
tool that can semi-automatically transform Google Gadgets, making them compliant to the Mashlight framework. The second is how to allow users to create
new compositions in a way that is powerful, yet easy. Mashlight already provides a rich environment for designing processes that users can adopt. However,
the paper has shown how it is possible to automatically generate new process
mashups through templates. This is an interesting innovation that moves in the
direction of letting users exploit applications that fully meet their needs without
programming them directly. We are currently investigating a scripting language
that designers can use to create new core templates and customized versions of
the core templates. In our future we will implement new widgets to cover more
disparate user needs, and provide further empirical evaluation of our approach.
We will also engage in lab-based studies to evaluate our tools' usability with
people that have varied degrees of technological awareness.

References

1. Google mashup editor, http://code.google.com/gme/index.html
2. Intel mash maker, http://mashmaker.intel.com/web/
3. Mozilla Labs Ubiquity,
   https://mozillalabs.com/blog/2008/08/introducing-ubiquity//
4. Yahoo pipes, http://pipes.yahoo.com/pipes/

5. Albinola, M., Baresi, L., Carcano, M., Guinea, S.: Mashlight: a Lightweight Mashup Framework for Everyone. In: 2nd Workshop on Mashups, Enterprise Mashups and Lightweight Composition on the Web, MEM 2009 (2009)
6. Andrews, T., Curbera, F., Dholakia, H., Goland, Y., Klein, J., Leymann, F., Liu, K., Roller, D., Smith, D., Thatte, S., Trickovic, I., Weerawarana, S.: Business Process Execution Language for Web Services, Version 1.1. BPEL4WS specification (May 2003)
7. Lizcano, D., Soriano, J., Reyes, M., Hierro, J.J.: EzWeb/FAST: Reporting on a Successful Mashup-based Solution for Developing and Deploying Composite Applications in the Upcoming Web of Services. In: Kotsis, G., Taniar, D., Pardede, E., Ibrahim, I.K. (eds.) iiWAS, pp. 15–24. ACM, New York (2008)
8. Griffin, E.: Foundations of Popfly: Rapid Mashup Development (Foundations)
9. Ennals, R.J., Garofalakis, M.N.: MashMaker: mashups for the masses. In: Proceedings of the 2007 ACM SIGMOD International Conference on Management of Data, p. 1118. ACM, New York (2007)
10. Daniel, F., Casati, F., Benatallah, B., Shan, M.: Hosted Universal Composition: Models, Languages and Infrastructure in mashArt. In: Laender, A.H., Fand Castano, S., Dayal, U., Casati, F. (eds.) ER 2009. LNCS, vol. 5829, pp. 428–443. Springer, Heidelberg (2009)
11. Daniel, F., Maristella, M.: Turning Web Applications into Mashup Components: Issues, Models, and Solutions. In: Gaedke, M., Grossniklaus, M., Díaz, O. (eds.) ICWE 2009. LNCS, vol. 5648, pp. 45–60. Springer, Heidelberg (2009)
12. Le Phuoc, D., Polleres, A.: Rapid prototyping of semantic mash-ups through semantic web pipes. In: Quemada, J., León, G., Maarek, Y.S., Nejdl, W. (eds.) WWW, pp. 581–590. ACM, New York (2009)
13. Kazhamiakin, R., Bertoli, P., Paolucci, M., Pistore, M., Wagner, M.: Having Services "YourWay!": Towards User-Centric Composition of Mobile Services. In: Domingue, J., Fensel, D., Traverso, P. (eds.) FIS 2008. LNCS, vol. 5468, pp. 94–106. Springer, Heidelberg (2009)
14. Turner, M., Budgen, D., Brereton, P.: Turning Software into a Service. Computer, 38–44 (2003)
15. van der Aalst, W.M.P.: Patterns and XPDL: A Critical Evaluation of the XML Process Definition Language. BPM Center Report BPM-03-09, BPMcenter. org (2003)

Telecommunication Mashups Using RESTful Services

Alistair Duke[1], Sandra Stincic[1], John Davies[1], Guillermo Álvaro Rey[2],
Carlos Pedrinaci[3], Maria Maleshkova[3], John Domingue[3], Dong Liu[3],
Freddy Lecue[4], and Nikolay Mehandjiev[4]

[1] BT Innovate & Design, British Telecommunications plc. Ipswich, UK
{alistair.duke,sandra.stincic,john.nj.davies}@bt.com
[2] iSOCO, Madrid, Spain
galvaro@isoco.com
[3] Knowledge Media Institute, The Open University, Milton Keynes, UK
{c.pedrinaci,m.maleshkova,j.b.domingue,d.liu}@open.ac.uk
[4] University of Manchester, Manchester M15 6PB, UK
f.lecue@mbs.ac.uk, nikolay.mehandjiev@manchester.ac.uk

Abstract. Evolution in the telecommunications sector has led to companies
within it providing APIs for their products and services, allowing others to build
communication services into their own service offerings. In order to support
mass adoption of this new approach, consumers of these APIs (many of which
are RESTful) must be supported by a reduction in the complexity involved with
describing, finding, composing and invoking them. Existing efforts to provide
automation have, in general, focused on WSDL services rather than REST
services. The paper explores the approach of the SOA4All project in supporting
interaction with REST services which is being applied in a telecommunications
focused case study.

Keywords: Web Services, Service Orientated Architecture, Semantic Web,
Web2.0, REST, Telecommunications.

1 Introduction

Telecommunication companies (telcos) are currently witnessing an erosion of their
customer base due to increased competition and the emergence of 'Over The Top'
(OTT) service providers – service and content providers that don't own the network
they use – who threaten to disintermediate telcos to the role of a commodity provider
(i.e. a supplier of 'dumb pipes'). In response to this threat, telcos are looking into
ways to generate further income by offering their services, e.g. voice, messaging, etc.
publicly on the web. Telcos have in this way the opportunity to reduce their costs, get
products to market quicker and provide customers with the flexibility they are
increasingly demanding. Furthermore the opportunity exists for telcos to transform
themselves by adopting new business models e.g. based on service platforms or by
utilizing the relationship they hold with their customers to create value.

A high proportion of these services are provided via RESTful services [1] (i.e.
services conforming to Representational State Transfer) rather than classical web

E. Di Nitto and R. Yahyapour (Eds.): ServiceWave 2010, LNCS 6481, pp. 124–135, 2010.
© Springer-Verlag Berlin Heidelberg 2010

services based on SOAP and WSDL. An internal BT survey found that 47% of providers supported REST whilst only 25% supported SOAP. The RESTful approach is generally simpler and aligns more closely with the web architecture. However, they are generally described in human readable web pages rather than machine readable XML files as is the case with WSDL. Thus enabling automated discovery and consumption of RESTful services is even more problematic than is the case with WSDL web services.

A further issue is the complexity of composing multiple services to meet a particular need (i.e. a mashup) or to integrate a service with an existing interface or system. As soon as a user has a need to go beyond what is offered by a single service (which they would typically interact with by filling in form fields and clicking a button), some development expertise is required.

SOA4All is an EU integrating project that supports the creation and proliferation of a "Service Web"—a Web where millions of parties are exposing and consuming millions of services seamlessly and transparently. A major outcome of the SOA4All project is SOA4All Studio, a set of online tools that cover the whole life-cycle of services from the end-user perspective: interaction with services is addressed from provisioning (where annotations are made on different types of services, and where they can be composed into more complex ones), consumption (where suitable services can be discovered and invoked) and analysis (where the execution of services can be monitored and analyzed at different levels).

By lowering the entrance barrier to the service world, SOA4All supports the "service prosumer", i.e., end-users who not only interact with services in a passive manner, consuming them, but are also able to create new ones or compose existing ones, etc. Telcos can leverage this fact by offering a set of base services that expose their telecommunications capabilities with which users can create new applications that make use of them, implementing new niche personalized services more easily.

This paper explores the SOA4All approach by describing a telecommunications-related scenario based on RESTful services and HTTP-based web APIs which is then implemented using SOA4All Studio through a process including description, discovery, composition, deployment and usage. In Section 2 we briefly describe the BT Ribbit API and identify the need for the SOA4All approach. The scenario and associated services are described in Section 3. The implementation of the scenario is described in Section 4 followed by an account of the next steps for the project in Section 5.

2   The Ribbit Vision

Ribbit (http://www.ribbit.com), a wholly-owned US-based BT subsidiary and a voice-oriented web company ('webco'), currently allows developers to consume voice services accessible via Adobe's Flex and Flash with a REST API currently in beta. The services that are exposed at the moment include voice calls, call routing, call management, third party call control, voice and text messaging, speech-to-text, VoIP and contact management, with more to come in the near future. Currently, users require detailed technical knowledge of the Flex, Flash or PHP programming languages to be able to access, combine and use Ribbit's web services. In the

SOA4All project, the use of contextual knowledge will support both the composition and provisioning of services in a customized manner. Using automation, we plan to shield service users from the complexities of creating such knowledge. We will also take advantage of semantic descriptions of services in building (semi-) automated provisioning, composition, consumption and monitoring tools. The next-generation platform we envisage will also enable inclusion of third party services. In addition, it will address several key issues for BT's transformation, including: (i) reducing time to market; (ii) enabling third-party services to be integrated into BT's portfolio; (iii) increasing so-called 'new wave' revenues from networked IT services; and (iv) extending BT's SOA to the public web.

The possibility of increased competition from the 'Over The Top' (OTT) service providers – service and content providers that don't own the network they use – highlights a risk that telcos could become 'disintermediated' from the digital supply chain. Webcos typically use advertising based business models, whereas telcos collect revenues through usage-based billing. As these two sectors converge, the challenge for telcos is to reconcile the two different business models, finding ways to generate revenue from advertising, while continuing to offer billable services where appropriate. Finally, other changes are apparent such as the rise in virtual social networking, the roll-out of alternative access networks such as WiMax and the emergence of enterprise mashups that use Web 2.0-style applications alongside more traditional IT assets.

Considering all these aspects, by appropriately positioning themselves in the Web 2.0 world, telcos will continue to evolve and transform themselves to providers of 'smart' pipes (connections backed by QoS guarantees and service level agreements), platforms that support an open service ecosystem and a range of telco and third-party applications that run on such platforms. Telcos will not only need to create new services to address the needs of the long tail (i.e. niche markets), but also allow third-party service providers to make use of telcos' underutilized operations and business support systems capabilities to create new service offerings, thereby creating new revenue streams.

3 Scenario Description

Our scenario describes a situation in which SOA4All technology is used for creating simple mash-ups of Ribbit services and other popular services on the Web. The aim is to make it easy for novice users to access Ribbit services and combine them with other services on the Web to create novel applications.

The focus of our scenario is on casual users building non-critical applications, and therefore involves minimal security or management infrastructure. In the scenario, a composition is created that allows one to organize a social meeting with a group of friends at short notice (as shown in Fig. 1).

The process is as follows: (i) Get list of friends from social networking site – in this example Last.fm was used, as it has a simple and open API to retrieve connections between users, and one of the options for meeting up is related to concerts, which are also available in Last.fm (ii) Find out which of the identified friends are currently close to the user's own current location using mapping sites such as FireEagle and Multimap (iii) Filter the meeting location list depending on reports from a weather service (iv) Find out travel information for the proposed meeting.

Send out invites and directions using Ribbit SMS to those users that are located within a defined range, customized depending on the weather information.

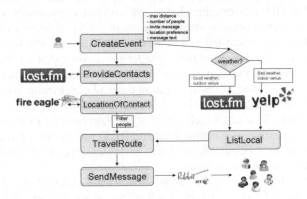

Fig. 1. Identifying service properties

For this scenario, several existing RESTful services and HTTP-based APIs were used. These use a range of authentication methods such as OUATH (http://oauth.net/). or API keys and return data as XML or JSON (JavaScript Object Notation).

4   Composition of Restful Services Using Soa4all Studio

In this section we briefly describe the SOA4All project and the SOA4All Studio and then illustrate the Studio's use in the implementation of the scenario.

The SOA4All project will help to realize a world where a massive number of parties expose and consume services via advanced Web technology. The outcome of the project will be a framework and software infrastructure that aims at integrating SOA and four complementary and revolutionary technical advances (the Web, context-aware technologies, Web 2.0 and Semantic Web) into a coherent and domain independent worldwide service delivery platform.

The aim of the SOA4All Studio is to provide an integrating interface for the various components developed in the SOA4All project, namely, service provisioning, consumption, process modelling, and analysis. It provides two levels of service i.e. infrastructure services such as storage, communication and user management and a UI Library containing widgets, templates and a dashboard. The latter provides the connection between users and the SOA4All run-time components. Further details about the studio are provided in [2].

4.1   Service Description

The services used within our scenario are RESTful services with API descriptions in HTML pages. In order that these services can be more easily discovered and used in a service composition, they need to be supplemented with semantic annotation of their properties. This additional semantic information supports the automation of discovery, composition and consumption tasks, which otherwise have to be performed completely manually. In addition, as opposed to WSDL services, there is no widely accepted structured language for describing RESTful services. As a consequence, in order to use RESTful services, developers are obliged to manually locate, retrieve, read and interpret heterogeneous documentation of RESTful services in HTML, and subsequently develop custom tailored software that is able to invoke and manipulate them. In SOA4All, a solution to these challenges is provided by the provisioning platform [2], which as the name suggests, provides tools and functionalities for supporting the provisioning of services and in particular, semantic Web services. The creation of semantic RESTful services is enabled through SWEET – the Semantic Web sErvice Editing Tool [3], which is part of the Provisioning Platform Prototype. It enables both the creation of machine-readable RESTful service descriptions and the addition of semantic annotations, in order to better support discovering services, creating mashups, and invoking them.

Therefore, the first step of the scenario is to use SWEET to create semantic descriptions of the RESTful services. Each of the service descriptions is annotated following these four main steps:

Identifying service properties - Insertion of hRESTS microformat tags in the HTML service descriptions in order to mark service properties (operations, address, HTTP method, input, output and labels). This is achieved by highlighting the relevant portion of the description and clicking on the appropriate hRESTS tag in the tool and is shown in Fig. 2.

Identifying suitable domain ontologies - Integrated ontology search for linking semantic information to service properties. The right of Fig. 2 shows a domain ontology being used to annotate a service property (password).

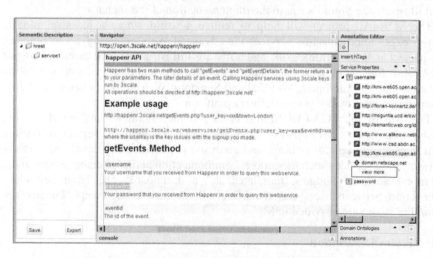

Fig. 2. Annotation of a service within the SWEET tool

Semantic annotation of service properties - Insertion of MicroWSMO [4] model reference tags, pointing to the associated semantic meaning of the service properties.

Saving the semantic RESTful services - Saving semantically annotated HTML RESTful service descriptions and automatic extraction of RDF MicroWSMO service descriptions based on the annotated HTML into the SOA4All repository.

In accordance with good practice, rather than create new ontologies, we re-used publically available widely used ontologies such as the W3C's GEO vocabulary for latitude and longitude, the FOAF vocabulary for personal profiles and the Kanzaki music vocabulary for music events information. An additional ontology was engineered for any missing properties.

When the user has finished annotating the HTML RESTful service description with hRESTS and MicroWSMO tags, the resulting annotated service can be saved, exported to RDF and / or uploaded to a service repository allowing service consumers to locate it.

4.2 Service Discovery

Service-orientation advocates the development of complex distributed applications based on the reuse and composition of existing functionality offered as services. Essential to this vision are the publishing and discovery of services. A number of repositories for WSDL services have been created to this end, e.g., UDDI [5], but they have failed to provide suitable support for publishing and querying them in an expressive and extensible manner. Research on SWS has devoted significant effort to enhancing service repositories with semantics in order to provide more accurate results or simply to automate the discovery of services to a greater extent, see for example [6] and [7]. Despite the efforts thus far, the largest public SWS repository is probably still OPOSSum, a test collection with less than 3000 service annotations [8]. Unfortunately, although useful for testing, OPOSSum does not represent nor does it aim to be a service repository supporting the publication and discovery of services.

In order to achieve the vision previously highlighted it is essential to have in place appropriate mechanisms for supporting the crawling, publication and querying services available on the Web, may they be WSDL-based on Web APIs.

To this end we have developed iServe [9], a platform for the seamless publishing of SWS. iServe addresses the publication of services from a novel perspective based upon 3 fundamental lessons learnt from the evolution of the Web of Data [10]: (i) lightweight ontologies together with the possibility to provide custom extensions prevail against more complex models, (ii) linked data principles are an appropriate means for publishing large amounts of semantic data, both for human and machine consumption and (iii) links between publicly available datasets are essential for the scalability and the value of the data exposed.

iServe (http://iserve.kmi.open.ac.uk) provides support for the seamless publishing of SWS defined in a variety of formats and according to different conceptual models, by transforming them into linked data that can easily be browsed, retrieved and querying by both humans and machines. The current version of iServe provides support for SAWSDL [11], WSMO-Lite [12], MicroWSMO [13], and (partially) OWL-S [14] descriptions. Taking the original descriptions, iServe automatically generates the appropriate RDF statements according to a common and minimal service model largely based on the one defined in WSMO-Lite, and exposes them as linked data in a manner that is suitable for the description and interlinking of services, people and data.

To facilitate the consumption and manipulation of the published linked data about services, iServe provides three interfaces: (i) a Web-based application, called iServe Browser, allowing users to browse, query and upload services to iServe, (ii) a SPARQL (the W3Cs RDF query language) endpoint where all the data hosted in iServe can be accessed and queried and (iii) a RESTful API that enables creating, retrieving and querying for services directly from applications.

Additionally, to further simplify the publication of services we provide two Web-based applications, SWEET (mentioned earlier) & SOWER supporting the annotation of Web APIs and WSDLs based on MicroWSMO and WSMO-Lite respectively, which directly provide the means for publishing the annotations in iServe.

4.3 Service Composition

SOA4All Studio contains a Process Editor tool which is used to link the different (annotated) services into the desired process (composition), also taking into account the restrictions that apply in the scenario. It is underpinned by the semantically powerful LPML [15] (Light-weight Process Modeling Language), yet the graphical interface users see is simplified for ease-of-use. The missing information is either supplied by users where they understand the underlying semantics, or by a reasoning engine which considers data types and activity specifications.

In this section, we first overview the underlying composition operators required to support the end-user in modeling her composition, Then, we briefly explain how expert and novice users interact with the process editor to model their composition using some specific composition operators.

4.3.1 Service Composition Constructs
Any process is composed of mashing data (i.e., data-flow based operators) from one service to another. For instance, the following illustrates the data-flow based operators used to model and design the composition of our scenario: (i) splitting data from the end user inputs e.g., "Location User" is reused in different points of the composition; (ii) merging data from different services' outputs e.g., the getLocalVenue and getLocalBar services provide multiple outputs that require merging for processing in the next step (by some following services); (iii) filtering data from the output of a service e.g., the SendSMS service will need only the first (closest) Location venue provided by the getLocalVenue service and getLocalBar service outputs; (iv) iterating processes on specific data controlled by some rules e.g., each element of the getFriend service needs to be processed by the getLocation service as inputs. The rule used is "Count Operator" with the "number of people" as variables; and (v) counting the number of outputs provided by a service e.g., the getLocation service iterates on a given number of outputs of a service, here a given number of friends.

In addition, the latter process is composed of one specific control flow construct supported by our ongoing work on LPML i.e. Conditional branching on services depending on the values of output data of services e.g., the getWeather service moves to getLocalVenue or getLocalBar depending on the data provided by getWeather service.

To this end, the scenario has been modelled and encoded using the LPML composition language. More specifically, the whole composition has been specified using a subset of the "Data Flow" operators (enabling modelling of a composition as a Mash-up of data) provided by the defined language: (i) Split Operator: This operator receives an input and splits it into two or more identical outputs. This operator can be used when the end-user wants to perform different operations on data from the same input (ii) Merge Operator: This operator takes an arbitrary number of inputs and produces an output, which is composed of the merge of its inputs. (iii) Filter Operator: This operator can be used to include or exclude items from an output of a service. Therefore, some rules can be created on top of the LPML language to compare the output of services to values that the end-user specifies. (iv) Loop Operator: This operator introduces the idea of sub-data processing. Any other operators could be inserted inside the Loop operator. An output of a service is provided to the Loop operator, the sub-data processing is run once for each item in the latter output. (v) Count Operator: This operator counts the number of items in the input and outputs that number. In addition, a subset of the "Control Flow" operators provided by the defined language i.e. If_Then_Else Operator: This operator enables branching from one service to another depending on some logical conditions.

4.3.2 Service Construction for Users

All the data flow operators above are supported by the process editor (Fig. 3) of our framework but they are not explicitly represented at the top representational level. Apart from a simple representation of boxes (activities) and arrows linking them (flow), their precise meaning is inferred or solicited at a later stage, depending on the skills level of the current user, in a process illustrated below.

The end-user is in charge of modelling her composition by dragging and dropping activities to the workspace page (see Start Activity in green, Activities in Orange and End activity in red – Fig. 3). Then, for each activity, the end user binds the service that fits her goals for this activity.

Once the activity and service selection is achieved, a chaining phase is required to connect services together and satisfy the data flow of the overall composition. To this end, two modes are possible, depending on the background of the end user.

In the case of an expert user, it is up to her to select the category of the data flow connection (Merge, Filter, Split ...) she expects between the services. For instance, between the getLocation (from FireEagle) and getDistance (from Multimap) operations, the user can filter the data coming from the getLocation operation, or merge data from this service and others to the getDistance operation. To this end, the end-user has access to data descriptions of services (at semantic and syntactic levels, depending on the services descriptions) and then could draw connections between services parameters sharing some similar or close descriptions. Then, background tools operate the final data connection between services by means of some Connectors (not described in this paper).

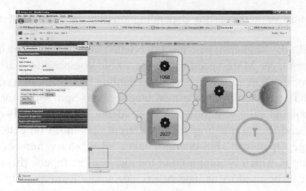

Fig. 3. Process Editor

Alternatively, in the case of non expert users, the process editor interacts directly with the reasoning engine (that comes with the SOA4All platform) to automatically infer the most appropriate connection between appropriate parameters of services, depending on the semantic descriptions the services expose. To this end, the process editor requires that connections between activities (and their services) are simply designed by the end-user. Obviously, the inferred connections can be subject to change if the user expects different data manipulation in the designed composition.

After the composition, its services binding, the control and the data flow designed on the workspace of the process editor, the composition can be saved (through a serialization in a service composition language a la BPEL4SWS [16], validated and finally executed by the execution engine of the SOA4All platform.

4.4 Service Execution

In SOA4All the execution of the service is handled by SPICES (Semantic Platform for the Interaction and Consumption of Enriched Services)[17]. SPICES will enable the composed service described in our scenario to be executed since it supports both WSDL and RESTful services (including combinations of the two).

The contribution of SPICES is in both supporting the end-users interaction with the service(s) and in supporting the consumption process itself which includes lifting and lowering between the conceptual level (which is tailored to humans) and the execution level (which is the actual service API).

The user is supported via the generation of appropriate user interfaces for the service. Typically, the user is presented with a set of fields which must be completed to allow the service to execute. Since the context of each field may not be obvious from a textual description attached to each field additional support is provided which allows the user to visualize the RDF graph appropriate for each input. This makes use of the ontological annotations referred to earlier which may include comments and relationships to other concepts and supports the user in understanding the context of the required input.

SPICES also provides support for the personalization of user interfaces. This makes use of individual user profiles to ensure that interfaces are built in accordance with preferences or contextual information e.g. language, currency, current location and to ensure information that is already in the profile is automatically entered so that the user is not asked to provide it again. This is supported via subsumption based reasoning to semantically compare the service descriptions and the profile and context descriptions associated with the user. Thus in the scenario, one required input is the mobile phone number of the user. Since this is contained in the user's profile, it can be automatically provided by SPICES.

The final area of user interaction support is that for authentication. In the scenario, a variety of authentication types are required to invoke a service including API keys (e.g. for Last.FM) which must be applied for and more general methods such as OAuth (e.g. for FireEagle). When the services are annotated the form of authentication is included and as a result SPICES is able to provide the required details from the user profile or support the user in obtaining the required details if the profile does not contain them.

From the service execution perspective, SPICES builds upon previous work on lifting and lowering [18] which supported WSDL services by moving from RDF instances to XML messages (lowering) and back again (lifting) to include support for RESTful services where XML is not required or applicable. With REST, an HTTP request needs to be built. To do this, SPICES uses UriTemplate [19] which allows HTTP requests to be built using a template with placeholders for variables which can be filled in with the appropriate values at run-time. The UriTemplate is stored with the service annotation. For example, a call to the Ribbit SMS service would be built from the following template:

```
http://ngwr.labs.bt.com/Ribbit/myapp/SendSMS.php?recipi
ent=tel:{mobile}&message={messageText}
```

where {mobile} and {messageText} are variable names which are populated by input or profile values. Further work is underway to cope with POST messages where the message body as well as request header must be modified.

Regarding lifting, services typically respond with XML or in some cases JSON. As such the lifting approach for WSDL services is applicable i.e. XSLT-based schema mapping (with appropriate prior conversion to XML for JSON-based responses).

SPICES includes service execution components for both WSDL and RESTful services. After lowering has taken place, the correct invoker is chosen (again using the service annotation) and called to interact with the target service. The response can then be passed on the lifting component.

5 Next Steps

In section 4 we described the various steps in the process of enabling mashups based on RESTful services using a telco related scenario. We have developed a prototype using SOA4All Studio which incorporates service description, discovery and composition. Service execution is under development and is our short-term focus.

In addition to this there are a number of other areas upon which we intend to focus. We are developing an additional scenario that fully reflects the business models described in section 2 i.e. where businesses (rather than casual users) are composing and consuming services from a variety of providers and offering these to their end customers with an appropriate 'service wrap' including billing, authentication, etc.

The first area we will address concerns the monitoring of services in order to be able to track certain non-functional properties such as the response time or the availability of services in order to provide a more adaptive environment. Both periodic batch as well as runtime monitoring will be carried out in order to gather information about services. This information shall be used for ranking when users are searching for services to use but also to support service providers to track the service delivery and take corrective measures if necessary. Rule engines shall be used to support the latter.

Finally, we will promote the creation of a community around services. This community will on the one hand create and share new composite services that will gradually enrich the available functionality providing added value solutions on an increasing complexity. On the other hand, members of the community will provide highly valuable information about the services themselves, may it be directly through ratings and comments, or indirectly through invocation. On the basis of this information the platform will support more accurate rankings of services and will include support for recommending services to users based on their profile.

Both of these latter areas will also be explored in our business reseller scenario.

6 Conclusions

Telecommunications companies are turning to web-based APIs as a way to allow direct access to their capabilities, many of which adopt a RESTful approach in order to create new revenue streams. In order to promote ease of use and enable mass market adoption the complexity involved with describing, finding, composing and using these services must be drastically reduced with a greater reliance on automation.

We have described the approach of the SOA4All project in providing support for RESTful services which until now have been largely neglected by efforts to deliver 'semantic web services'. The application of this approach to the Telecommunication domain is expected to enable a greater level of adoption of such services by both expert and novice users for both personal consumption and for the creation of new business opportunities.

References

1. Pautasso, C., Zimmermann, O., Leymann, F.: RESTful Web Services vs. Big Web Services: Making the Right Architectural Decision. In: 17th International World Wide Web Conference (WWW 2008), Beijing, China (2008)
2. Domingue, J., Fensel, D., González-Cabero, R.: SOA4All, Enabling the SOA Revolution on a World Wide Scale. In: Proceedings of the 2nd IEEE International Conference on Semantic Computing ICSC. IEEE Computer Society Press, Los Alamitos (August 2008)
3. Maleshkova, M., Pedrinaci, C., Domingue, J.: Supporting the Creation of Semantic RESTful Service Descriptions Workshop: Service Matchmaking and Resource Retrieval in the Semantic Web (SMR2). In: 8th International Semantic Web Conference (October 2009)

4. Vitvar, T., Kopecky, J., Viskova, J., Mocan, A., Kerrigan, M., Fensel, D.: Semantic Web Services with lightweight descriptions of Services, Advances in Computers, vol. 76. Elsevier, Amsterdam (2009)
5. Clement, L., Hately, A., von Riegen, C., Rogers, T.: UDDI Specification Version 3.0.2. Technical report, OASIS (2004)
6. Srinivasan, N., Paolucci, M., And Sycara, K.: Adding OWL-S to UDDI: Implementation and throughput. In: Proceedings of 1st International Conference on Semantic Web Services and Web Process Composition (2004)
7. Verma, K., Sivashanmugam, K., Sheth, A., Patil, A., Oundhakar, S., Miller, J. M.-S.: WSDI: A Scalable P2P Infrastructure of Registries for Semantic Publication and Discovery of Web Services. International Journal of Information Technologies and Management 6(1), 17–39 (2005)
8. Küster, U., König-Ries, B.: Towards Standard Test Collections for the Empirical Evaluation of Semantic Web Service Approaches. International Journal of Semantic Computing 2(3) (December 2008)
9. Pedrinaci, C., Domingue, J., and Reto Krummenacher: Services and the Web of Data: An Unexploited Symbiosis, Linked AI: AAAI Spring Symposium "Linked Data Meets Artificial Intelligence", Standford, USA, March (2010)
10. Bizer, C., Heath, T., Berners-Lee, T.: Linked data - the story so far. International Journal on Semantic Web and Information Systems, IJSWIS (2009)
11. Farrell, J., Lausen, H.: Semantic Annotations for WSDL and XML Schema. January 2007. W3C Candidate Recommendation 26 January (2007), http://www.w3.org/TR/sawsdl/
12. Vitvar, T., Kopecky, J., Viskova, J., Fensel, D.: Wsmo-lite Annotations for Web Services. In: Hauswirth, M., Koubarakis, M., Bechhofer, S. (eds.) Proceedings of the 5th European Semantic Web Conference. LNCS, Heidelberg (June 2008)
13. Maleshkova, M., Kopecky, J., Pedrinaci, C.: Adapting SAWSDL for Semantic Annotations of Restful Services. In: Workshop: Beyond SAWSDL at OnTheMove Federated Conferences & Workshops (2009)
14. Martin, D., Burstein, M., Lassila, O., McDermott, D., McIlraith, S., Paolucci, M., Parsia, B., Payne, T., Sirin, E., Srinivasan, N., Sycara, K.: OWL-S: Semantic Markup for Web Services (2004), http://www.daml.org/services/owl-s/1.0/owl-s.pdf
15. Schnabel, F., Xu, L., Gorronogoitia, Y., Radzimski, M., Lecue, F., Ripa, G.: Advanced Specification Of Lightweight, Context-aware Process, SOA4All Deliverable D6.3.2, http://www.soa4all.eu/file-upload.html?func=fileinfo&id=127
16. Nitzsche, J., Norton, B.: Ontology-based Data Mediation in BPEL. In: BPM Workshops, pp. 523–534 (2008)
17. Álvaro, G., Martínez, I., Gómez, J., Lecue, F., Pedrinaci, C., Villa, M., di Matteo, G.: Using SPICES for a Better Service Consumption. In: Poster at Extended Semantic Web Conference (2010)
18. Kopecky, J., Roman, D., Moran, M., Fensel, D.: Semantic Web Services Grounding. In: Proc. of the International Conference on Internet and Web Applications (2006)
19. Gregorio, J., Hadley, M., Orchard, D.: URI Template. IETF Draft (2008), http://tools.ietf.org/html/draft-gregorio-uritemplate-0

Web Services for Analysing and Summarising Online Opinions and Reviews

Dwi A.P. Rahayu[1], Shonali Krishnaswamy[1], Cyril Labbe[2], and Oshadi Alhakoon[1]

[1] Centre of Distributed System and Software Engineering, Monash University, Australia
[2] University of Genoble, France
dwi.ap.rahayu@gmail.com,
{Shonali.Krishnaswamy,Oshadi.Alhakoon}@monash.edu.au,
Cyril.Labbe@imag.fr

Abstract. Review mining is a part of web mining which focuses on getting main information from user review. State of the art review mining systems focus on identifying semantic orientation of reviews and providing sentences or feature scores. There has been little focus on understanding the rationale for the ratings that are provided. This paper presents our proposed RnR system for extracting rationale from online reviews and ratings. We have implemented the system for evaluation on online reviews for hotels from TripAdvisor.com and present extensive experimental evaluation that demonstrates the improved computational performance of our approach and the accuracy in terms of identifying the rationale. We have developed a web based system as well as web service based application to provide flexibility of accessing the rationale. Web based version of RnR system is available for testing from http://rnrsystem.com/RnRSystem. RnR system web service is available from http://rnrsystem.com/axis2/services/RnRData?wsdl.

Keywords: Review mining, online web reviews, web services, information extraction.

1 Introduction

The phenomenal growth of online social networking and Web 2.0 has led to an unprecedented increase in opinions/reviews on a wide range of topics, products and services being available and accessible both through websites or reviews from service APIs. In fact, these reviews and opinions are now a *de facto* basis and contributing factors for a range of daily activities such as buying products (e.g. electronic goods), choosing restaurants, booking hotels and planning holidays. Thus, there is an increasing reliance on online opinions for selection of product and services. This in turn is leading to an increasing focus in the area of opinion/review mining. The main of aim of review/opinion analysis is to firstly identify the product/service and its key features and then to distill whether a review expresses positive/negative sentiments towards the object that is being reviewed [1].

In this paper, we contend that in addition to feature identification and sentiment analysis, online review/opinion mining must also focus on explicating rationale [2]

E. Di Nitto and R. Yahyapour (Eds.): ServiceWave 2010, LNCS 6481, pp. 136–149, 2010.

and reasoning that underpins an opinion expressed with respect to a product/service or its specific features. This can be easily justified as follows. Consider the example of a hotel which has very clean rooms, with a good view – but which is rather small in size. It is quite possible that for a certain users, this hotel could be rated very positively because of the cleanliness or the view. However, it is also possible that some users have negative opinions based on the size of the room. Thus, it is important to understand what drives users to rate things differently since this makes selections based on such reviews more personalized and appropriate.

It is interesting to note that while many online reviews/opinions typically have a rating to specify the extent of positive or negative affinity for the product/service. We take the position those ratings (when available) along with textual descriptions provide a holistic representation of the opinion. Together, they combine an objective/directly measurable opinion along with a subjective/qualitative view which underpins the rationale for the opinion [2]. We also take the view that in opinion analysis, "positive" opinions that indicate certain negative aspects or "negative" opinions that bring to the positive features are significant and worthy of highlighting. Finally, we take the position that in analyzing reviews/opinions, it is important to factor in the changing views over time. This temporal dimension captures the essential improvement or decline in the general perception of a product or service.

In this paper, we present our RnR system for extracting rationale from online reviews/ratings. The system captures and summarizes the key rationale for positive and negative opinions expressed in a corpus of reviews. It highlights the negative features among positive reviews and vice versa. It also displays the changing perceptions of reviewers over time with respect to the entity that is being reviewed. We have developed as part of the RnR approach, techniques that leverage support metric in conjunction with a domain ontology to improve the computational overheads associated with sentiment identification. We have implemented the RnR system for a hotel review mining application. The RnR system uses reviews in the TripAdvisor.com as its corpus. The system can be accessed for trial at website http://rnrsystem.com/RnRSystem and can be embedded into other website using http://rnrsystem.com/axis2/services/RnRData?wsdl.

This paper is organized as follows: Section 2 provides background and analysis of current review mining systems. Section 3 presents the RnR system architecture and the algorithms for review analysis and extraction of rationale from reviews. Section 4 presents the implementation and extensive experimental evaluation of RnR in terms of computational performance and accuracy of representation. Section 5 concludes this paper.

2 Current Review Mining System

Review/opinion mining is a part of web mining which focuses on information and knowledge extraction from online user reviews [3]. Review/opinion mining can be done at three different types of granularity [1]: *document level, sentence level*, and *feature level*. Our focus in this paper is on feature-based review mining [4-9] which is generally seen as the preferred approach for extracting detailed knowledge/ information.

Feature level review mining commonly involves three steps. The first step is *feature and opinion word identification*. Feature identification refers to the process of finding important key words within a product of service that can be used to measure its performance. Typical approaches for feature and opinion word identification [4-6,9-10] use part-of-speech (POS) tagging. While POS based feature identification has been shown to be highly effective in terms of accuracy, it is nevertheless a time consuming and computationally intensive process since the POS of every word of the review has to be identified. In RnR, we propose the use of domain ontologies along with a metric to identify and prune the key features. This approach enables us to achieve substantial reduction in computational overhead associated with the POS tagging of the entire corpus.

The second step is *semantic analysis*. Opinion Observer [4,5] classifies opinion sentences into positive and negative opinion sentences using lexicon-based method. OPINE [6] determines the semantic orientation using a relaxation labeling method. PULSE [7] uses machine learning techniques. Zhao and Li [9] build movie ontology and score its nodes as positive, negative, and neutral using opinion sense scores. Thumbs up and thumbs down [10] get the semantic value by aggregating Pointwise Mutual Information of opinion words within the reviews. In our approach, in order to identify the semantic orientation, we use a lexicon-based POS approach with WordNet. However, since we considerably reduce the size of the corpus to be tagged, we achieve substantial reductions in overhead and consequently significant improvements in overall response time.

The third step is *opinion summarization* and *feature scoring*. There are two common outputs in review mining. *Opinion Summarization* results in simplified sentences that aim to concisely capture the gist of the main concerns of the review. *Feature scoring* aims to identify the polarity of review content in terms of whether it is positive or negative and to support this with a score. Most review mining systems [4-10] use score as output of their system. However, OPINE [5] provides a list of opinions in addition to the score. In [11], the system produces short sentence that contains information about the features but the target is for sound based review summary. While state-of-the-art review mining systems will be able to analyze reviews to establish correctly the positive semantic orientation of this feature, they do not infer the underpinning rationale that has led to this being seen as a positive feature. We contend that this rationale is an important aspect of a review or an opinion and one that can have a significant input into user's personal choices/selections based on online reviews. We do acknowledge that some of the systems[4-7] provide a list of supporting sentences if a user wants to know more about a feature score, but these do not constitute a systematic and holistic reasoning of the rationale for the score or the feature itself.

Many review mining systems focus on the content of the opinions without considering the additional semantics that ratings provide in the context of certain areas. Red Opal [8] is one of the review mining systems that uses ratings as one of scoring components beside the occurrence of feature in review. However this system does not consider semantic orientation that is usually recognized using opinion words. We contend that a review mining system must have the flexibility of leveraging ratings when they are available and be able to function effectively in contexts where they are not available.

Finally, we also contend that in extracting information from online reviews, it is also important to consider a temporal dimension of the semantic orientation. For instance, in reviews pertaining to certain product or service, the changing semantic orientation of reviews of time may be an important indicator of improving (or declining) perception of the product/service or its key features.

3 RnR System

3.1 System Overview

The RnR conceptual architecture is shown in Fig. 1. RnR is implemented as a wcb based system as well as a web service application. Users can access the system using web based application or embed RnR system in their websites using web service. The user enters the product/service name, for which a performance summary based on online customer reviews is determined, either using RnR webpage or RnR service request. RnR main system connects to and accesses a corpus of previous reviews for the queried product/service. RnR system has a local cache for recently retrieved reviews. If the cached data is valid (in terms of being recent, as determined by a user threshold), and valid for the query, then the cached data is used rather than performing an online crawling and retrieval. Otherwise, the query is sent to an external site where online reviews are maintained (e.g. TripAdvisor.com, Expedia.com.au) via their service API. The retrieved set of reviews is then locally processed to extract the requisite rationale.

There are three processing stages in the RnR main system that we propose and develop: computing support for product features using a domain ontology to support feature identification; identifying the opinion words that describe the features and their semantic orientation to extract rationale for the ratings/reviews; and performing a regression analysis of the changing nature of reviews on a temporal dimension. Those three processing stages produce both feature based general opinion summaries and a temporal based performance analysis chart. This information is combined together and returned to the user. The algorithms, for the above three steps of the RnR approach, are discussed in depth in the following sub-sections.

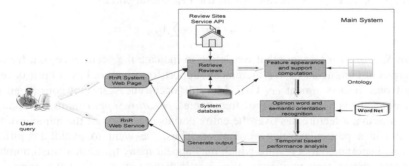

Fig. 1. RnR system architecture

3.2 Support Metric Computation

This step focuses on identifying key/significant features that have been the *raison d'être* for the opinion formation. In our approach, we first identify features within the comments using a domain ontology. We also develop a metric termed *Support* which establishes the impact of a given feature in the corpus of reviews. In the next step (detailed in Section 3.3), we use the metric to extract adjectives related to each feature. The feature identification and support computation is explained in the following discussion.

Let Q be a query for which a set of reviews R is returned. Let R consists of m individual reviews, $R = \{r_1, r_2, \dots r_m\}$. Each individual review r_i has the following information: a user given rating (t), date of stay (d), and the comment sentences themselves (c). Each individual review r_i is denoted by the triple $r_i<c_i,t_i,d_i>$. We define a threshold GT to distinguish between positive and negative reviews. If $t_i < GT$ then r_i is a negative review. If $t_i > GT$ then r_i is a positive review. Therefore all reviews in R can be grouped as positive and negative reviews sets R_{pos} and R_{neg} respectively.

Each comment c_i within a review r_i consists of several sentences that contains unnecessary words (stopwords) such as articles and common words. We remove all stopwords, and leave the full stop ('.') and comma (',') characters. These characters show the punctuation of the sentences. We stem the remaining words within each comment and put them in a new *set* $C = \{cc_1, cc_2, \dots, cc_m\}$. Each review has exactly one comment.

Unlike typical review mining systems which use POS tagging over the entire corpus [4-7,9-10], we use a domain ontology as a features dictionary. The use of ontology in feature identification has the impact of reducing computational overhead significantly as shown in our experimental evaluation. Since the RnR system aims to produce feature level granularity, we focus on the features that are represented by the ontology terms. Those features are clustered into several groups that are represented by ontology classes. Let $F = \{f_1,f_2, \dots ,f_n\}$ be a set of n features. The features are categorized into y groups $G = \{g_1,g_2, \dots ,g_y\}$ (i.e $g_z \subseteq F$, $1 \leq z \leq y$). The sets g_z ($1 \leq z \leq y$) have the following property: $\Rightarrow g_a \cap g_b = \emptyset$, $a \neq b$, $1 \leq a \leq y$, $1 \leq b \leq y$

Having identified features with the use of domain ontology, the next step is to define a metric that determines the level of support for each of the features in the set $C = \{cc_1, cc_2, \dots, cc_m\}$. We define this metric FeatureSupport as:

$$FeatureSupport_{f_j} = \sum_{k=1}^{m} 1_{\{f_j \in cc_k\}}$$

FeatureSupport is a measure that we define to indicate the occurrence of a feature in the corpus of comments C. We increment support for a feature based on it occurring at least once in a comment $cc_k \in C$. Multiple occurrences are not considered since *FeatureSupport* is not a measure of frequencies. *FeatureSupport* aims to capture the importance that a feature has over the entire corpus regardless of the number of times it occurs in a particular review/comment. Thus, we want to avoid the pitfall of assigning importance to a feature which may appear many times in a small number of comments, and in turn may skew the overall picture. We extend the computation of *FeatureSupport* for individual features f_i to compute *GroupSupport* for a group of features g_z

Given a set of stemmed comments C and set of features F, the system records position of each feature f_i within each comment cc_k as $pos_{f_i}^{cc_k}$ and counts how many comments cc_k contains each f_i as *FeatureSupport(f_i)* where $1 \le i \le n$ and $1 \le k \le m$ as well as *GroupSupport(g_z)* where $f_i \in g_z$.

An example snapshot of the output produced by this algorithm in terms of feature identification and calculation of *FeatureSupport* for both features and groups is shown in Fig. 2.

Group	Group Support	Inverted List Word
G(1) : Rooms	32	
...		
G(y) : Attractions	6	

Feature	Feature Support	Feature Position List
f_1 : room	31	1@35 2@25 ...
f_2 : bed	2	2@90 3@40 3@60
...		
f_{n-1} : city	4	7@13 10@15 ...
f_n : park	2	2@75 4@36

Feature	OpinionList
f_1 : room	{(small,12), (little,3), (comfortable,2), (smallish,2), ... }
f_2 : bed	{(comfortable,5), (great,1), (excelent,1), (foldaway,1), ...}
...	...
f_{n-1} : city	{(free,2), (great,1), (good,1), ... }
f_n : park	{(near,1), (fantastic,1), (down,1), ...}

Fig. 2. Data structure of ontology based feature support

Fig. 3. Opinion list of each feature

As can be seen in Fig. 2, each feature f_i may appears once or more in a comment cc_k but not every feature f_i appears in every comment cc_k. Feature "room" appears in 31 comments and "bed" appears in 2 comments. Feature "bed" appears once in cc_2, and two times in cc_3, but this duplication of "bed" in comment cc_3 is not reflected in the *FeatureSupport* = 2. Feature "room" and "bed" are in the same subset g_1 which has a *GroupSupport* of 32.

We focus on determining the rationale underpinning the principal features that have led to the review, therefore we define a support threshold ST. Each f_i in group g_z that has *FeatureSupport(f_i)/GroupSupport(g_z)* $< ST$ is eliminated from further consideration. The purpose of feature pruning is twofold. Firstly, it implies that if a feature has not been referred to by a specified minimum number of reviews, then it is not one of the defining features that have contributed significantly to the underpinning rationale for the opinions or reviews and rating. Secondly, this further helps to improve the computational performance. If it is deemed that all features must be accounted for in a particular analysis, this control threshold can be set to 0. This support metric computation process is done for both R_{Pos} and R_{Neg} groups separately.

3.3 Opinion Word and Semantic Orientation Recognition

Having identified set of positions for each feature in the comments, we iterate through the position list to identify the adjectives associated with that feature in that position. It is here that our approach deviates from existing techniques. We only use POS tagging for a small subset of *neighbor-words*. *Neighbor-words* are words surrounding the feature occurrences. This results in substantial reduction of computational overhead since POS tagging is known to be expensive and time consuming.

For a given feature f_i, we iterate each positions *Pos* within *PosList(f_i)* to identify adjectives associated to the feature. We have two steps in identifying related adjectives within the neighbor-words:

1. We search for all previous adjectives until a non-adjective or full stop ('.') is encountered.

    e.g: in the phrase "work big comfortable bed .", the adjectives of bed are big and comfortable.
2. We search for all following adjectives until a non-adjective or full stop ('.') is encountered with the exception of adverbs and negative words such as not. When an adverb is encountered, we continue the process of looking for the adjectives and ignore the adverb itself. If a negative word is encountered and its following word is an adjective, we get the antonym of that adjective word.

    e.g: "room very dirty not big .", the adjectives of room are dirty and small (antonym of big).

The extracted adjectives for each feature are stored in *OpList[f_i]* in a list of <opinion, frequency> tuples as shown in Fig. 3. There are some adjectives that have similar meanings (synonyms). We propose to integrate (merge) synonyms together in order to construct a less fragmented opinion before we rank them. As an example, in feature "room", since small, little, and smallish are synonyms (small, 12), (little, 3) and (smallish, 2) can be grouped as (small, 15). In a *OpList[f_i]*, there are certain adjectives that only occur occasionally, we treat these rare adjectives as noise and ignore them. We eliminate opinion words that have fewer occurrence/frequency than a specified opinion threshold (*OpT*). Again, if for a specific case, all opinion words need to be considered, *OpT* can be set to a 0 so as to include all opinion words.

Unlike most review mining systems, we do not focus on only determining an overall score to specify whether a feature is positive or negative. We aim to highlight those features that have a positive opinion associated with it, while being part of a review which belongs to R_{neg} group (and vice versa). This capability allows users to quickly absorb the standout features, both positive and negative. The orientation of each adjective whether it is positive or negative is determined using OrientationPrediction [4].

3.4 Temporal Based Performance Analysis

Another complementary analysis that our approach focuses on is the capturing of the "trend" in reviews over time. The aim is to show whether there is an increasing trend of positive reviews, an increasing trend of negative reviews, or unchanging trends, as well as highly variable trends. This is done using either the ratings as the basis. The RnR system generates a scatter plot chart of each rating (t_i) correspondence to its date (d_i). We use linear regression to calculate the perception change over time. Linear regression results in the generation of a straight line trend with a specific degree of curvature. In general, there are three types of trend lines: *increasing, decreasing* and *stable*.

4   Implementation and Evaluation

4.1   Implementation

The discussed algorithms have been implemented for a hotel review domain. The system queries and accesses reviews available at TripAdvisor.com and generates the summary, rationale and trends for hotels that are queried. The implementation of RnR has been done and the system is available for access and trial at: http://rnrsystem/RnRSystem. RnR service is also available in http://rnrsystem.com/axis2/services/RnRData?wsdl

In order to keep RnR as efficient as possible, RnR stores crawled reviews in a local database. RnR also stores review's metadata such as: hotel name, date of retrieval, and number of retrieved reviews. Since new reviews do not often enter the stream, we assume that the number of reviews does not change much within a day. Therefore, at query time, if the last date of retrieval, for this particular hotel, is not older than one day, RnR uses locally cached data. Otherwise, RnR accesses TripAdvisor, retrieves new reviews, if available, and appends those new reviews into previously retrieved reviews.

TripAdvisor rating range is 1-5, the group threshold is fixed to *3 (GT=3)*. RnR uses this threshold to groups the reviews into two groups based on rating: positive reviews R_{pos} and negative reviews R_{neg}. By grouping those reviews, RnR shows the main reasons why a person gives bad ratings or good ratings. RnR is also able to highlight positive comments in negative reviews, as well as negative comments in positive reviews.

The next step is to remove all stop words and stem the resting words within each review comment. RnR uses stop words library provided by [12]. RnR system implements well known porter stemming algorithm [13] to reach root form of remaining words. We leave full stop characters '.' and commas ',' in the comment to keep the sentence structure and avoid overlap adjectives recognition.

As explain in 3.2, to keep processing time as efficient as possible, RnR uses a domain specific ontology to find features of hotels. In this experiment, we use Hotel Domain Ontology (HDO) [14]. HDO was developed based on the question and answer section in Yahoo!Answer and some other websites. Thus it can be seen as highly relevant for review mining. This ontology is built on the OWL platform, which has three main components: class, property and individuals. Classes are *site (location), attraction, room, public amenity, means of transportation, services,* and *bathroom amenity*. Individuals are instances of these classes. For instance, the class *services* has various individuals such as *laundry* and *exchange*. RnR considers classes as groups. It considers subclasses, together with the individuals, as features. The algorithm in 3.2 is used to compute *FeatureSupport* and *GroupSupport*. RnR consider that a feature is relevant if its *FeatureSupport* is high enough relatively to its *GroupSupport*. If the *FeatureSupport(f_i)/GroupSupport(g_z) > ST* then f_i is relevant. In all experiments presented here *ST=0.2*.

In opinion word recognition process, RnR checks the features neighbor-words POS and find synonym of adjectives using WordNet [15] through Java WordNet Library (JWNL) based on the method discussed in section 3.3. Again a measure of importance has to be used to identify most common opinion on a feature. In RnR, if the opinion frequency (*fo*) for a feature is high enough, the opinion is considered as representative for a feature. Importance of an opinion word for a feature is given by the following quantity: *I(o)=(fo/FeatureSupport(f_i))*. An opinion threshold (*OpT*) is used to select only relevant opinions. In the following experiment *OpT=0.15*. RnR also displays a temporal view of rating. The purpose is to give the users evolution trends of hotel performances. This chart is generated using JFreeChart.

Fig. 4 shows the output of the system. Information is summarized in four main quarters. Top left quarter shows the general/summarized overview of the hotel. It provides the total number of review and the number of positive and negative reviews. For example the, hotel in Fig. 4 has 119 retrieved reviews, 44 of them are positive, 39 are negative. Then most frequent opinions within each group are presented. In Fig. 4, 38 people giving positive reviews write about *rooms*, most of them write about *small room* and *comfortable bed*. The most common issue spotted by negative reviewer is *small room* and *tiny bed*.

The two bottom sections give detailed rationale of each positive (left hand side) and negative (right hand side) groups of reviews. An important feature of RnR is to identify "good" opinions in the negative group and "bad" opinions in the positive group. So, it can be expected to find negative opinions on the right and positive opinions on the left. RnR system gives grey highlights to negative adjectives within positive group and positive adjectives within negative group.

The top right column contains the time based performance chart. Each point represents one rating given for a date of stay. The straight line within the scattered chart is the linear regression line showing the trend of performance. In Fig. 4, the trend of performance is slightly decreasing indicating a small drop in hotel quality based on reviews' ratings.

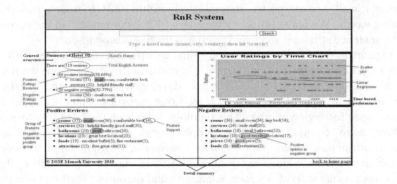

Fig. 4. RnR Result page

However, RnR can also operate without considering ratings. In this case we merely work with semantic orientation of features.

4.2   Experiments and Evaluation

As stated before, we conducted the experiments using reviews from the TripAdvisor hotel review site (www.tripadvisor.com). TripAdvisor provides a service API which returns a list of reviews for its business partners. However, during the experiments we were unable to get access to the API despite several requests, and finally decided to crawl the reviews from the website. We retrieved reviews from 24 hotels for evaluation. The number of reviews per hotel ranged from 37 up to 289 individual reviews. However, some reviews were written in languages other than English, which we discarded. The number of crawled reviews per hotel ranged from 32-271 and each comment within an individual review had 173 words on average.

There are three main evaluations which we perform:

1. We identify the performance in terms of time of the different computation parts of the RnR approach. Thus, the aim is to identify the cost of accessing and retrieving reviews from TripAdvisor and the cost of the processing computations of the RnR approach.
2. We compare the performance of the RnR approach, which limits the extent of POS tagging of the corpus, with a typical review mining system that performs similar tasks as RnR and has been tested in the hotel review domain. We choose the OPINE [6] system. This evaluation is essential to quantify the significant reduction in overhead that we are able to achieve compared with systems that do POS tagging over an entire corpus. In addition, we recognize that while the need for such tagging is inevitable in certain domains, the comparison made with OPINE is purely because it is in the same application domain as RnR.
3. We evaluate the quality of the summary generated by RnR, This evaluation assesses whether the summary is indeed representative of the reviews.

4.2.1 RnR Performance

In this evaluation we record time for crawling the data from the review site and the time for complete RnR processing to generate the summary and the regression analysis over time.

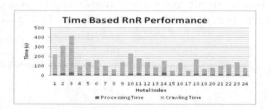

Fig. 5. Time based RnR performance

As can be seen in Fig. 5, the overall processing time is clearly dependent on the number of reviews as expected. However, it also clearly evident that the crawling time is significantly more than the processing time. Crawling data from the review site is time consuming. It takes on average 85.4% of the total time. The crawling process uses 127 seconds on average and reviews processing which is the core of system take 16 seconds on average per hotel. This clearly indicates the computational efficiency of the RnR approach, but also necessitates the use of local caching/storage of data to reduce the crawling costs. Thus, if a query is posed for a hotel that has already had a previous request, in a recent timeframe, then the local version of the stored reviews will be used to generate the summary and this will be considerably faster than the first time a query is posed, where crawling will be necessary for retrieval.

4.2.2 Other System Comparison

We now further demonstrate the efficiency of RnR by comparison with a similar analysis system operating in the same application domain, OPINE [6]. OPINE and RnR are similar in that both systems produce summaries of each hotel feature. OPINE also retrieves data from Tripadvisor. Fig. 6 below shows a snapshot of OPINE taken from OPINE website [16] (Note: OPINE is not currently available for trial via the webpage). OPINE lists all identified features and lists of opinion of each feature. The number in the bracket shows the number of sentences containing those opinion phrases. As can be seen in Fig. 4, RnR also provides feature based summary, but in our case the number in the bracket within the RnR summary represents the number of reviewers that have written about that feature. Furthermore, we also have the changing temporal perspective of the reviews, as well as the highlighting of positive aspects of negative comments and vice-versa.

The first operational step of OPINE is POS tagging using Minipar [19]. In order to affect a fair comparison, we implement the Minipar tagging for the corpus and compare this with the RnR approach for POS tagging. The comparative performance results are shown in Fig. 7. Minipar POS tagging needs on average 74.6 seconds to tag all words within each review. In comparison, the RnR system with its Wordnet based reduced POS tagging needs 9.6 seconds to finish the process. The difference in POS tagging times between OPINE (and other such similar systems that tag the entire corpus) and RnR is due to the number of tagged words. OPINE uses Minipar to get POS tagging for all words in comments. On the other side, RnR only checks neighbor words of each feature occurrence. Moreover, RnR has previously pruned the features using the *FeatureSupport* metric and support threshold *ST*. As a comparison, while RnR on average checks POS of 1,380 words, OPINE tags 15,425 words per hotel.

Fig. 6. OPINE snap shot

Fig. 7. RnR vs Minipar POS tagging time Accuracy/Quality

4.2.3 Accuracy/Quality

The RnR system produces two kind of information - summary and time-based performance chart. Fig. 4, 8 and 9 show the system output for three different hotels. The first and second hotels have similar number of both positive and negative groups, and third hotel has a significant number of positive reviews.

The general overview of each hotel is represented in top left quadrant. In hotel 10 (Fig. 4), the most positive reviewers are about rooms and service. However, even with the largely positive perception of the rooms, the size of the room being small (i.e. a negative opinion) is extracted and highlighted. Most negative reviewers also write about the small rooms. Such indicators are useful and are self-validating. A similar phenomenon appears in the hotel 14 result (Fig. 8). Both of the groups confirm that the hotel has comfortable beds, although they disagree about room size. The general overview of hotel 4 (Fig. 9) shows different significant features for each group. Most reviewers in positive groups write about comfortable beds and friendly staff. On the other hand, negative reviewers are more concerned about superior rooms.

The top right quadrant shows the scatter plot chart of the ratings given by reviewers, and a linear regression analysis shown as a line on top of the scatter plot chart. This line shows the changing perception of the reviews over time. Hotel 10 has a tendency of slight performance decline, while Hotel 4's reviews indicate a signficant improvement in perception. Hotel 14 has a stable performance over time.

The RnR system does not provide a score for each feature, or judge that a specific feature is bad or good. Instead, it represents the rationale for a feature being suitable for some reviews and not so much for others. The RnR system shows all opinions attached to the feature. Specific and detailed opinion about each feature is provided in the bottom quadrants. These snapshots show how different features are emphasized in different hotels, and also shows how the negative opinions in positive reviews (and vice versa) are highlighted.

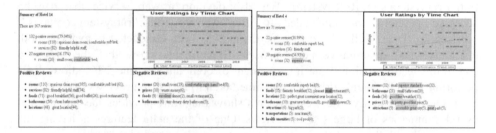

Fig. 8. Hotel 14 result page   **Fig. 9.** Hotel 4 result page

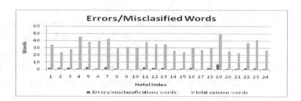

Fig. 10. Misclasified words statistic

The RnR system aims to provide a representative and objective summary and changing trend in terms of perception of the reviews over time. However, as with any such automated system, there are certain errors in summarising/sentiment detection that do occure. We term these as errors in the analysis. For instance, in one case, we encountered the term "free city" which actually comes from a sentence "free city circle tram". Since city is one of the feature in the domain ontology, the system treats this as a noun and attaches 'free' as its adjective. For the 24 hotels that were evaluated, we undertook a manual check to identify such erroneous /meaningless words in the summary. These error levels are shown in Fig. 10. It can be seen that the occurrence of such errors is quite low. It is on average 5% of the adjectives contained within an entire hotel summary and generally does not affect the overview generated by the system.

5 Conclusion

RnR provide detailed and fair aggregation of opinion, and highlight both the strengths and weaknesses of products or services. Thus, RnR allows users to find products or services according to their special needs and helps providers to identify their main weakness. A set of methods is proposed to provide such an aggregation. First, a domain ontology is used to identify the features in the reviews. Second, text around the occurrence of features is analyzed to extract opinion about features. Third, metrics based on the support of features and opinions are proposed to identify the most important features and most frequent opinions.

The proposed methods have been implemented and tested in a web based system (http://rnrsystem.com/RnRSystem). We also develop a web service that can be accessed publicly and embedded to user website (http://rnrsystem.com/axis2/services/RnRData?wsdl). A set of experiments has been conducted to evaluate both qualitative and quantitative performances. Experiments show that the proposed algorithms lead to a significant improvement of computation time. This allows RnR performance to be mainly driven by the time taken to access the reviews (web service call). On the qualitative side, experiments show that RnR provides meaningful and useful summaries of large sets of reviews. One of the main features is having the capacity to highlight negative opinions in positive reviews and vice versa.

References

[1] Hu, M., Liu, B.: Mining opinion features in customer reviews. In: Proceedings of National Conference of Artificial Intelligent, pp. 755–760. AAAI Press, San Jose (2004)

[2] Sherchan, W., Loke, S.W., Krishnaswamy, S.: Generating Web Services Ratings and Reputation Rationale for Explanation-Aware Service Selection. In: Service Oriented Computing and Applications (SOCA), November 4, vol. 2, pp. 203–218. Springer, Heidelberg (2008) (to appear)

[3] Kosala, R., Blockeel, H.: Web mining research: A survey. ACM SIGKDD Explorations Newsletter 2(1), 1–15 (2000)

[4] Hu, M., Liu, B.: Mining and summarizing customer reviews. In: Proceedings of the Tenth ACM SIGKDD International Conference on Knowledge Discovery and Data Mining, pp. 168–177. ACM, Seattle (2004)

[5] Liu, B., Hu, M., Cheng, J.: Opinion observer: analyzing and comparing opinions on the Web. In: Proceedings of the 14th International Conference on World Wide Web, pp. 342–351. ACM, Chiba (2005)

[6] Popescu, A.-M., Etzioni, O.: Extracting Product Features and Opinions from Reviews. In: Proceedings of the Conference on Human Language Technology and Empirical Methods in Natural Language Processing, pp. 339–346. Association for Computational Linguistics, Vancouver (2007)

[7] Gamon, M., Aue, A., Corston-Oliver, S., Ringger, E.: Pulse: Mining Customer Opinions from Free Text. In: Famili, A.F., Kok, J.N., Peña, J.M., Siebes, A., Feelders, A. (eds.) IDA 2005. LNCS, vol. 3646, pp. 121–132. Springer, Heidelberg (2005)

[8] Scaffidi, C., Bierhoff, K., Chang, E., Felker, M., Ng, H., Jin, C.: Red Opal: product-feature scoring from reviews. In: Proceedings of the 8th ACM Conference on Electronic Commerce, pp. 182–191. ACM, San Diego (2007)

[9] Zhao, L., Li, C.: Ontology Based Opinion Mining for Movie Reviews. In: Karagiannis, D., Jin, Z. (eds.) KSEM 2009. LNCS, vol. 5914, pp. 204–214. Springer, Heidelberg (2009)

[10] Turney, P.: Thumbs up or thumbs down? Semantic orientation applied to unsupervised classification of reviews. In: Proceedings of the 40th Annual Meeting of ACL, pp. 417–424. Association for Computational Linguistics, Philadelphia (2002)

[11] Nguyen, P., Mahajan, M., Zweig, G.: Summarization of multiple user reviews in the restaurant domain (2007), http://research.microsoft.com/apps/pubs/default.aspx?id=70488 (retrieved on February 5, 2010)

[12] Weiss, S.M., Indurkhya, N., Zhang, T., Damerau, F.J.: Text Mining Predictive Methods for Analyzing Unstructured Information. Springer, New York (2005)

[13] Porter, M.: The porter stemming algorithm,(2006), http://tartarus.org/~martin/PorterStemmer/ (accessed February 5, 2010)

[14] Yoo, D., Kim, G., Suh, Y.: Hotel-Domain Ontology for a Semantic Hotel Search System. Information Technology & Tourism 11(1), 67–84 (2009)

[15] Fellbaum, C.: WordNet: An electronic lexical database. MIT Press, Cambridge (1998)

[16] Dekang, L.: Dependency-based evaluation of MINIPAR. In: Proceedings of the Workshop on the Evaluation of Parsing Systems, Granada, Spain, pp. 298–312 (1998)

A Frame of Reference for SOA Migration

Maryam Razavian* and Patricia Lago

Department of Computer Science, VU University Amsterdam, The Netherlands
{m.razavian,p.lago}@few.vu.nl

Abstract. Migration of legacy systems to service-based systems constitutes a key challenge of service-oriented system engineering, namely
rehabilitation of pre-existing enterprise assets while conforming to service engineering principles. Over a decade there has been an increasing
interest in the approaches addressing SOA migration. These approaches
mainly differ in 'what is migrated' and 'how the migration is performed'.
Such differences aggravate achieving a general understanding of 'what
SOA migration entails'. To solve this problem, we conducted a systematic review that extracts main migration categories, called SOA migration families, from the approaches proposed in the research community.
Based on the results of the systematic review, we describe eight distinct
families along with their characteristics and goals. These families represent a first frame of reference for SOA migration which brings order and
enhances understanding on how migration can be carried out.

1 Introduction

One of the key promises of service oriented paradigm is facilitating reuse of enterprise assets in legacy systems [1]. Migration of legacy systems to service-based
systems enables achieving advantages offered by SOA while still reusing the embedded capabilities in the legacy systems. Since the early use of SOA, migration
of legacy systems to SOA has caught a lot of attention. Various studies present
an approach for such migration. These studies mainly differ in the way they
provide solutions for two challenging problems of what can be migrated (i.e. the
legacy elements) and how the migration is performed (i.e. the migration process). As an example, some studies address implementation aspects of migration
by providing methods for altering segments of the legacy code to web services.
On the other hand, other studies focus on refactoring the legacy architecture
to a service-based architecture based on business drivers such as business rules,
benefits and risks. Such differences can hinder achieving a general understanding
of 'what SOA migration entails' and therefore making it difficult to determine
how to migrate.

---

* This research has been partially sponsored by the Dutch Joint Academic and Commercial Quality Research and Development (Jacquard) program on Software Engineering Research via contract 638.001.206 SAPIENSA: Service-enAbling PreexIsting
ENterprISe Assets; and the European Community's Seventh Programme FP7/2007-
2013 under grant agreement 215483 (S-Cube).

E. Di Nitto and R. Yahyapour (Eds.): ServiceWave 2010, LNCS 6481, pp. 150–162, 2010.

To obtain such understanding, we conducted a systematic review that extracts main migration categories existing in the field. Due to its methodological rigor, we chose systematic review as our research method in aggregating existing SOA migration approaches. Furthermore, the strength of systematic reviews in minimizing the bias in the review process enhances the extraction of sound and meaningful migration categories. By devising a coding procedure, we analyzed the studies and extracted eight distinct categories. As an answer to the question of 'what SOA migration entails', this paper describes these eight categories, called *SOA migration families*. Using a holistic conceptual framework that reflects distinct conceptual elements involved in the migration process, SOA migration families are typified in a unified manner. As such, these families act as a frame of reference for SOA migration which brings order and enhances understanding in how such migration can be carried out. Accordingly, this frame of reference increases awareness of the ways in which a legacy system can be migrated to SOA.

2   Research Method

We followed a formal systematic literature review process based on the guidelines proposed in [2,3]. As part of the process, we developed a protocol (described in the following) that provided a plan for the review in terms of the method to be followed, including the research questions and the data to be extracted.

2.1   Review Protocol

Research Questions. In order to answer the question of 'what SOA migration entails', we seek for extracting the types of SOA migration approaches regarding their solution for migration. The systematic review envisions providing an evidence base of existing SOA migration approaches and further categorizing them. To achieve this goal, we define the following research questions:

What methods/techniques/processes/approaches regarding legacy to SOA migration, have been proposed in research community so far? In particular, the following aspects facilitate characterizing the approach: (a) what are the activities carried out? (b) what artifacts are used or produced? (c) what are the knowledge elements used within different activities?

Search Process. As the first step of systematic search, three main keywords are built from our research question, namely: *migration, legacy systems* and *SOA*. Considering the related terms for the keywords, we defined the following search string:

(SOA or 'service-oriented' or 'service-computing' or 'service-based' or 'service-centric' or 'service' or 'service-engineering' or SOSE) AND ('legacy code' or 'legacy system' or 'existing system' or 'legacy component' or 'existing code' or 'existing asset' or 'existing component' or 'pre-existing code' or 'pre-existing system' or 'pre-existing component' or 'legacy software' or 'existing software' or 'pre-existing software') AND (migration or modernization or transformation or

reengineering or re-engineer or evolving or reuse or 'service mining' or 'service identification' or 'service extraction')

We used the following libraries as main resources: IEEE Explore, ACM Digital Library, ISI Web of Knowledge, SpringerLink, ScienceDirect, and Wiley Inter Science Journal Finder. As major venues on service-oriented systems like ICSOC started in 2003, we decided to set 2000 as the start date to minimize the chance of overlooking relevant studies [1]. We applied the search terms to titles and abstracts considering that they provide a concise summary of the work. This decision was assessed by running the search string on data sources and checking if the pilot studies are retrieved.

Selection of Primary Studies. Peer-reviewed articles in the field of software engineering that satisfy the following inclusion criteria are selected as a primary study. I1) A study that is about migration *to services*. Rationale: studies which support migration to other types of target systems (not to service-based) should be excluded. I2) A study that addresses migration *from existing legacy assets*. I3) A study which proposes *a solution for migration*. Rationale: studies that not specifically provide a solution for the migration problem should be excluded. For instance, studies presenting challenges on SOA migration are out of scope of this work.

2.2 Data Analysis

As mentioned, this study seeks for achieving a general understanding of 'what SOA migration entails' by *categorization* and *comparisons* of the approaches. The question that we faced is how to systematically analyze the primary studies, in such way that the meaningful categorizations are determined. We chose coding as our qualitative analysis method, since we were seeking for the conceptualization of data, not actual data per se. According to [4], one method of creating codes is to have an initial set of codes, called 'start-list', that is refined during the analysis. Our start-list stems from a SOA migration framework (called SOA-MF), proposed in earlier work [5]. The comprising conceptual elements of SOA-MF, described in Section 2.3, provide pieces of information to position each migration approach into SOA-MF. Hence, by coding the primary studies their associated mappings on SOA-MF is achieved. Similar to searching process, in order to carry out the analysis systematically, its procedure has to be made explicit. Inspired by the procedure proposed by Lincoln and Guba [4], we devised the following coding procedure for our purpose: *(1) Filling in/Surfacing activities involved in migration:* coding activities and refining the codes labeling activities, identifying the new activities. *(2) Filling in/Surfacing process:* coding the inputs and outputs of an activity, identifying the sequence of activities. *(3) Surfing knowledge elements:* Identifying the knowledge elements as well as the level of abstraction in which they reside. *(4) Bridging/Observations:* Identifying patterns, goals and gaps in the migration process.

---

[1] We cannot be certain that we have covered all studies with a publication date in 2009, since studies may not have been indexed yet at the time we conducted our review (Jan 2010).

2.3   The SOA Migration Framework

The SOA migration framework [5], called SOA-MF, is a skeleton of the holistic migration process along with the distinct conceptual elements involved in such a process (see Fig. 1.I). The framework consists of three sub-processes: reverse engineering, transformation and forward engineering. SOA-MF follows a horseshoe model by first recovering the lost abstractions and eliciting the legacy fragments that are suitable for migration to SOA (reverse engineering), altering and reshaping the legacy abstractions to service based abstractions (transformations), and finally, renovating the target system based on transformed abstractions as well as new requirements (forward engineering). Reverse engineering starts from existing implementation and continue with extracting the design entities (*code analysis*), recovering the architecture (*architectural recovery*) and recapturing abstractions in requirements or business models (*business model recovery*). Within the transformation sub-process the activities of *design element transformation, composition transformation* and *business model transformation*, respectively, realize the tasks of reshaping design elements, restructuring the architecture and altering business models and business strategies. The forward engineering sub-process involves the activities of *service analysis, service design* and *service implementation*. Finally, the framework covers different levels of abstraction including *concept, composite design element, basic design element* and *code*.

3   Results

By applying the search query defined in Section 2.1 to the selected data sources, we obtained 258 articles whose titles or abstracts contained the keywords specified in the search query. After applying the inclusion/exclusion criteria, 51 were considered relevant for our study. Although we identified 51 articles by this search process, some articles were earlier or short versions of other articles. Thus, we ended up with 44 unique primary studies. Using the procedure explained in Section 2.2, we coded the primary studies and consequently obtained their mappings on SOA-MF. Although initially we had 44 primary studies, the analysis resulted in 39 different mappings on SOA-MF. This was because in five studies the description of the migration approach was too general or vague, for us to be able to codify them. By thoroughly analyzing the mappings, we identified a set of meaningful relationships among the approaches with similar coverage patterns and their migration objectives and solutions. More precisely, thanks to SOA-MF, the migration approaches that pursue a common migration goal using conceptually similar activities and artifacts, have graphically similar coverage pattern as well. Accordingly, by considering similar SOA-MF coverage patterns, out of 39 different mappings eight distinct families of SOA migration approaches were extracted. Fig. 1.III illustrates the schematic form of distinguished mappings that are dedicated to each family. As an example, F4.b is a schematic form of the mapping shown in Fig 1.II. Section 3.1 describes each family in the following way: 1) the *family at a glance* provides a general description of the

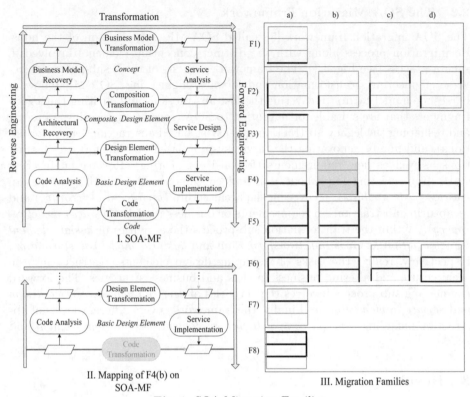

Fig. 1. SOA Migration Families

implications of each family, illustrated in Fig. 1.III 2) the *observations* include analytical explanation of 'what migration entails' in each family[2].

3.1 Families of SOA Migration Approaches

Code Translation Family (F1). *Example Members:* [6,7]. *Family at a glance:* The mapping of the approaches of this family on SOA-MF (simplified in Fig 1.F1(a)), reflects the following feature: out of the three sub-processes, the migration process is limited to transformation at system level in which the existing legacy code is transformed to service-based implementation.

Observations: Migration, in code translation family, entails moving the legacy system as a whole to a service-oriented platform or technology, without decomposing the existing system. We identified two main categories in this family: (1) translating the whole code to web services, and (2) wrapping the whole application as a web service. The problem addressed by the first category is to translate a legacy code to a web service implementation. The second category embraces

---

[2] Due to space constraints, not all members of each family are introduced. The full list of the primary studies distributed among the families is available at http://www. few.vu.nl/~mrazavi/SOAMigrationAppendix.pdf

encapsulating the interfaces of the existing application to a (web) service interface. In our view, this category is in line with classical black-box reengineering techniques, that integrate systems via adaptors and allow the application to be invoked as a service. We also found that the members of this category are common in altering the legacy interaction protocol from synchronous communication to asynchronous communication, mostly using Enterprise Service Bus (ESB).

Service Identification Family (F2). *Example Members:* [8,9,10,11]. *Family at a glance:* In this family, the transformation sub-process is not covered, meaning that reshaping of the legacy elements to service-based elements is not realized. The reverse engineering sub-process is carried out in all family members, while forward engineering occurs only in some (Fig 1.F2(c,d)). Reverse engineering, here, embraces the activities of 'code analysis' and 'architectural recovery' and forward engineering is limited to the 'service analysis' activity.

Observations: This family of approaches focuses on the identification of the candidate services in the existing legacy system. *Migration, here, is limited to 'what is migrated', whereas 'how migration is performed' is not addressed.* The legacy elements realizing the candidate services are identified using reverse engineering techniques. This implies that, by extracting system's functionality, structure, or behavior, the legacy elements suitable for migration are identified. Based on the criteria guiding the service identification, we extracted two main categories in this family: in the first category, (Fig 1.F2(a,b)), which just covers the reverse engineering sub-process, the identification of the candidate services is guided by a set of constraints characterizing a service (e.g., [8,12]). These constraints are inherently features, requirements or properties characterizing a service or service composition. As an example in [8], higher level representations of the legacy system are extracted aiming at identification of legacy elements (e.g. components, modules) that are 'cohesive' and are 'loosely coupled'. The second category (Fig 1.F2(c,d)) mostly focuses on locating a specific business functionality in the legacy code. While sets of constraints drive the service identification in the first category, it is a set of desired *business functionalities* that guide this task in the second category (e.g., [9,10,11]). The business functionalities are codified using sets of structural representations such as business ontology or business service model. We found that service identification, here, is realized by mapping the desired business functionalities (extracted within forward engineering sub-process) on a model representing the legacy system.

Business Model Transformation Family (F3). *Example Members:* [13,14,15]. *Family at a glance:* In this family, the reverse engineering and the forward engineering sub-processes are not covered. This means that recapturing the abstractions of the existing legacy system as well as development of the service based system is not addressed by these family members. Migration is realized by the transformation sub-process, carried out at concept level.

Observations: Based on the types of transformation at concept level, we found two main categories in this family: (1) approaches providing a meta-process for migration, e.g., [14,15], and (2) approaches with business process reengineering e.g., [13]. The main goal of the meta-process category is to *support the decision regarding 'how to perform migration'*. The constituent activities of these approaches support decision making on the migration process itself. Due to its orthogonal view on the migration process, we recognize this category as a 'meta-process'. a) information representing the As-Is state of the legacy system (i.e. existing capabilities and constraints) and b) information about the To-Be state of the service based system (i.e. target capabilities and constraints). The output, extracted based on a comparison among the As-Is and To-Be states, constitutes a roadmap shaping the migration process.

Despite having the same coverage pattern on SOA-MF, we found that the business process reengineering category of this family reflects a different perspective on SOA migration: *altering the business process of the existing legacy system to serve as a basis for top-down service development*. We found that the main focus of this category is quite similar to business process management techniques that address reengineering the existing business processes based on the new requirements and goals. The difference among these two categories motivates a refinement to SOA-MF that is further discussed in Section 4.

Design Element Transformation Family (F4). *Example Members:* [16,17,18].*Family at a glance:* According to coverage of this family members on SOA-MF, the common feature is that the transformation sub-process only occurs at 'basic design element' level. Similarly, reverse and forward engineering sub-processes, if covered, are also limited to this level.

Observations: Migration in this family is limited to reshaping the existing legacy elements to the service-based elements. More precisely, a set of legacy elements, extracted by means of the 'code analysis' activity or simply known beforehand, are transferred to a set of services or service-based elements. For instance, a 'component specification' is altered to 'service specification' [17], or a 'module' is reshaped to a 'service' [18] or 'segment of code in the persistence layer' is transformed to a 'data service' [16]. We found that the understanding of the existing system proceeds until its constituting structural (e.g. components or modules) or behavioral elements (e.g. interaction models) are extracted. Afterwards, these elements are reshaped to the associated element in the service-based system, and further implemented. Most of the wrapping approaches fall in this family.

Forward Engineering with Design Element Transformation Family (F5). *Example Members:* [19,20]. *Family at a glance:* This family fully covers the forward engineering sub-process, whereas transformation and reverse engineering sub-processes occur at 'basic design element' level.

Observations: The main focus of this family is on development of service-based systems starting from the desired business processes. These processes need to be designed in terms of constellations of interacting services obtained from both 'migrated' and 'newly designed' services. Here understanding of the existing legacy system (within the reverse engineering sub-process) is limited to locating the required functionalities in the target service based system. *The migration here entails Top-Down service-based development while locating the realization of the required business functionalities and transforming them to services.*

Design and Composite Element Transformation Family (F6). *Example Members:* [21,22,23]. *Family at a glance:* The three migration sub-processes occur in the two levels of the 'basic design element' and 'composite design element', meaning that the members include both design element and composition transformations.

Observations: What characterizes this family is having transformation in both levels of 'basic design element' and 'composite design element'. This entails altering legacy elements to services (i.e. design element transformation) as well as reshaping the structure and the topology of legacy elements to realize new service compositions (i.e. composition transformation). Prior to refactoring the architecture and reshaping the legacy elements, the legacy architecture is recovered during reverse engineering sub-process. Architectural recovery, here, is guided by a set of service-specific constraints (e.g. high level of granularity, autonomy) and the desired functionalities (e.g. business services). We also observed that refactoring architecture (i.e. composition transformation), triggers the lower level transformations (i.e. design element transformation and translation). As shown in Fig. 1.F6, the forward engineering sub-process is not similarly covered in all members. In some members [23,22] (Fig. 1.F6(b)), forward engineering includes both design and development of the services based on the service compositions, extracted from architectural refactoring. While, in other members such as [21] (Fig. 1.F6(a,c,d), this sub-process is limited to implementation of the wrapped services. To sum up, *migration embraces recovering and refactoring of the legacy architecture to the service-oriented architecture as well as reshaping the legacy elements to service-based elements.*

Pattern-Based Composition Transformation Family (F7)
Example Members: [24,25]. *Family at a glance:* Migration only includes the transformation sub-process at 'composite design element' level. This implies that the architecture of the existing system is altered or configured into the service based architecture.

Observations: A common feature in this family is using 'patterns' for transforming the existing architecture to service-based architecture. Patterns are inherently reusable solutions, that are here used to extract services or facilitate transformations of legacy elements to services. We found two main types of patterns used by the members of this family: application-specific (e.g. reference architectures or workflow patterns) and application-generic (e.g. Facade, Mediator, and Chain of responsibility) used. The application-specific patterns mainly represent common structure of a domain, while workflow patterns represent business or workflow processes in an application domain. We argue that the recurring nature of the transformation problem, initiated the need for patterns that codify reusable solutions. *Migration here entails pattern-based architectural transformation to SOA.*

Forward Engineering with Gap Analysis Family (F8). *Example Members:* [26]. *Family at a glance:* The transformation sub-process, in this family, occurs in the three tiers of 'concept', 'composite design element' and 'basic design element'. As shown by (Fig. 1.F8(a)), the forward engineering subprocess covers the activities of 'service analysis' and 'service design' whereas the reverse engineering sub-process is not covered.

Observations: This family mainly focuses on top-down service development, starting from extraction of the business model of the target system and further designing service compositions and services. What distinguishes this family from pure top-down service development approaches is that at each abstraction level (including concept, composition and design level) a comparison (a gap analysis) among the new and pre-existing artifacts occurs. This comparison serves to assess how the desired business services can be realized by exploiting pre-existing capabilities. We observed that the gap analysis at the highest level indicates the discrepancies among business model the existing and the target system. This comparison further triggers design decisions regarding how the new service functionality can be obtained by reusing or revamping pre-existing assets. This implies that transformation at the highest level guides the transformations at composition and basic design element levels. *The migration here entails Top-Down service development while assessing the reuse opportunities in all abstraction levels.*

4   Discussion

In the following we discuss the possible threats to validity of our analysis and our findings.

Threats to Validity. One of the threats to validity of the study is that the review is mainly conducted by a single researcher. However, subjective interpretations are mitigated by both following a systematic protocol, checked and validated by senior researchers experienced in software engineering, systematic reviews and SOA and validating it further using a pilot study. Additionally, we explicitly included only publications whose objective is to present a solution for migration. It is possible that a publication proposes also a solution for migration blended with other objectives, so that the contribution on migration is not clearly represented. To mitigate this threat, we added some more generalized keywords such as 'reuse' in the search terms.

Threat to validity of the analysis is in the general applicability of the codes used for characterizing and classifying migration approaches. An assuring factor in this regard is that the start-list of codes is extracted from a conceptual framework published in a service-oriented computing forum, after being peer reviewed by experts in the field [5]. This framework stems from existing theory on reengineering and architectural recovery while it is constantly refined through our coding procedure. This further consolidates its general applicability.

Finally, the scope of our review is restricted to the scientific domain. The threat here is that very relevant migration approaches originated in industry, if not described in scientific publications, are not covered. To fill this gap, we are carrying out a survey focusing on how SOA migration is performed in industrial practice.

Refinements to SOA-MF. As described in Section 2.2, code refinement constitutes a key part of our coding procedure. As codes stem from the original SOA-MF, refinements to code entails changes to SOA-MF as well. In other words, the need for refining the codes reflects the relevant changes to the framework which enhance it's ability for characterizing different approaches. Below, two examples of the findings motivating refinements to SOA-MF are presented: 1) In the initial version of SOA-MF framework [5] the 'code translation' activity did not exist, since it was originated from the existing theory on architectural recovery [27] that did not consider transformation at code level. During the early stages of this analysis, we observed that there are some migration approaches that translate the legacy system code to web services. In order to characterize such approaches a code called 'code translation activity' was added. Eventually, the 'code translation activity' was added to the transformation sub-process of SOA-MF as well. 2) As mentioned, we observed that the two categories of 'meta-process' and 'business process reengineering' in the business model transformation family, are so different in their objectives that do not resemble members of the same family. This suggests that the current framework does not fully highlight their differences. Although the 'meta-process' category is positioned on the concept level, its 'meta' characteristic suggests the need for an orthogonal dimension on the current two-dimensional SOA-MF. The third dimension reflects the decision making process, orthogonal to migration process itself. This motivates further research on refining SOA-MF to a three-dimensional framework.

Synthesis of Findings. In summary, our study yields two main findings:

(I) The description of the families suggests the following two themes in the objectives of SOA migration approaches: modernizing the legacy system and facilitating reuse during service-based development. *1) Migration for modernization:* In a set of families (i.e. F1, F2, F4, F6 and F7) the migration aims at renovating the existing legacy system to reconstitute it in the new form of SOA. Consequently, they mainly focus on how to adapt the legacy systems to the SOA environment. To this end, the reverse engineering sub-process realizes understanding of the existing system, transformation sub-process specifies how to restructure the legacy systems, while forward engineering sub-process realizes the restructuring. *2) Migration for reuse in service-based development:* in some families (i.e. F5 and F8) the main goal of migration is to facilitate reuse in building new service-based systems. This goal changes the order in which the three sub-processes are carried out. Accordingly, the forward engineering sub-process realizes the service-based development; to do so, the reverse engineering sub-process facilitates identifying reusable legacy assets and the transformation sub-process reshapes the legacy elements to service-based elements. Note that F3 provides a 'meta process' view on the whole migration approach that pertains to both themes and is therefore not categorized in the two themes. Identifying these two themes can help the designers better select the appropriate approach for SOA migration.

(II) Considering the abstraction levels, SOA-MF presents four levels of 'code', 'basic design element', 'composite design element' and 'concept'. The 'code' level deals with the actual running system, the 'basic design element' and 'composite design element' levels represent the design solution, whereas the 'concept' level represents the problem. In a number of primary studies, design solution artifacts reflect two layers of atomic element (e.g. modules), and composite element (e.g. architecture). In the same vein, we expected to observe the similar layering scheme for the concept level artifacts. For instance, having two layers of business services (i.e. atomic element) and business processes (i.e. composite element). This layering scheme, for example, has been leveraged in [1], in which business services play a mediator role to articulate business processes, with the underlying solution services. However, only one of the primary studies distinguished the abstraction levels in the concept level [26]. This motivates further research since the importance of having different abstraction levels at 'concept level' has been considerably acknowledged in practice.

5   Conclusion

It is hard to gain insightful understanding of how to perform migration in an emerging and still fuzzy research field like SOA migration. To reach such understanding, this paper has presented a frame of reference for SOA migration by defining eight distinct families. To identify these families, we mapped each study on SOA-MF and clustered them into different families based on the similarity of their mappings. By analyzing the migration approaches, a more profound description for migration families was obtained that characterizes each family from the two following aspects: *what* is the main objective of migration and *how* this objective is pursued by different categories of solutions. By describing the families, this paper brings order on the existing SOA migration approaches and consequently provides a "bird's-eye" view of 'what SOA migration entails'.

By positioning a migration approach on these families, insight in the following aspects can be achieved: to what extent the reverse engineering, transformation and forward engineering occur, what activities are carried out, what artifacts are used or produced, what abstraction levels are covered, what is the main objective of migration, and finally, what are the available solutions.

During the course of the systematic review, we observed different types of knowledge that guide each of reverse engineering, transformation and forward engineering sub-processes. As our future work, we will further analyze the results of this study to identify the types of knowledge driving SOA migration. In addition, we are conducting a follow-up study targeting at SOA migration approaches in practice to examine what migration families are used in practice and what is the gap among the migration families in academia and industry.

References

1. Papazoglou, M.: Web Services: Principles and Technology, 1st edn. Prentice-Hall, Englewood Cliffs (2007)
2. Kitchenham, B.: Procedures for performing systematic reviews. Technical report, Keele University (TR/SE- 0401) and National ICT Australia Ltd. (2004)
3. Dyba, T., Dingsoyr, T., Hanssen, G.K.: Applying systematic reviews to diverse study types: An experience report. In: 1st Int. Symposium on Empirical Software Engineering and Measurement, pp. 225–234. IEEE Computer Society, Los Alamitos (2007)
4. Miles, M.B., Huberman, M.: Qualitative Data Analysis: An Expanded Sourcebook, 2nd edn. Sage Publications Inc., Thousand Oaks
5. Razavian, M., Lago, P.: Towards a conceptual framework for legacy to soa migration. In: Fifth International Workshop on Engineering Service-Oriented Applications, WESOA 2009 (2009)
6. Bodhuin, T., Tortorella, M.: Using grid technologies for Web-enabling legacy systems. In: 11th Workshop on Software Technology and Engineering Practice, pp. 186–195 (2003)
7. Zhang, B., Bao, L., Zhou, R., Hu, S., Chen, P.: A black-box strategy to migrate GUI-based legacy systems to web services. Service-Oriented System Engineering, 25–31 (2008)
8. O'Brien, L., Smith, D., Lewis, G.: Supporting migration to services using software architecture reconstruction. In: Software Technology and Engineering Practice, pp. 81–91 (2005)
9. Chen, F., Zhang, Z., Li, J., Kang, J., Yang, H.: Service identification via ontology mapping. In: Computer Software and Applications Conference, pp. 486–491 (2009)
10. Sindhgatta, R., Ponnalagu, K.: Locating components realizing services in existing systems. In: Services Computing, pp. 127–134 (2008)
11. Ilk, N., Zhao, J., Hofmann, P.: On reuse of source code components in modernizing enterprise systems. In: Advanced Management of Information for Globalized Enterprises, pp. 1–5 (2008)
12. Li, S., Tahvildari, L.: E-BUS: a toolkit for extracting business services from java software systems. In: ICSE Companion 2008: Companion of the 30th international Conference on Software Engineering, pp. 961–962. ACM, New York (2008)
13. Lavery, J., Boldyreff, C., Ling, B., Allison, C.: Modelling the evolution of legacy systems to web-based systems. Journal of Software Maintenance and Evolution: Research and Practice 16, 5–30 (2004)
14. Lewis, G., Smith, D.: Developing realistic approaches for the migration of legacy components to service-oriented architecture environments (2007)
15. Umar, A., Zordan, A.: Reengineering for service oriented architectures: A strategic decision model for integration versus migration. Journal of Systems and Software 82(3), 448–462 (2009)
16. del Castillo, R.P., García-Rodríguez, I., Caballero, I.: PRECISO: a reengineering process and a tool for database modernisation through web services. In: Jacobson Jr., M.J., Rijmen, V., Safavi-Naini, R. (eds.) SAC 2009. LNCS, vol. 5867, pp. 2126–2133. Springer, Heidelberg (2009)

17. Li, S.H., Yen, D.C., Chang, C.C.: Migrating legacy information systems to web services architecture. Journal of Database Management 18(4), 1–25 (2007)
18. Sneed, H.M.: Integrating legacy software into a service oriented architecture. In: Conference on Software Maintenance and Reengineering, pp. 3–14 (2006)
19. Cetin, S., Altintas, N.I., Oguztuzun, H., Dogru, A.H., Tufekci, O., Suloglu, S.: A mashup-based strategy for migration to service-oriented computing. In: IEEE International Conference on Pervasive Services, pp. 169–172 (2007)
20. Chen, F., Li, S., Yang, H., Wang, C.H., Cheng-Chung Chu, W.: Feature analysis for service-oriented reengineering. In: Software Engineering Conference (2005)
21. Canfora, G., Fasolino, A.R., Frattolillo, G., Tramontana, P.: A wrapping approach for migrating legacy system interactive functionalities to service oriented architectures. Journal of Systems and Software 81(4), 463–480 (2008)
22. Liu, Y., Wang, Q., Zhuang, M., Zhu, Y.: Reengineering legacy systems with RESTful web service. In: Computer Software and Applications, pp. 785–790 (2008)
23. Zhang, Z., Yang, H., Chu, W.: Extracting reusable object-oriented legacy code segments with combined formal concept analysis and slicing techniques for service integration. In: Quality Software, pp. 385–392 (2006)
24. Arcelli, F., Tosi, C., Zanoni, M.: Can design pattern detection be useful for legacy system migration towards SOA? In: Workshop on Systems Development in SOA Environments, pp. 63–68 (2008)
25. Pahl, C., Barrett, R.: Layered patterns in modelling and transformation of service-based software architectures. In: Gruhn, V., Oquendo, F. (eds.) EWSA 2006. LNCS, vol. 4344, pp. 144–158. Springer, Heidelberg (2006)
26. Nguyen, D., van den Heuvel, W., Papazoglou, M., de Castro, V., Marcos, E.: GAMBUSE: A Gap Analysis Methodology for Engineering SOA-Based Applications. In: Borgida, A.T., Chaudhri, V.K., Giorgini, P., Yu, E.S. (eds.) Conceptual Modeling: Foundations and Applications. LNCS, vol. 5600, pp. 293–318. Springer, Heidelberg (2009)
27. Kazman, R., Woods, S.G., Carrière, S.J.: Requirements for integrating software architecture and reengineering models: CORUM II. In: Working Conference on Reverse Engineering (1998)

A Comparative Study: Service-Based Application Development by Ordinary End Users and IT Professionals

Abdallah Namoun, Usman Wajid, and Nikolay Mehandjiev

Manchester Business School, The University of Manchester, Manchester, M13 9SS, UK
firstname.lastname@mbs.ac.uk

Abstract. Service-Oriented Architecture enables users, both ordinary end users and IT professionals, to be part of the development cycle of interactive service-based systems in order to fulfil their desired needs. In this paper we explore and compare the mental model of two different categories of users towards the idea of "service composition by end users". Participants' responses are concluded from 5 separate focus groups, including a total of 64 participants. Results have shown that both groups of users are highly interested in the composition of service-based systems; however, privacy and security concerns and technical complexity of current approaches and service composition environments hinder the diffusion of service-based technologies among users. In this respect, this paper proposes a preliminary model of service composition uptake by end users and discusses user views and requirements to facilitate service composition.

Keywords: EUD, risks and benefits, user study, services, service composition.

1 Introduction

Current trends in Software Engineering, Human Computer Interaction, and Service and Components Research emphasise the need to create software artefacts that are easy to develop and customize [6]. In our view, computer users can be categorised according to their jobs into two major groups, a small proportion of expert software developers whose primary job is to create sophisticated software artefacts and a large proportion of ordinary end users who use those artefacts in support of their jobs. The former group includes people who are skilful programmers and problem-solving experts whereas the latter group includes people who are programming and modelling inept but they maybe domain experts. Thus, the research challenge is to equilibrate this imbalance by empowering ordinary end users, especially domain experts, to uptake software development activities via suitable tools so they can easily develop and customise software artefacts based on their goals and changing requirements.

To address this challenge, service-oriented architecture (SOA) offers suitable means of loosely coupling software services to produce augmented service-based applications through the so called process of "service composition" [1]. Composing services requires specifying what and how services are executed in a composition and

E. Di Nitto and R. Yahyapour (Eds.): ServiceWave 2010, LNCS 6481, pp. 163–174, 2010.

how data is passed between them using complex composition languages and tools. This process is time consuming and requires considerable modelling and programming knowledge even for experienced programmers. In this respect, it is vital to simplify the composition process for both groups of users, firstly by offering user-friendly service composition tools, and secondly by reducing the programming efforts and activities usually associated to software development. Such research promises to promote the reuse of web services, especially by ordinary end users.

When creating a user-friendly interface for a service composition system, we need to consider user expectations regarding the trade-off between the costs of learning new tools and the benefits they expect to get from using them. The balance between costs and benefits is likely to differ for different groups of users and different target domains (e.g. [9], [14]), yet we believe that identifying user attitudes and expectations towards service composition is a key to predicting successful uptake of service composition [9], [14] and [15].

In this paper, we endeavour to capture and contrast mental models of both ordinary end users and IT professionals about web services and service composition, their perception of end user development risks and benefits, and requirements in order to build user-friendly composition tools that account for the differences and special needs of each user category. This comparison produced differing requirements for end user composition.

2   Composition of Service-Based Systems

Service Composition is broadly supported by two main approaches: workflow-based scripting of service components, and AI-based automatic composition of service components reasoning with pre- and post-conditions. Further details are available elsewhere [4] and [13].

Professional programmers are supplemented with specialized composition languages (BPML, BPEL4WS, WSCDL ... etc) to construct service-based systems. However, developing composite services using text and XML editors is complex, error-prone, and time consuming. Therefore, several visual representations for service composition and interaction have been proposed with the aim to make the composition more user-friendly (e.g. Zenflow [7]). However, most of them are *ad hoc*, i.e. they use technology-led representations and metaphors, which are not derived from user studies. Only a few of them have been evaluated in terms of usability and cognitive effectiveness. For example, Lets Dance [16] has been evaluated using the framework of Cognitive Dimensions [2], but iterative testing and enhancement have not been documented in the related references. Another example is Vitabal WS [5], which is a version of an earlier visual language tuned to the needs of web service composition. It has been evaluated using the cognitive dimensions framework, yet it targets experienced web service developers only.

Opening up service use and development to people who are not professional programmers (i.e. end users) requires the delivery of user interfaces that are task-oriented rather than technology-oriented; that is, they should be tuned to the expected skills and foreseen tasks of our target users. Activities such as service construction and composition involve non-trivial problem-solving in a context called End User

Development (EUD) [6, 15]. EUD research provides an insight into the type of software interfaces and motivational factors likely to support end user activities.

Sutcliffe *et. al.* [14] see the trade-off between expected benefits and learning costs as a main determinant of uptake of an EUD tool by users. Risks and benefits of EUD have been used to underpin a number of quantitative studies in concrete domains, aiming to elicit the likelihood of uptake for end user development ideas in the specific context of that domain (e.g. [9]). The workshops reported here are examples of an application of this approach to the target domain of SOA4All[1], an EU-funded project that aims to open up service composition to everyone.

Several research studies have attempted to explore end user perception of software development, for instance: McGill and Klisc [8] argue that end users in the Internet domain are aware of the associated risks and benefits and thus it is crucial to involve them in the development of Internet application development approaches to minimize risks. Due to the difficulty of learning traditional programming languages, Myers *et al* [11] report on a number of studies aiming to elicit understanding of how people think about a particular task, natural programming languages and design environments that support the way end user developers are thinking. The generated data about user behaviour is used to build intuitive and usable programming environments. More recently, Namoune *et. al* [12] summarised potential problems of service composition showing that end users have difficulty connecting various services and understanding specialized service-related terms such as: operations, parameters etc. Overall, review of existing literature reveals that research in end user development of service-based systems is very rare and most studies are in their infancy.

3 Procedure and Materials

To acquire a better understanding of end users' perception about service composition and their likelihood for uptake of application development, we have conducted *five separate* focus groups; *three focus groups* with students and University staff and *two focus groups* with IT specialists who come from IT companies and research labs from various EU-countries). The focus groups included a total of 64 participants. Of those, 35 represented the mix expected by general consumers of services (range 19 to 40 years, mean 26 years) and further 29 were selected as representative of the specialist application fields like telecoms, where the majority did have IT expertise (range 23 to 60 years, mean 35 years).

Focus groups were used as a self-contained method to perform this study since no interactive prototype was available to evaluate at this early stage and to collect detailed insights into mental models, opinions and experiences of participants [10]. A qualitative research methodology was followed since we had no hypotheses or knowledge about our end users' perception towards service composition. Each focus group lasted for approximately one hour; participant responses were recorded using audio recorders and questionnaires. The overall strategy was to introduce participants to the topic of *"web service composition by end users"* through a presentation, followed by capturing their subjective judgment about the topic through a

---

[1] www.soa4all.eu

questionnaire, and finally discuss several themes in small groups. In details, our participants performed the subsequent tasks.

1. Define software services and fill in a participant background form
2. Listen to a 20-minute presentation to familiarize themselves with software services and service composition; this was facilitated by examples and figures (detailed in section 3.1). It is important to note here that the authors did not, in anyway, present or discuss the merits, drawbacks, or technical details of service composition; they mainly explained the meaning of '*service composition*'
3. Complete a subjective service composition questionnaire to capture initial opinions and rating of service composition aspects (detailed in section 3.2)
4. Discuss the potential risks and benefits of service composition by users and anticipate any composition-related problems; this was carried out in small discussion groups containing 5 participants each
5. Suggest potential solutions to overcome the identified problems

3.1 Service Composition Introductory Presentation

The introductory presentation "The Internet of Services", presented by one author, aimed to introduce the concept of web services along with examples of service composition. It started by explaining the difference between conventional services (human-performed services), software services and hybrid services. The influence of current Web 2.0 technologies was argued to enable end users to take part in the development of the web, and the idea is to move this influence to the Internet of Services. Following this, Yahoo! Pipes (a mash-up tool) was used as an illustrative example of service composition (Figure 1). Next, the motivation behind the SOA4All project was explained to the attendees, with the project aiming to transform the current web of information into a web of services through which users of services could also become producers of services. Then the scenario about the creation of a *Meet Friends* composite service was introduced to drive further discussions. This hypothetical composite service, which contains four atomic services, allows users to organize a meeting with friends at a short notice. Finally, the presenter showed mockups of a future authoring service composition tool, SOA4All Studio (Figure 2).

Fig. 1. Yahoo! Pipes as an elaborating example (left)

Fig. 2. SOA4All Studio – a composition tool under development – (right)

3.2 Service Composition Questionnaire

The service composition questionnaire used in our study consisted of three main parts. Part one captured users' service composition experience and the composition languages and systems they have used. Part two captured users' rating of various aspects of service composition. Part three rated users' opinions on ways for supporting service composition. Questions were rated on a five-point Likert scale where 1 corresponds to "*Disagree*" and 5 corresponds to "*Agree*".

Although the questionnaire contained some questions which are difficult to assess at this stage, for example, it is rather hard to judge whether "composition by end users is easy to achieve" without actually trying it, the principal aim was to drive initial impressions about service composition and check users' acceptability of this innovative idea. Furthermore, the results of this questionnaire provide a reference point to future evaluation stages of our composition authoring tool (SOA4All Studio).

4   Results

We first report on the background of our participants and then on the study results which are divided into three main themes: service perception, risks and benefits of "service composition by users" (for short SCU), and service composition problems.

4.1 Background of Target User Groups

As previously mentioned, two categories of users participated in our study: end users and IT professionals. Analysis of variance (ANOVA) tests (following the Games-Howell procedure since it does not assume sample sizes are equal) showed that IT professionals' experience in software development (f(1, 62)= 54.64, p<0.001), web service development (f(1, 62))= 24.06, p<0.001), with analysis and design notations (f(1, 62)= 14.32, p<0.001), and in service composition (f(1, 61)= 9.15, p<0.01) were all significantly higher than end users. This is a rather predictable result since 75% of IT professionals had IT-focused degrees. The groups of general end users had few IT-students but with no working experience with software services. Table 1 summarises the background and skills of each of the two user groups.

Table 1. End Users and IT Professionals Background

Criterion	Ordinary End Users	IT Professionals
Number of participants	35 (13 males, 22 females)	29 (27 males, 2 females
Experience in software development	2.31[2]/5 (std= 1.13)	4.07/5 (std=0.65)
Experience in service development	2.11/5 (std= 1.15)	3.44/5 (std=0.98)
Experience with analysis and design notations	2.28/5 (std= 1.31)	3.48/5 (std=1.18)
Experience in service composition	2.34/5 (std=0.93)	3.10/5 (std=1.06)
Service composition languages and systems used before	Facebook, iGoogle	Yahoo!Pipes, OWL-S, BPEL4WS, BPML

---

[2] Ratings were performed on a 5-point Likert scale, where 1= disagree and 5= agree.

4.2   Users' Mental Models of Software Services and Service Composition

The qualitative analysis of end users responses revealed 30 user-oriented definitions and only 1 technical definition of web services; no programming-oriented terms were used to define services. Users' definitions of web services varied between: *"online information and service provisioning to people* (39% of the responses)", *"features assisting users to accomplish their tasks and satisfy their needs* (29%)", *"software that enable service composition* (6%)", and *"reusable components* (3%)".

In general, end users' definitions concentrated on two main aspects, (1) describing specific interactions with users in the form of service consumption, such as: providing users with information and delivering expertise, (2) describing attributes/features of services such as: services are intangible and they have a back end. Four end users were not able to provide any definition or examples of web services.

As for IT professionals, 21 definitions were provided. 76% of which were very technical such as: *"reusable network-based components"*, *"self-contained units provided by software"* … etc. Only 14% of the responses perceived web services as *"online software"*, whilst the remaining 10% described the business aspects of web services (e.g. *"pay as you go software"*). Eight IT professionals did not provide any definition for web services. Table 2 summarizes the perspectives of both user groups and highlights the implications for the design of development environments.

Table 2. Users' Mental Model of Software Services

Criterion	Ordinary End Users	IT Professionals
Level of understanding	Basic, general	Complex, detailed
Details	User oriented, simple terminology	Technical, specialized terms e.g. self-contained units
Features	Interaction, Consumption. Information-oriented, User Interface	Reusability, software components, functionality-oriented, business model
Level of abstraction	High level of abstraction	Low level of abstraction
Implications for service composition platforms	Services should be presented in a *visual form* and *abstracted* from their technical aspects. Use familiar terminology and enable graphical development of service-based systems.	Complex properties of service composition and of services such as input and output parameters, and operations should be revealed to users who are willing to modify them.

Subjective rating of several service composition questions revealed that both user groups are highly interested in service composition (end users (4.20/5), IT professionals (4.32/5)). Similarly, they agreed that service composition is highly useful (end users (4.44/5), IT professionals (4.44/5)), as well as efficient in promoting the accomplishment of online activities (end users (4.12/5), IT professionals (3.86/5)).

ANOVA tests (the Games-Howell procedure) showed a significant difference in the perception of easiness ($f(1, 61)) = 10.87$, $p<0.01$) and error proneness ($f(1, 60)) = 18.26$, $p<0.001$) of service composition (Figure 3). Indeed, *"service composition by users"* was regarded easier (3.32/5) by end users than IT professionals (2.37/5). However, IT professionals perceived the composition as more likely to make errors (3.55/5) than end users (2.54 /5). Interestingly both groups agreed that service composition can break organizational rules and policies (end users (3.50/5), IT professionals (3.51/5)) which suggests worries about loss of personal information.

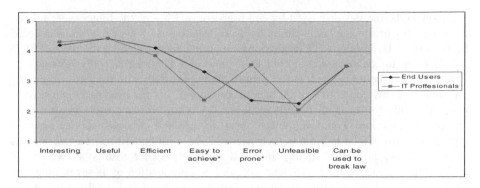

Fig. 3. Rating of Service Composition aspects by end users and IT professionals, * refers to questions that were rated significantly different according to ANOVA tests

In regard to ways of supporting and encouraging service composition, ordinary users rated that "successful examples (4.69/5) and training courses (4.38/5) could encourage people to be actively involved in the composition of service-based applications" significantly higher than IT professionals (4.34/5 and 3.55/5 respectively), as shown by the ANOVA tests (f(1, 60)) = 4.88, p<0.05, and f(1, 61)) = 15.24, p<0.001 respectively). End users strongly thought that quality standards and testing will decrease risks of service composition (4.32/5), whilst IT professionals were less convinced (3.71/5), ANOVA tests were significant (f(1, 60)) = 8.30, p<0.01). Both groups agreed that recognising and rewarding service composition efforts will increase people's willingness to uptake development activities (end user (4.15), IT professionals (3.82)).

In summary, both end users and IT professionals were highly interested in composing services and strongly agreed that service composition is possible and useful, but expressed uncertainty about the difficulty and potential misuse of service composition by the general public. It is notable that IT professionals view in respect to the idea of '*service composition by end users*' was more critical and realistic than ordinary end users. They were less convinced that examples and training classes could help uptake of service development activities by users, probably owing to their awareness of the difficulty programmers encounter when developing composite services. The implication for service composition platforms is *to identify techniques that simplify the composition process for non-programmers, protect end users from making mistakes and help them localize faults, guide users actions during service composition proactively, and provide realistic examples, tutorials and demos about service composition and its concepts.*

4.3 Risks and Benefits of Service Composition

The ongoing research in this area aims to analyze the factors which impact the balance of perceived risks and perceived benefits based on [9], [14] and [15], and to discover organizational and technical strategies which aim to tip the balance in favour of the benefits, thus supporting the uptake of such technologies. We used *the thematic analysis technique* to create risk and benefit categories from the collected data [2].

Amongst the themes discussed by end users, only 7.2% of the topics were related to the benefits of service composition by users, whereas 25.5% of the topics covered the risks of SCU. Similarly, IT professionals mainly concentrated on the risks of SCU (37.7% of the topics discussed), giving less attention to the benefits (only 7.5%).

In terms of benefits, end users mainly focused on the usefulness of reusing composition knowledge (40% of all benefit responses), and the time users can save as a result of this (30% of all benefit responses). Giving ordinary users control over service composition would empower them to produce various service-oriented applications that can be tailored to their needs (15% of all benefit responses), such as meta-search engines, thus saving time and obtaining richer results. However, IT professionals argued for the efficiency of service composition as it saves time and efforts (41.6% of all benefit responses). Service composition can also be used to generate income (25% of all benefit responses) e.g. *"you need to create a business model around that and you would need to generate income somehow"*.

In terms of risks, end users' biggest fear was about losing control over personal information (46% of all risk responses), especially when the effect is mediated through the effect of social interactions (e.g. friends exposing your information), or through the service provider, which may pass personal information (e.g. phone number) to other sub-contracting services e.g. *"I would be concerned whether the details are given to third parties"*, which may or may not be bound to the data protection principles. Technical difficulty imposed by service composition was also amongst the top concerns for end users (17% of all risk responses) e.g. *"to build a system that can include all those different services and provide an interface for them is quite difficult"*. Errors in putting information together were also possible, especially when the composition is performed by inexperienced users and un-trusted third parties. Moreover, users felt that services may no longer be there when they need them, and that any recommendation support for services may be biased to a set of services. Likewise, service developers specified that their major concerns were about data privacy (21% of all risk responses) e.g. *"once you start allowing components to exchange information, there goes privacy"*, followed by security issues when using infected (e.g. virus) or compromised services (18.33% of all risk responses), and trust issues when using services from unknown service providers (6.66% of all risk responses), e.g, *"there can be trust security and trust issues involved using someone else's services"*.

We have categorized the risks identified by our users according to two factors: likelihood of occurrence (very likely, likely, unlikely, and highly unlikely) and severity of results if a specific risk occurs (slightly harmful, harmful, and very severe). These two factors determine the probability and seriousness of a risk and its influence and enable us to prioritize and concentrate our efforts on the probable incidents. At the time of focus groups we were not aware of the potential risks of service composition, thus we were not able to ask our users to classify the risks. However, during the analysis process we referred to users' comments to inform our categorisation. Table 3 organizes the potential risks of service composition.

End users and IT professionals also discussed what could be the social and organizational support for user-based service development. For instance:

- "Go with the flow" – once everybody is doing it, people will join, mirroring success in other technologies;

- Efficient examples of successful use will also help (to sell benefits), this was felt quite strongly;
- Community-level control mechanisms, such as feedback, would ensure validation of services and, together with a validating body/watchdog may help to ensure the trust, which is considered vital for uptake of user-driven service composition.

Table 3. Risk categorization according to severity of outcomes and likelihood of occurrence

		Severity of outcome		
		Slightly harmful	Harmful	Very severe
Likelihood of occurrence	Very likely		Technical difficulty (*end users*)	
	Likely		-Errors in putting information together (*end users*) -Trusting unknown services (*IT professionals*) - Awareness of implications of actions (*Both*)	-Privacy of personal information (*end users and IT professionals*) -Security of services (*IT professionals*)
	Unlikely	Biased recommendation of services (*end users*)	Unavailability of desired services (*end users*)	
	Highly unlikely			

4.4 Problems of Service Composition

Although both categories of users favoured the idea of assembling services to produce interactive applications that fulfil their special needs, several service composition-related issues were raised, in particular:

- *Services complexity*: services are usually represented using their functional elements (operations and parameters) which are often not understood by ordinary web users. End users are not willing to learn complex concepts in order to be able to compose services; they prefer instead traditional and easy-to-use alternatives.
- *Services compatibility*: users expressed frustration in regards to aggregating heterogeneous services from different service providers. How do they ensure the business services they are trying to combine together are technically compatible with each other?
- *Composition steps*: users agreed that it might be problematic to define the single steps required to combine services together and the order in which these services should be executed due to their lack of technical knowledge and modelling skills. This issue becomes more complicated in the case of many services (for example: 100 atomic services). For an ordinary end user or a domain expert, it is quite challenging to identify the right service that fulfils a specific task and the best way to connect the relevant services.
- *Composition for everyone*: users reported worries about designing composition development environments which target all users; this might not work due to diversity of users' experience, requirements, and computing expertise. The 'one size fits all' metaphor does not hold anymore in the evolving world of Internet.

- Other less aggravated *user interface-related concerns* cantered around the service composition editor e.g. direct manipulation of web services (i.e. selection, deletion, etc) within the design space could be the main source of frustration.

In terms of technical support which can be provided by the composition authoring tool, the following themes emerged:

- The difference between novice and professional users was perceived to lie partially in the awareness about the consequences of one's actions
- Full automation such as Google search results will frustrate owing to lack of control by the end users, a balance should be maintained;
- Tools should offer clarity of process in respect to building and using (i.e. context and personalisation, reuse of designs);

5 Discussion

The comparison between the results of end users and IT professionals yielded very interesting findings. End users showed either no or a very limited knowledge of the technical aspects of services. This is anticipated because this target group has no specialist technical skills, as demonstrated by the background questionnaires. Essentially, end users perceived services as elements which deliver online services (be it information, help, solutions ... etc) to fulfil specified user needs. This view necessitates that services should to be *highly abstracted* from their technical complexity and presented in ways that efficiently describe their purpose and functionality. On the contrary, IT professionals showed a high level of understanding of the technical features of services which can be attributed to their profound knowledge about programmable aspects of services.

Both target groups showed a high likeability towards the idea of "composing services into personalized interactive applications", confirming [12]. This agrees with the current trends that end users are becoming proactive about developing the web. IT professionals perceived service composition as more difficult to achieve than end users since they are more aware of the underlying technical issues. They also thought service composition is likely to cause errors more than end users, which can be associated to the programming (compilation and debugging) problems they regularly encounter. This finding urges to develop composition tools that facilitate development tasks and manage development issues for IT professionals.

End users and IT professionals showed high levels of awareness of the risks and benefits of service composition by users which agrees with [8]. Their greatest concerns in regard to service composition revolved around data privacy and security issues. Hence, for people to uptake development activities high levels of data security and privacy policies must be guaranteed.

In regard to perceived benefits, users argued that service composition will save time and enable them to develop applications on the fly through a straightforward process. Hence, it is important that end users are enabled to compose services without the need to learn programming languages and modelling notations.

A Preliminary Model of Service Composition Uptake: figure 4 summarizes the relationship and interaction between user mental model, perceived risks and benefits, and service composition. In principal every user has initial expectations about service composition and is directly affected by what they know, their abilities, domain and working experience. This mental model is improved via practice after users get involved into building service-based applications. Sadly our findings suggest that the risks associated to service composition outweigh the benefits, as perceived by end users. It is thus essential to implement accurate measurements to resolve this unbalance in users' perception because simply this is the first step towards realizing successful service composition by and for everyone.

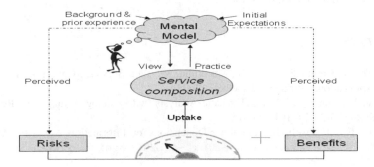

Fig. 4. A preliminary model of service composition uptake by end users

To restore the balance between perceived risks and benefits and overcome the above service composition problems, various tentative remedies are proposed.

Guideline 1'Promote service composition awareness': composition editors should clearly communicate "the composition aspect" of services. Users' awareness of the possibility to develop service-based applications should be elevated via the right amount of publicity to familiarize ordinary people with SOA technologies.

Guideline 2'Simplify service composition': it is crucial to simplify service composition by hiding the technical aspects of services from users. Composition should be as easy as dragging and dropping a service into a design space, followed by creating connections between the selected services.

Guideline 3'Guide service composition': users should be supplied with wizards, tutorials, help messages, and composition templates to guide them through the service composition process within an easy to use composition tool. The provisioning of examples and training is also important to support and encourage SCU.

Guideline 4 'Specialize service composition platforms': for each category of users with a particular set of characteristics and skills, specialized composition platforms which employ appropriate visual paradigms and metaphors should be offered.

6 Conclusion

This paper summarizes the results of five focus groups aiming to gauge and compare perceptions of two different target user groups, end users and IT professionals, on software services and their willingness to uptake service composition activities. In general both groups of users showed a high willingness to develop interactive service-oriented applications, but expressed concerns that relate to privacy, security, and complexity underlying the composition process and to the knowledge required to build software applications. These concerns should be addressed well in order to restore the balance between perceived risks and benefits (as shown by our preliminary model) and thus motivate and involve ordinary end users in the development of service-based systems. In future research, various composition design approaches of different complexity levels will be offered to accommodate users with various skills and backgrounds levels within an easy to use online service composition tool, formally known as SOA4All studio.

References

1. Alonso, G., Casati, F., Kuno, H., Machiraju, V.: Web Services: Concepts, Architectures, and Applications. Springer, Heidelberg (2004)
2. Braun, V., Clarke, V.: Using Thematic Analysis in Psychology. Qualitative Research in Psychology 3(2), 77–101 (2006)
3. Green, T., Blackwell, A.: Cognitive Dimensions of Information Artefacts: A Tutorial (1998), http://www.cl.cam.ac.uk/~afb21/CognitiveDimensions/CDtutorial.pdf
4. Jinghai, R., Xiaomeng, S.: A Survey of Automated Web Service Composition Methods. In: Cardoso, J., Sheth, A.P. (eds.) SWSWPC 2004. LNCS, vol. 3387, pp. 43–54. Springer, Heidelberg (2005)
5. Li Na-Liu, K.: Visual Languages for Event Integration Specification. PhD Thesis, University of Auckland, Department of Computer Science (2008)
6. Lieberman, H., Paterno, F., Wulf, V. (eds.): End User Development. Springer, Germany (2005)
7. Martinez, A., Patino-Martinez, M., Jimenez-Peris, R., Perez-Sorrosal, F.: ZenFlow: A Visual Web Service Composition Tool for BPEL4WS. In: Proceedings of the IEEE Symposium on VLHCC, pp. 181–188. IEEE Computer Society, Washington (2005)
8. McGill, T., Klisc, C.: End User Perceptions of the Benefits and Risks of End User Web Development. Journal of Organizational and End User Computing 18(4), 22–42 (2006)
9. Mehandjiev, N., Stoitsev, T., Grebner, O., Scheidl, S., Riss, U.: End User Development for Task Management: Survey of Attitudes and Practices. In: Proceedings of IEEE Symposium on VLHCC. IEEE Press, Los Alamitos (2008)
10. Morgan, D.L.: Focus Groups as Qualitative Research. Sage Publications, California (1997)
11. Myers, B., Pane, J. F., Ko, A.: Natural Programming Languages and Environments. Communications of the ACM (Special issue on End-User Development) 47(9) (2004)
12. Namoune, A., Nestler, T., Angeli, A.D.: End User Development of Service-based Applications. In: 2nd Workshop on HCI and Services at HCI 2009, Cambridge (2009)
13. Papazoglou, M.P., Traverso, P., Dustdar, S., Leymann, F.: Service-Oriented Computing: State of the Art and Research Challenges. Computer 40(11), 38–45 (2007)
14. Sutcliffe, A., Lee, D., Mehandjiev, N.: Contributions, Costs and Prospects for End-User Development. In: Proceedings of HCI International. Lawrence Erlbaum Associates, Inc., New Jersey (2003)
15. Sutcliffe, A., Mehandjiev, N.: Introduction: Special Issue on End User Development. The Communications of ACM 47(9), 31–32 (2004)
16. Zaha, J., Barros, A.P., Dumas, M., ter Hofstede, A.H.M.: Let's Dance: A Language for Service Behavior Modeling. In: Meersman, R., Tari, Z. (eds.) OTM 2006. LNCS, vol. 4275, pp. 145–162. Springer, Heidelberg (2006)

Using a Lifecycle Model for Developing and Executing Adaptable Interactive Distributed Applications

D. Meiländer[1], S. Gorlatch[1], C. Cappiello[2], V. Mazza[2],
R. Kazhamiakin[3], and A. Bucchiarone[3]

[1] University of Muenster (Germany)
[2] Politecnico di Milano (Italy)
[3] Fondazione Bruno Kessler (Italy)

Abstract. We describe a case study on using the generic Lifecycle Model developed in the S-Cube project for a novel class of Real-time Online Interactive Applications (ROIA), which include distributed simulations (e.g. massively-multiplayer online games), e-learning and training. We describe how the Lifecycle Model supports application development by addressing the specific challenges of ROIA: a large number of concurrent users connected to a single application instance, frequent real-time user interactions, enforcement of Quality of Service (QoS) parameters, adaptivity to changing loads, and competition-oriented interaction between users, other actors, and services. We describe the implementation aspects of the application development and adaptation using the RTF (Real-Time Framework) middleware, and report experimental results for a sample online game application.

Keywords: Service-Oriented Architecture, Service Engineering, Real-Time Online Interactive Applications, Adaptation, Real-Time Framework (RTF).

1 Introduction

Service-oriented applications are developed for constantly changing environments with the expectation that they will evolve over time. Several service-oriented system engineering (SOSE) methodologies have been proposed aiming at providing methods and (sometimes) tools for researchers and practitioners to engineer service-oriented systems. SOSE methodologies are more complex than traditional software engineering (TSE) methodologies: the additional complexity results mainly from open world assumptions, co-existence of many stakeholders with conflicting requirements and the demand for adaptable systems. A number of service lifecycle models have been proposed by both industry and academia. However, none of the proposed models has either reached a sufficient level of maturity or been able to fully express the aspects peculiar to SOSE. The S-Cube project [1] combines existing techniques and methodologies from TSE and SOSE to improve the process through which service based applications will be developed.

This paper describes an industrial-strength case study for the S-Cube Lifecycle Model in the emerging and challenging area of Real-time Online Interactive Applications (ROIA) which include such popular and socially important applications

E. Di Nitto and R. Yahyapour (Eds.): ServiceWave 2010, LNCS 6481, pp. 175–186, 2010.

as multi-player online computer games, high-performance simulations, e-learning, etc. ROIA pose several new challenges: thousands of users connect simultaneously to one application instance and frequently interact with each other, system must adapt to changing loads, maintaining QoS requirements, etc. Within the European edutain@grid project [2], a service-oriented architecture including a novel RTF (Real-Time Framework) middleware was implemented which focuses on the main challenges of ROIA.

The paper studies how the application of the S-Cube Lifecycle Model to the applications on top of the edutain@grid architecture enables the designer to identify suitable adaptation mechanisms and design patterns for the challenging area of ROIA.

We briefly introduce the S-Cube Lifecycle Model for SOSE in Section 2, followed by a description of the edutain@grid architecture and RTF in Section 3. We describe the application of the Lifecycle Model on the case study scenario from edutain@grid in Section 4 and report experimental results of a sample ROIA application based on RTF in Section 5. Related work is finally discussed in Section 6.

2   The Lifecycle Model for Service-Oriented Applications

The S-Cube Lifecycle Model for adaptable Service Based Applications (SBAs) (see Figure 1) comprises two main cycles: (i) a design-time iteration cycle that leads to the explicit re-design of the application in order to adapt it to new needs (i.e., *evolution*), and (ii) an *adaptation* cycle at runtime that is used when the adaptation needs are addressed on-the-fly. The two cycles coexist and support each other during the lifetime of an application [5].

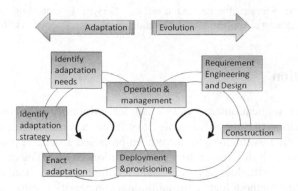

Fig. 1. The S-Cube Lifecycle Model

The development of an SBA starts with the former cycle that inherits some common aspects from the traditional software lifecycle but is modified in order to deal with specific adaptation issues. In case of ROIA, already in the *Requirements Engineering & Design* phase it is necessary to identify monitoring and adaptation requirements and methods to guarantee high update rates.

The *Construction* phase of an SBA is often performed in the form of a service composition. The construction can be manual (service integrator defines an executable process composed of concrete and abstract services), model-driven (service orchestration models are generated by abstract models) or automated (starting from service models, the executable SBA is automatically generated). For ROIA, it is necessary to implement suitable parallelization, adaptation and scalability mechanisms. Then, after the *Deployment and Provisioning* phase in which the application is introduced to customers, the *Operation and Management* phase relies on the monitoring activities that use the monitored properties to derive the status of the application and detect changes in the context or in the system that require adaptation or evolution. Starting from this phase, ROIA developers can decide to execute the right-hand side of the lifecycle if an evolution of the application is required (redesigning the application offline, making it temporarily unavailable to customers), or otherwise the ROIA is managed online by enacting adaptation actions at runtime (executing the left-hand side). E.g., an iteration of the evolution cycle may become necessary if the application is facing new attacking mechanisms by fraudulent users or in case of changing user requirements, since there may be a need to define additional sensors and monitors, as well as to change adaptation strategies.

In the adaptation cycle, it is important to define the adaptation needs that can be caused by: changes in the functional and non-functional aspects (e.g., unreliable hoster resources cannot preserve QoS requirements) or changes of the context in which the application is running (e.g., increasing user numbers in the evening hours creating peak load). In the domain of ROIA, adaptation mechanisms need to be proactive and transparent to users in order to adapt the application during runtime.

3   A Service-Oriented Architecture for ROIA

In this section, we describe the specific features of Real-time Online Interactive Applications (ROIA) and express their major design and execution aspects in the context of the S-Cube Lifecycle Model. ROIA pose many new challenges for SOSE including: large number of concurrent users connecting to a single application instance, frequent real-time user interactions, enforcement of precise QoS parameters, adaptivity to changing loads, and competition-oriented interaction between users and services.

Within the edutain@grid project, a distributed service-oriented architecture (see Figure 2) was implemented that is based on the interaction of four actors [10]: (1) *End-user* accesses ROIA sessions through graphical clients, typically purchased as a DVD; (2) *Scheduler* negotiates on behalf of the end-user appropriate ROIA sessions based on the QoS requirements (e.g. connection latency); (3) *Hoster* is an organisation that provides a computational and network infrastructure for running ROIA servers; (4) *Resource broker* provides a mechanism for application Schedulers and Hosters (and possibly other actors) to find each other in a large-scale environment and negotiate QoS relationships.

The service-oriented edutain@grid architecture encompasses stateful web services, ontologies, business and accounting models, as well as a flexible and generic communication API for ROIA. In the following, we use the application area of online gaming to identify suitable services for the implementation of the adaptation cycle in the S-Cube Lifecycle Model (Figure 1).

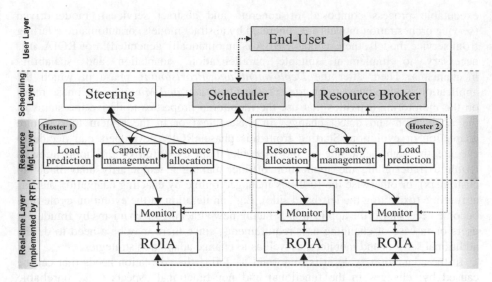

Fig. 2. The edutain@grid architecture for ROIA

Scheduling Service. The web service-based Scheduler receives from the user QoS requirements which can be performance-related (e.g., maximum allowed latency, minimum bandwidth) or application-specific (e.g., game genre, minimum number of users) and negotiates with existing hosters. The result is a contract, called *service level agreement (SLA)*, for the interaction of the end-user with the application. The mapping of users to game servers, as well as the allocation of Hoster resources to game servers, takes place as a distributed negotiation between the Scheduler and Hosters. The result is a performance contract that the Scheduler offers to the end-user and which does not necessarily match the original QoS request. The user can accept the contract and connect to the proposed session, or reject it.

Runtime Steering Service. During the game session, situations may occur which affect the performance, such that the negotiated SLAs cannot be maintained. Typical perturbing factors include external load on shared resources, or overloaded servers due to an unexpected concentration of users in "hot spots". The steering component is a web service which interacts at runtime with the monitoring service of each Hoster for preserving the negotiated QoS parameters for the duration of the session. A violation of a QoS parameter triggers appropriate adaptive steering or rescheduling using the API of the real-time layer. Thereby the Runtime Steering Service contributes to the "Identify Adaptation Needs" and "Identify Adaptation Strategy" phases of the adaptation circle of the Lifecycle Model.

Resource Allocation Service. Typically, each Hoster owns a Resource Allocation service responsible for allocating local resources to the clients. This web service receives from the Scheduler connection requests formulated in terms of QoS requirements, such as minimum latency or maximum bandwidth, and returns a positive answer if it can accomodate them. Online games are characterized by a large number of users that share the same application instance and interact across different game servers. The atomic resource allocation units for users are, therefore, no longer coarse-grain processes, but rather fine-grained threads and memory objects, which are more sensitive to external perturbations.

Capacity Planning Service. The load of a game session depends heavily on internal events, e.g. interactions of avatars. Also external events may occur, such as the user fluctuation over the day or week [9]. Hence, it is crucial for a Hoster to anticipate the future game load. The Capacity Planning web service predicts future load of Hoster resources by employing neural networks [10] and thereby contributes to the "Identify Adaptation Needs" and "Identify Adaptation Strategy" phases of the Lifecycle Model.

The real-time layer of edutain@grid is implemented by the *Real-Time Framework (RTF)* [3] that distributes game state calculations among the participating servers. Instead of using web services and SOAP-encoded communication messages which are not suitable for fast real-time communication, RTF uses TCP/IP sockets internally. RTF provides efficient parallelisation and adaptation concepts and implements suitable monitoring capabilities, which we explain in the following.

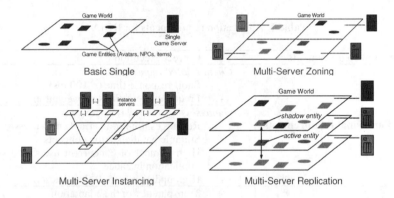

Fig. 3. Adaptation strategies of RTF via (re)distribution

Real-Time Adaptation Service. To enable the service scalability to a high number and density of users, RTF distributes game sessions adaptively, based on several adaptation strategies illustrated in Figure 3. *Zoning* [8] distributes the game world into disjoint zones, each zone being assigned to one server. *Instancing* uses multiple, independently processed copies of highly frequented subareas of the game world, each copy processed by one server: if an avatar moves into one frequented subarea, it is assigned to one of the available copies. Different copies are not synchronized since users in disjoint copies cannot interact with each other. *Replication* [13] assigns multiple servers to a zone with a high load; the responsibility of computing in that zone is divided equally among the servers. RTF's adaptation strategies are used in the "Enact Adaptation" phase of the Lifecycle Model as explained in Section 4.

Monitoring Service observes the QoS parameters negotiated by the Hoster. Several monitoring parameters are summarized in profiles which support monitoring of low-level QoS parameters, as well as of game-related metrics (like entity positions, messages sent or received, or end-user activity information) crucial for an adequate game experience of the users. RTF's monitoring services are used by the steering and capacity planning services.

4 Using the Lifecycle Model for Developing ROIA

In this section, we demonstrate how the Lifecycle Model of Section 2 is applied to ROIA applications by exploiting the edutain@grid architecture of Section 3. The lifecycle is based on various adaptation- and monitoring-specific actions and related design artifacts. The main aspects for designing an adaptive application are: the *application requirements*, the *adaptation strategies*, and the *adaptation triggers*.

Our analysis of ROIA applications has identified the application requirements shown in Table 1. Besides the functional and non-functional application requirements described in Section 3, it is also important to identify the requirements to be considered for the design of adaptation actions. In the case of ROIA, the mechanisms for monitoring and adaptation should be non-intrusive, i.e., take place in parallel with the application execution, and users not aware of changes inside the application. Since the considered system must guarantee the QoS requirements, proactive adaptation should be supported in order to prevent QoS violations.

Table 1. Application requirements for ROIA

Functional Requirements	- Correct execution
Non Functional Requirements	*Client related requirements* - Short response time (< 100 ms) - Frequent interactions between users
	Game session-related requirements - Resources use for a variable # of users - Suitable parallelization concepts - High number of concurrent users in a single application instance - High update rate (5-100 updates/s)
Adaptation Requirements	- Transparency of the adaptation - Instance-specific adaptation during runtime - Need for proactive adaptation - Autonomy (self-adaptability) - Efficiency of adaptation actions

The application requirements drive the selection of the adaptation strategies. According to the Lifecycle Model, we identify the following five adaptation strategies for ROIA applications on top of the edutain@grid architecture:

(1) *User migration*: users are migrated transparently from an overloaded server to an underutilized server which is replicating the same zone.

(2) *Zoning*: new zones are added during runtime and assigned to additional game servers. Zoning provides the best scalability of all adaptation strategies, but is not transparent to users (since the geography of the virtual world is changed), so it is generally used for high numbers of users that cannot participate otherwise.

(3) *Replication*: new game servers are added transparently during runtime in order to increase computation power for highly frequented zones. When replicating a zone, a number of users are migrated to the replica and initiate workload redistribution. However, replication implies an additional inter-server communication and thus, its scalability is limited. To address the demand for autonomic and self-adaptable

applications, the number of active replicas for a particular zone is monitored to decide whether activating additional replicas is feasible.

(4) *Instancing*: creates a copy of a zone which is processed by a different server than the original zone. Since users in different copies of the same zone cannot interact with each other, replication is generally preferred to instancing in order to support high interactivity between users. However, instancing as an adaptation strategy is useful if the overhead of replication would be too high.

(5) *QoS negotiation* with several distributed hosters which includes (i) adaptation of existing contracts, or (ii) negotiation of contracts with new hosters. Typical scenarios include the usage of stronger resources of the same hoster (QoS adaptation) or leasing cheaper resources from a new hoster. QoS adaptation can be an alternative to replication by allocating more powerful resources to serve more users. Since QoS adaptation needs a longer time, replication and instancing provide better scalability, but QoS adaptation can be used to overcome small peaks in resource shortage.

For designing adaptable SBAs, adaptation strategies must be related to adaptation triggers. Adaptation triggers and suitable trigger rules are defined considering all scenarios at runtime in which application requirements may be violated. For ROIA, adaptation triggers are related to changes in Service Quality, in the computational context and in users' requirements, unexpected increment of the users' accesses, and specific users' needs. In the edutain@grid architecture, proactive adaptation is planned on the basis of predicted values from the capacity planning service. For example, load balancing may anticipate increasing user numbers in the evening hours and request appropriate resources. Then, the adaptation trigger (predicted increase in user numbers) is related to the change in the context (i.e., time period).

Adaptation triggers provide to the application designers the variables to be monitored at runtime and thereby drive the design of the monitoring mechanism. In ROIA, monitored properties include CPU/memory load on hoster resources, the number of concurrent users in an application instance, bandwidth capacity etc.

By considering the application requirements and the adaptation strategies, we distinguish the following scenarios for triggering adaptation in ROIA applications:

(1) *Change in Quality of Service*: QoS violations which were not expected and predicted, e.g., caused by unreliable hoster resources. In this scenario, user migration, replication or instancing is used for adaptation in order to overcome performance bottlenecks. We decide which of the three adaptation mechanisms to use depending on the amount of free resources and number of active replicas: in order to minimize costs for the application provider, migrating users to underloaded resources is preferred if the additional load can be compensated by running resources; otherwise replication is preferred to instancing in order to support a high level of interactivity between users; if activating additional replicas implies too high communication overhead, instancing is used.

(2) *Change in computational context*: a change in the costs of calculating the application state, e.g., caused by increasingly or decreasingly frequent interactions between users. To prevent QoS violations, one of the adaptation strategies is used: user migration, replication or instancing (depending on free resources and number of replicas).

(3) *Change in business context*: a change in user preferences which was not predicted in advance, e.g., many new users connecting to the application. In this scenario, user migration, replication or instancing (depending on the amount of free resources and number of replicas) are used for adaptation.

(4) *Prediction results*: The capacity planning service gathers information about the users' preferences and triggers adaptation proactively and autonomously. Depending on the predicted number of additional users, either QoS negotiation, replication or adding new zones at runtime are used for adaptation since predicted adaptations can be planned ahead. If the maximum number of replicas is already reached, then instancing can be chosen.

Table 2 shows how the described adaptation triggers and adaptation strategies are linked together, and provides examples for trigger rules and monitored values:

Table 2. Relationship between Adaptation Triggers and Adaptation Strategies

Adaptation Trigger	Monitored variable	Adaptation Trigger rule	Adaptation Strategy
Change in Quality of Service	response time, throughput, resource usage, average packet loss, connection latency, update rate, service availability	update rate < 25 updates/s	user migration, replication or instancing
Change in comput. context	CPU and memory load, incoming/outgoing bandwidth	CPU load > 90%	user migration, replication or instancing
Change in business context	number of concurrent users, number of requests per application	number of concurrent users > Σ user capability of application servers	user migration, replication or instancing
Prediction values from capacity planning service	number of users/hour, number of requests per application	predicted users > current users + △ (threshold)	QoS negotiation, replication or instancing/zoning

We observe that for each adaptation trigger, various adaptation strategies may be suitable. A ROIA application is realized in the *Construction* phase of the Lifecycle Model in order to include all the monitoring features and technical infrastructure needed for proactive adaptation. The design patterns and distribution concepts offered by RTF support developers designing and implementing efficient ROIA; application development on top of RTF was described in [18]. The need for proactive adaptation has a strong impact on the design and realization of the monitoring mechanisms. Since ROIA applications are very dynamic, not all failures/critical situations can be identified at design time. Therefore, there is a need to continuously update the knowledge about the behavior of the system.

After the construction phase, the application is deployed, i.e. it is ready to be executed and managed. During the *Operation and Management* phase, the application is running and all the previously designed adaptation triggers are monitored to detect changes in the context or in the system that could require adaptation or evolution. Starting from this phase, the application is managed online by enacting adaptation actions during runtime; if evolution is required, the right-hand side of the lifecycle is executed again conforming to the specific implementation issues for ROIA.

5   State of Implementation and Experimental Results

In order to test the effectiveness of system design using the Lifecycle Model, we perform some experiments with the central part of the edutain@grid architecture, responsible for real-time services for ROIA. In particular, we study the suitability of the zoning and replication adaptation strategies for ROIA. We have implemented the Real-Time Framework (RTF) [18] as a C++ based library, since C++ is currently the language of choice for ROIA applications in industry. Using RTF as a development framework and runtime middleware, we developed several applications, some of them jointly with industrial partners, from three areas: online computer games [16], e-learning systems [11], and crowd simulation [19]. We use one such application for our experiments.

Fig. 4. Screenshot of RTFDemo (avatars managed by different servers have different colours)

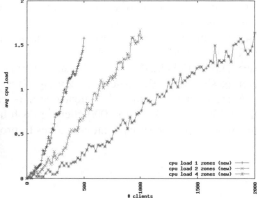

Fig. 5. CPU load for zoning adaptation

The *RTFDemo* application is an industrial-strength, fast-paced online game that takes place in a zoned 3D world and is built on top of RTF. RTFDemo is a representative of the first-person shooter game category, the most demanding class of online games requiring a very high state update rate, interactivity and frequent message exchange. A user participates in RTFDemo by controlling a robot avatar in a 3D virtual world and interacting with avatars controlled by other users. The characteristics of RTFDemo correspond to a modern commercial online game: the game state is updated 25 times per second, both seamless migration between different zones and interactions across zone borders are supported. Fig 4 shows a screenshot of the RTFDemo game.

We conducted experiments that test the zoning and replication adaptation strategies implemented in RTFDemo. We use a pool of homogeneous PCs with 2.66 GHz, CoreDuo 2 CPUs, and 4 GB RAM in a LAN. A static setup of zones and servers was started with multiple computer-controlled clients (bots) that continuously sent inputs to their servers. The average CPU utilization was measured on the servers as the metric to be evaluated. Clients were allowed to move between zones and thereby generate higher load on some of the servers.

In the experiments with adaptation by zoning, each zone was assigned to a different server. Figure 5 shows the measured number of players that were able to participate fluently in the game for one, two and four zones, respectively. We observe that the zoning adaptation scales almost linearly.

Our second set of experiments aims at the replication adaptation strategy: we replicate the computation of a single zone on up to four servers. Figure 6 shows the measured results for the CPU load. One server is able

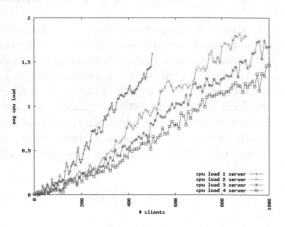

Fig. 6. CPU load for replication adaptation

to serve up to 450 clients at a CPU load of 120% (each core has a load below 100%), which is similar to the results of zoning. But if more servers are added to the processing of a large zone, the client numbers can be increased from the previous limit of 450 clients to up to 1000 clients in a four-server setup. This shows that the replication adaptation strategy allows games to provide a higher level of interactivity.

6 Related Work

Initial SOSE methodologies directly derived from traditional software engineering (TSE) methodologies, but over time, the need for dealing with new challenges led to the development of specific approaches (e.g., [5],[14],[15]).

Several approaches (e.g., [4],[6]) deal with the design and realization of service-based applications. Most of them are not flexible since they base the execution of service-based applications on static rules that trigger the execution of a pre-defined adaptation action only when some specific and known events happen. In fact, applications could address adaptation issues by using built-in adaptation or dynamic adaptation, but it is suitable when all the adaptation configurations are known at priori. In such kind of applications, specification is performed by extending standard notations or using ECA-like rules [7] or aspect-oriented approaches [12]. The main disadvantage of such adaptation approach is the impossibility to react to unforeseen events. This paper studies challenging cases in which the adaptation needs are dynamic and not all the system characteristics are known a priori, i.e. the adaptation actions cannot be completely defined at design time. Some approaches address this issue by proposing an abstraction-based adaptation through which at design time, the adaptation strategies are defined while the concrete mechanism is defined only at run-time. For example, in [17] the design of the application is based on the abstract definition of service. Only at run-time the services are effectively selected on the basis of the situation and context in which the execution is required. The S-cube lifecycle enables both the built-in and the abstraction adaptation, but it also addresses the dynamic adaptation, for which it is possible to provide mechanisms that select and instantiate adaptation strategies depending on a specific trigger and situation [5].

7 Conclusions and Future Work

The main contribution of this paper is the industrial-strength case study in which we applied the generic Lifecycle Model for developing adaptive service-based applications to the novel, emerging class of ROIA (Real-Time Interactive Applications). We demonstrated how the specific, challenging features of ROIA can be met during the evolution and the adaptation cycles of the application development. In particular, we identified the adaptation triggers and adaptation strategies that help to develop high-quality, scalable ROIA applications. We show the effetiveness of the proposed lifecycle for ROIA applications in which proactive adaptation is mandatory.

Our experimental results confirm the feasibility of applying the S-Cube Lifecycle Model and identified adaptation mechanisms to developing demanding applications. In addition to the RTFDemo game described in the paper, we have implemented several industrial applications using RTF: a multi-server port of the commercial action game Quake 3 [16], the 3D game *Hunter* developed by the game company *Darkworks,* and the remote e-learning framework *edutain@grid Virtual Classroom* [11] developed by the environmental consulting company *BMT Cordah Ltd.*

Our future work will include implementing the adaptation triggers identified in Section 4, developing design patterns for the described adaptation scenarios, as well as further joint experiments with industrial partners. The adaptation capabilities of our system can be naturally complemented by the advantages of Cloud Computing offering virtually instantly available, pay-per-use compute resources. We plan to further enhance our system in order to provide ROIA on Clouds.

References

[1] The S-Cube project (2010), http://www.s-cube-network.eu/
[2] The edutain@grid project (2009), http://www.edutaingrid.eu
[3] The Real-Time Framework, RTF (2010), http://pvs.uni-muenster.de
[4] Baresi, L., Guinea, S., Pasquale, L.: Self-healing BPEL processes with Dynamo and the JBoss rule engine. In: ESSPE 2007: International Workshop on Engineering of Software Services for Pervasive Environments (2007)

[5] Bucchiarone, A., Cappiello, C., Di Nitto, E., Kazhamiakin, R., Mazza, V., Pistore, M.: Design for Adaptation of Service-Based Applications: Main Issues and Requirements. In: Proc. of the Fifth International Workshop on Engineering Service-Oriented Applications: Supporting Software Service Development Lifecycles, WESOA (2009)

[6] Canfora, G., Di Penta, M., Esposito, R., Villani, M.L.: An approach for QoS-aware service composition based on genetic algorithms. In: GECCO 2005: Proc. of the 2005 Conference on Genetic and Evolutionary Computation (2005)

[7] Colombo, M., Di Nitto, E., Mauri, M.: Scene: A service composition execution environment supporting dynamic changes disciplined through rules. In: Dan, A., Lamersdorf, W. (eds.) ICSOC 2006. LNCS, vol. 4294, pp. 191–202. Springer, Heidelberg (2006)

[8] Cai, W., Xavier, P., Turner, S.J., Lee, B.-S.: A scalable architecture for supporting interactive games on the internet. In: 16th Workshop on Parallel and Distributed Simulation, Washington, DC, USA, pp. 60–67. IEEE Computer Society, Los Alamitos (2002)

[9] Feng, W.-C., Brandt, D., Saha, D.: A long-term study of a popular MMORPG. In: NetGames 2007. ACM Press, New York (2007)

[10] Gorlatch, S., Glinka, F., Ploss, A., Müller-Iden, J., Prodan, R., Nae, V., Fahringer, T.: Enhancing Grids for Massively Multiplayer Online Computer Games. In: Luque, E., Margalef, T., Benítez, D. (eds.) Euro-Par 2008. LNCS, vol. 5168, pp. 466–477. Springer, Heidelberg (2008)

[11] Gorlatch, S., Glinka, F., Roreger, H., Rawlings, C.: Distributed e-Learning using the RTF middleware. In: Proc. of the 2nd Annual Forum on e-Learning Excellence (2009)

[12] Kongdenfha, W., Saint-Paul, R., Benatallah, B., Casati, F.: An aspect-oriented framework for service adaptation. In: Dan, A., Lamersdorf, W. (eds.) ICSOC 2006. LNCS, vol. 4294, pp. 15–26. Springer, Heidelberg (2006)

[13] Müller-Iden, J., Gorlatch, S.: Rokkatan: Scaling an RTS game design to the massively multiplayer realm. Computers in Entertainment 4(3), 11 (2006)

[14] Papazoglou, M.P., Van Den Heuvel, W.J.: Service-oriented design and development methodology. International Journal of Web Engineering and Technology 2(4), 412–442 (2006)

[15] Pernici, B.: Methodologies for Design of Service-Based Systems. In: Nurcan, S., Senesi, C., Souveyet, C., Ralyté, J. (eds.) International Perspective of information Systems Engineering. Springer, Heidelberg (2010)

[16] Ploss, A., Wichmann, S., Glinka, F., Gorlatch, S.: From a Single- to Multi-Server Online Game: A Quake 3 Case Study Using RTF. In: ACE 2008: Proccedings of the 2008 Int. Conference on Advances in Computer Entertainment Technology (2008)

[17] Verma, K., Gomadam, K., Sheth, A.P., Miller, J.A., Wu, Z.: The METEOR-S Approach for Configuring and Executing Dynamic Web Processes. Technical report (2005)

[18] Glinka, F., Ploss, A., Gorlatch, S., Müller-Iden, J.: High-Level Development of Multiserver Online Games. Int. Journal of Computer Games Technology 2008(5), 1–16 (2008)

[19] Scharf, O., Gorlatch, S., Blanke, F., Hemker, C., Westerheide, S., Priebs, T., Bartenhagen, C., Ploss, A., Glinka, F., Meiländer, D.: Scalable Distributed Simulation of Large Dense Crowds Using the Real-Time Framework (RTF). In: D'Ambra, P., Guarracino, M., Talia, D. (eds.) Euro-Par 2010. LNCS, vol. 6271, pp. 572–583. Springer, Heidelberg (2010)

Immersive Collaboration Environment

Maarten Dumont, Steven Maesen, Karel Frederix,
Chris Raymaekers, Philippe Bekaert, and Frank Van Reeth

Hasselt University — tUL — IBBT,
Expertise Centre for Digital Media
Wetenschapspark 2, 3590 Diepenbeek, Belgium
`firstname.lastname@uhasselt.be`

Abstract. We integrate multitouch interaction, free-viewpoint video and a multiprojector system to develop a more natural and immersive collaboration environment.

1 Introduction

People use many forms of communication to collaborate in meetings. Voice communication is very important, but also pieces of paper are used to sketch ideas. Furthermore, non-verbal communication such as facial expressions contribute to the meeting, as it shows how people feel about the various points that are presented. However, when collaborating over a distance, much of this information is lost. Current Computer-Supported Collaborative Work (CSCW) applications and video conferencing solutions only provide limited human interaction possibilities.

2 Demo Description

Our demo shows how to create an immersive virtual office, where people that are not co-located can meet. Users can collaborate by using a multitouch interface to exchange ideas. Moreover, free-viewpoint video allows users to have eye-gaze corrected face-to-face communication. Finally, a multiprojector system is used to realize an immersive feeling of working together. We show how the integration of these technologies results in an office-of-the-future setup [1]. The accompanying video can be found at `http://research.edm.uhasselt.be/~mdumont/ServiceWave2010`

2.1 Collaborative Multitouch

We provide users with a multitouch table for collaboration. Such a table supports a natural way of interacting, since users can manipulate information (e.g. pictures, documents, schematics, . . .) using their hands. As we have developed a framework for collaborative multitouch applications, it is possible for users to collaboratively manipulate information, each using their own separate multitouch table as if it were one virtual table. Actions on objects are distributed over the network, while users still have their own view of the information [2].

E. Di Nitto and R. Yahyapour (Eds.): ServiceWave 2010, LNCS 6481, pp. 187–188, 2010.

2.2   Free-Viewpoint Video

One major drawback of current video-conferencing systems is the fact that the user is not able to simultaneously look at the screen and into the camera. This leads to a loss of eye contact, which is an important factor in non-verbal communication.

We utilise free-viewpoint video, where the user is filmed by multiple cameras. By interpolating between the images of the cameras, every viewpoint in range of these cameras can be shown. This range also includes an eye-gaze corrected viewpoint that enables remote users to directly look into each other's eyes [3].

2.3   Multiprojector

A true immersive feeling can only be achieved by providing a sufficiently large projection of the remote environment. Our system uses several projectors to compose this large picture and to show a surround image of the remote site.

Manually aligning several projectors is a tedious job. We have therefore automated the projector calibration by using structured light. Our calibration process compensates for misalignment of the projectors, color difference in the images and the geometric structure of the projection surface. This allows us to project on arbitrary surfaces, including corners of a room.

3   Integration

These different technologies, which are on itself novel, are integrated in order to form an office-of-the-future setup. Users in this virtual office can collaborate using multitouch interaction. Meanwhile, free-viewpoint video offers natural eye-gaze corrected face-to-face communication. Finally, the multiprojector system completes the illusion of full immersion into the virtual office.

Acknowledgments

This work was funded by IBBT through the Hi-Masquerade, QoE and SEGA projects and by the EU FP7 IP "2020 3D Media" project.

References

[1] Raskar, R., Welch, G., Cutts, M., Lake, A., Stesin, L., Fuchs, H.: The Office of the Future: A Unified Approach to Image-Based Modeling and Spatially Immersive Displays. ACM SIGGRAPH (1998)
[2] Cuypers, T., Frederix, K., Raymaekers, C., Bekaert, P.: A Framework for Networked Interactive Surfaces. In: 2nd Workshop on Software Engineering and Architecture for Realtime Interactive Systems, SEARIS@VR 2009 (2009)
[3] Dumont, M., Rogmans, S., Maesen, S., Bekaert, P.: Optimized two-party video chat with restored eye contact using graphics hardware. Springer Communications in Computer and Information Science 48(11), 358–372 (2009)

ecoBus – Mobile Environment Monitoring

Srdjan Krco, Jelena Vuckovic, and Stevan Jokic

Ericsson Serbia
srdjan.krco@ericsson.com

Abstract. In this paper, the ecoBus system, a smart city service built according to the FP7 SENSEI architecture design is described.

Keywords: M2M, Internet of Things, smart city.

1 Introduction

The ecoBus system is a FP7 SENSEI project field trial designed to enable evaluation of the main technical features of the SENSEI architecture [1] as well as to showcase the potentials of such systems and explore the exploitation opportunities in a real environment.

The system utilizes public transportation vehicles (buses and trolleybuses) to carry a set of sensors across the city of Belgrade to observe a number of environmental parameters as well as events and activities in the physical world (average speed, number of stops along a route, duration of each stop, etc.). Each device is equipped with gas sensors (CO, CO_2, NO_2), weather sensors (temperature, air pressure, humidity), location (GPS) and a mobile network interface (GPRS).

The main users of the demo system are the citizens and the city government agencies responsible for environment protection and traffic management. They can interact with physical resources in real time via a web or a mobile application. The system is open and other users can easily access the same physical resources and integrate available sensor information in their services. The following services are included in the trial:

- Continuous monitoring of environmental parameters across the city
- Management of public transportation system
- Provision of services to the citizens (bus arrival time to a bus stop).

2 System Overview and Implementation

The main system components (Figure 1) are the following: Resource Directory (RD), resources (sensors), end user applications, a database and the SMS module. The resources use Resource Publication Interface (RPI) to publish their descriptions in the RD. The resource descriptions describe the sensor, measurements and the context as well as the URL where the so called Resource End Point (REP) is located. The REPs are access points to the resources and they

E. Di Nitto and R. Yahyapour (Eds.): ServiceWave 2010, LNCS 6481, pp. 189–190, 2010.
© Springer-Verlag Berlin Heidelberg 2010

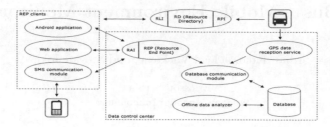

Fig. 1. System overview

provide the Resource Access Interface (RAI) for querying the sensors. The applications first use the Resource Lookup Interface (RLI) to query the RD and discover resources available at a given time and with the required characteristics. Then, the resources are queried using the RAI. All interactions between the components are REST based. The web and mobile applications are used by the end users to interact with the resources and to visualize the obtained measurements. The SMS module interacts with the mobile operators to enable efficient SMS processing for a SMS based bus arrival time service. In the demo, all data will come from live sensors deployed on 20 buses. One additional device will be deployed in the demo booth. Both web and mobile ecoBus applications will be available on site. A video outlining the main functions is available at the following address: http://195.178.44.184/demo/.

3   Summary of Novel Characteristics

Instead of building closed vertical systems, the demo utilizes the SENSEI framework as a horizontal layer allowing multiple user applications to interact with the heterogeneous physical resources via a set of standardized interfaces. The resources are discoverable dynamically, are accessible by any user with appropriate access rights and can be used in various services and applications.

Acknowledgment

This paper describes work undertaken in the context of the SENSEI project (www.ict-sensei.eu), supported by the European 7th Framework Programme, contract number: 215923.

Reference

[1] Tsiatsis, V., Gluhak, A., Bauge, T., Montagut, F., Bernat, J., Bauer, M., Villalonga, C., Barnaghi, P., Krco, S.: Real World Internet Architecture. In: Towards the Future Internet - Emerging Trends from European Research. IOS Press, Amsterdam (April 2010)

Demonstration of the SmartLM License Management Technology for Distributed Computing Infrastructures

Hassan Rasheed[1], Angela Rumpl[1], Wolfgang Ziegler[1], and Miriam Gozalo[2]

[1] Fraunhofer Institute SCAI, Department of Bioinformatics,
53754 Sankt Augustin, Germany
{Hassan.rasheed,angela.rumpl,wolfgang.ziegler}@scai.fraunhofer.de
[2] Gridcore AB, Göteborg, 411 33, Sweden
miriam.gozalo@gridcore.se

Abstract. Current praxis of software licensing has been identified as major obstacle for Grid computing a couple of years ago already. Recent surveys of Clouds indicate that the same holds true for Cloud computing. As a consequence, using commercial applications that require access to a license server for authorisation at run-time has been quite limited until recently in distributed computing environments. Due to the mandatory centralised control of license usage at application run-time, e.g. heartbeat control by the license server, traditional software licensing practices are not suitable especially when the environment stretches across administrative domains. In this demonstration we present a novel approach for managing software licenses as web service resources in distributed service oriented environments. Licenses become mobile objects, which may move to the environment where required to authorise the execution of a license protected application. The SmartLM solution decouples authorisation for license usage from authorisation for application execution. All authorisations are expressed and guaranteed by Service Level Agreements.

1 Introduction

So far, commercial software is rarely used in Grids and Clouds due to the limitations both with respect to the license management technology and the missing business models of the independent software vendors (ISV) for using their software in the Grid.

The license management technology for software licenses is still based on the model of local computing centres providing both resources for computation and the software used for simulations together with the required licenses locally. Thus, these licenses are provided on the basis of named users, hostnames (IP-addresses), or sometimes as a site license for the administrative domain of an organisation. Using this software in a distributed service oriented infrastructure is impossible using resources that are spread across different administrative domains, that do not host the application's license server. The licenses usually are

E. Di Nitto and R. Yahyapour (Eds.): ServiceWave 2010, LNCS 6481, pp. 191–192, 2010.

bound to hardware within the domain of the user and do not allow access from outside, e.g. due to firewalls, thus, enforcing local use of the protected applications only.

The European project SmartLM has developed a new technology to protect applications from unauthorised use without the restrictions that existing license technologies impose on the end-user and its home organisation. Moreover, thanks to the ISVs participating in the project SmartLM developed new business models, which can easily be realised with new technology achieving a win-win situation between software vendors and software users.

2   SmartLM Innovations

The SmartLM solution realises software licenses as mobile objects in Distributed Computing Infrastructures (DCI). Detaching the license from the license server allows to move the license in form of a token to the Grid or Cloud resource used for the execution of the application. Along with this basic mechanism SmartLM provides sophisticated security mechanisms to protect the token from being misused. Besides the basic technology SmartLM provides a number of innovations that will be demonstrated:

- Licenses can be used on the fly as with existing license management technologies but also reserved in advance to have a guarantee for license availability at a certain time.
- Security mechanisms establishing a chain of trust from the ISV to the application to be executed.
- Both the ISV and the local administrator can define policies governing license usage, e.g. to control the number of licenses used by a certain department.
- The user is informed about the cost of using a specific license prior to license usage.
- License usage is subject to a Service Level Agreement between the user and the license service transparently managed in the background.
- The site administrator can define budget limits for users or user groups thus ensuring that licenses are available to all users or groups according to e.g. the business value of their work.
- Using SmartLM in Grids or Clouds is supported by an orchestrating service that organises co-allocation of computing resources and licenses.
- An optional accounting and billing service for license usage

3   Demonstration

The demonstration will show

- The SmartLM basic mechanisms when used locally
- Using the orchestrator for job submission in a Grid
- Accounting and billing
- Security mechanisms

A high-level video can be found here: www.smartlm.eu

Experimenting with Multipath TCP

Sébastien Barré[1], Olivier Bonaventure[1], Costin Raiciu[2], and Mark Handley[2]

[1] Université catholique de Louvain
B-1348 Louvain-la-Neuve
firstname.lastname@uclouvain.be
[2] University College of London
{c.raiciu,m.handley}@cs.ucl.ac.uk

1 Introduction

Today, most smartphones support at least 3G and 802.11, and so do tablet PCs like Apple's iPad. This has increased interest in using several access mediums in the same connection, so that it becomes possible to transparently change from one medium to another in case of failure. Further, using several paths *simultaneously* can improve end-to-end throughput.

The transport layer is the best place to implement multipath functionality because of the high amount of information it collects about each of the paths (delay/bandwidth estimation), and its knowledge of the application byte stream. The network may know path properties, but simply scattering packets of a single transport connection over multiple physical paths will typically reorder many packets, confusing the transport protocol and leading to very poor throughput. The apps could implement multipath, but such changes are not easy to get right. If we simply switched from TCP to multipath TCP while maintaing the reliable byte stream semantics, unmodified apps could benefit immediately.

The desire to use multiple paths at the transport layer is not new, and has been already the subject of several research papers, some based on TCP [4,2,5], others based on modifications to the SCTP protocol [3]. However, to the best of our knowledge, none of these research efforts have produced a real-world implementation despite the importance of such an implementation for verifying how a multipath transport solution behaves in real usage scenarios (except a recent implementation of [3] for FreeBSD).

There is currently fresh interest in making multipath TCP real, as the IETF has created a multipath working group. We believe an in-kernel implementation of multipath can serve many purposes, chief among which is experimentation in the Internet. It helps show the benefits and drawbacks of using multipath TCP for real applications; it offers a better understanding of how multipath TCP competes with TCP in the Internet; it can highlight errors and gaps in protocol design; it helps test deployability and find unexpected middlebox behaviour. Finally it allows running realistic experiments (e.g. with link speeds of 1 Gbps and up). Our contribution is to fill this gap by providing a functional implementation of MPTCP, the IETF multipath solution [1][1]. We propose to concretely demonstrate the potential of that solution by showing a media transfer (e.g. video streaming) over multipath TCP between a remote server (http://mptcp.info.ucl.ac.be) and a Nokia N900 device.

---

[1] http://inl.info.ucl.ac.be/mptcp

E. Di Nitto and R. Yahyapour (Eds.): ServiceWave 2010, LNCS 6481, pp. 193–194, 2010.

2   MPTCP Implementation

All legacy TCP applications directly benefit from the added multipath capability. When a new TCP flow is started multipath TCP adds a new option to the SYN packet to announce it multipath capability. If the endpoint replies with a SYN/ACK containing the multipath capable option, this connection is multipath from now on. Initially there is a single TCP socket opened (the master socket), corresponding to the first subflow in the connection. When additional subflows are opened, new socket structures are created and associated to the meta-socket. The master socket is a special socket as it is the only connection to the application. Application writes to this socket are redirected to the meta-socket which segments the bytestream and decides which subflow should send each segment. Application reads from this socket are serviced from the meta-socket's receive buffer. Data arriving on the subflows is serviced by the master and slave sockets (checking for in-order, in window sequence numbers, etc.), and passed to the meta-socket once it is in order at subflow level. Here the data is reordered according to the connection sequence number, which is carried in each TCP segment as an option. Retransmissions are driven only by the subflow sequence number; hence MPTCP avoids problems due to connection level reordering of packets. Additional subflows are only opened after the initial handshake succeeds. The stack checks to see if it has multiple addresses that have routes to the destination; if so it will try to open subflows using currently unused addresses.

Conclusion. While simulations are useful to evaluate large scale behaviours of a protocol, a fundamental change like MPTCP requires careful evaluations of its behaviour in real world situations. An implementation can shed light on protocol behaviours and corner cases that cannot be observed with simulators. While several previous works have produced code that take benefit of multiple paths, this implementation is, to the best of our knowledge, the first one that works across the Internet (as opposed to local networks), and that allows unmodified applications to benefit. Our current work uses this implementation to analyse the behaviour of MPTCP in a number of real-life scenarios, including datacenters, mobile communications and multi-homed networks.

Acknowledgements. The research results presented herein have received support from the Trilogy (http://www.trilogy-project.eu) research project (ICT-216372), partially funded by the European Community under its Seventh Framework Programme. The views expressed here are those of the author(s) only. The European Commission is not liable for any use that may be made of the information in this document.

References

1. Ford, A., Raiciu, C., Handley, M.: TCP Extensions for Multipath Operation with Multiple Addresses. Internet draft, draft-ietf-mptcp-multiaddressed-01.txt, Work in progress (July 2010)
2. Hsieh, H.-Y., Sivakumar, R.: pTCP: An End-to-End Transport Layer Protocol for Striped Connections. In: ICNP, pp. 24–33. IEEE Computer Society, Los Alamitos (2002)
3. Iyengar, J., Amer, P.D., Stewart, R.R.: Concurrent multipath transfer using SCTP multihoming over independent end-to-end paths. IEEE/ACM Trans. Netw. 14(5), 951–964 (2006)
4. Magalhaes, L., Kravets, R.: Transport Level Mechanisms for Bandwidth Aggregation on Mobile Hosts. In: ICNP, pp. 165–171. IEEE Computer Society, Los Alamitos (2001)
5. Rojviboonchai, K., Osuga, T., Aida, H.: R-M/TCP: Protocol for Reliable Multi-Path Transport over the Internet. In: AINA, pp. 801–806. IEEE Computer Society Press, Los Alamitos (2005)

REMICS- REuse and Migration of Legacy Applications to Interoperable Cloud Services

REMICS Consortium

Parastoo Mohagheghi[1], Arne J. Berre[1], Alexis Henry[2],
Franck Barbier[3], and Andrey Sadovykh[4]

[1] SINTEF, Norway
[2] BLU AGE Software - Netfective Technology, France
[3] Univ. of Pau - Netfective Technology, France
[4] SOFTEAM, France
{Parastoo.Mohagheghi,Arne.J.Berre}@sintef.no

Abstract. The main objective of the REMICS project is to specify, develop and evaluate a tool-supported model-driven methodology for migrating legacy applications to interoperable service cloud platforms. The migration process consists of understanding the legacy system in terms of its architecture and functions, designing a new SOA application that provides the same or better functionality, and verifying and implementing the new application in the cloud. The demonstrations will show the support for two tasks in this migration: recovery process with the BLU AGE tool and the use of SoaML and forward engineering with Modelio tool.

Keywords: Cloud computing, service-oriented architecture, legacy systems, ADM, SoaML.

1 REMICS Approach and Demonstrations

The REMICS[1] project will provide tools for model-driven migration of legacy systems to loosely coupled systems following a bottom up approach; from recovery of legacy system architecture (using OMG's ADM-Architecture Driven Modernization) to deployment in a cloud infrastructure which allows further evolution of the system in a forward engineering process. The migration process consists of understanding the legacy system in terms of its architecture, business processes and functions, designing a new Service-Oriented Architecture (SOA) application, and verifying and implementing the new application in the cloud. These methods will be complimented with generic "Design by Service Composition" methods providing developers with tools simplifying development by reusing the services and components available in the cloud.

In order to instrument the migration process, the REMICS project will integrate a large set of metamodels and will propose several dedicated extensions. For the

---

[1] http://remics.eu/; funded by the European Commission (contract number 257793) within the 7th Framework Program.

E. Di Nitto and R. Yahyapour (Eds.): ServiceWave 2010, LNCS 6481, pp. 195–196, 2010.
© Springer-Verlag Berlin Heidelberg 2010

architecture recovery the REMICS will extend the KDM metamodel. On Platform Independent Model (PIM) level, the components and services are defined using SoaML (SOA Modeling Language[2]) which is developed in the SHAPE project[3]. The REMICS project will extend this language to address the specific architectural patterns and model driven methods for architecture migration, and to cover specificities of service clouds development paradigm. In particular, the PIM4Cloud Computing, model-driven Service Interoperability and Models@Runtime extensions are intended to support the REMICS methodology for service cloud architecture modeling.

Furthermore, REMICS will investigate existing test notations such as the UML2 test profile (UTP) for their application to the SOA and Cloud Computing domain and refine and extend them.

The project will focus on open source metamodels and models with an emphasis on Open Models for standards and will be actively involved in the standardization process of the related standards for cloud computing, business models, SOA, service interoperability, knowledge discovery, validation and managing services.

REMICS targets the following main impact objectives:

- REMICS will preserve and capitalize on the business value engraved in legacy systems to gain flexibility brought by Service Clouds, lower the cost of service provision and shorten the time-to-market.
- REMICS research will provide innovations in advanced model driven methodologies, methods and tools in Software as a Service engineering.
- REMICS will provide standards-based foundation service engineering and will provide a suite of open ready-to-use metamodels that lowers barriers for service providers.

REMICS started in September 2010 and will run for three years while it builds on the results of several on-going or finished EU projects such as SHAPE and MODELPLEX[4] (both finished recently) with focus on model-driven development of applications, MOMOCS with focus on model-driven modernization, and SOA4ALL and RESERVOIR with focus on service-oriented development. The relevant results of previous projects will therefore be discussed and extensions planned in REMICS will be presented. The presentation will also discuss collaboration areas which should be of interest to other projects and conference participants.

The demonstrations will show the support for two tasks in this migration: recovery process using BLU AGE[5] tool and the use of SoaML and forward engineering with Modelio[6] tool. Both tool providers are participating in the REMICS project.

---

[2] http://www.omg.org/spec/SoaML/
[3] http://www.shape-project.eu/
[4] https://www.modelplex-ist.org/
[5] http://www.bluage.com/; a solution for both reverse and forward engineering fully based on MDA and ADM principles.
[6] http://www.modeliosoft.com/

Service Compositions for All*

Nikolay Mehandjiev, Freddy Lécué, Usman Wajid,
Georgia Kleanthous, and Abdallah Namoun

Centre for Service Research, University of Manchester,
Manchester, UK
`firstname.lastname@manchester.ac.uk`

Abstract. We have developed a tool to allow users who are not programmers to assemble non-trivial service compositions. The tool uses templates and background reasoning to reduce the mental effort needed by users when they compose services, and provides immediate feedback about the consequences of any decisions made by its users. We will demonstrate the tool on a number of scenarios aiming to illustrate these novel characteristics.

Keywords: service composition, semantic services, end user development.

1 Introduction

Empowering users who are not programmers to compose and modify their own service-based applications is a key step to the general uptake of service-oriented computing. Many composition environments, some also known as "mashup tools", have appeared aiming to facilitate the consumption and assembly of software services. They often use diagrammatic languages designed to represent technical dependency details.

In contrast to these, we started with our target service producers and consumers. We studied the core requirements and problems standing in the way of people without programming background when they attempt to assemble services into meaningful applications. Our results suggest we need to make the composition as transparent as possible, hide any technical details which are not relevant to the task of the user, and provide immediate feedback in respect to any design decisions by end users.

2 Our Approach

The findings from our user-centric studies motivate our transparent, task-oriented approach to service composition, where software takes over technical details of no interest to the end user such as aligning service inputs and outputs. We use "best-practice" templates of successful service compositions, and make different degrees of customisation available for users with different skills and technology aptitudes. Given an abstract description of any service composition in a template, the "assisted composition" approach, shown in Fig. 1 supports all end users in creating actual service compositions. Non-technical users should be shielded from the details of such service assembly, so we hide dependencies (control and data) between tasks within the template processes. These aspects are instead considered behind the scene using semantic reasoning.

---

* Supported by the European Commission Framework VII Project SOA4All.

E. Di Nitto and R. Yahyapour (Eds.): ServiceWave 2010, LNCS 6481, pp. 197–198, 2010.

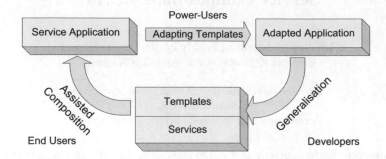

Fig. 1. Lifecycle of user-developed service applications

Our approach also includes stages of customisation and generalisation. In the former, "Power users" will be able to change service compositions thus creating innovative variations of standard service composition tasks. These innovations would then be generalised into reusable templates by software developers, ensuring the growth of the overall system, learning from innovative compositions and offering them for reuse by non-technical users. In our demonstration we will focus on users binding concrete services to reusable templates, but we will also be able to demonstrate the link to the execution environment, and the composition customisation activity.

3   Key Innovations and Features of the Tool

The demonstration will illustrate the following innovative features of the approach:

1. The overall template-based process for user composed services, which involves three stages: assisted composition, template adaptation and learning (generalising user-adapted innovative applications into templates).
2. A semantic technique of service alignment, alleviating the need for data integration between constituent services, and shielding users from inter-service dependencies and the technical complexity of service technology.

Demonstration of the tool can be seen on the following link:

`http://www.servicedesign.org.uk/assistedComposition`

The tool has been evaluated by a focus group with 13 non-technical users and compared to Yahoo!Pipes within a set of six observation experiments. These demonstrate that our non-technical end users understood the principles of the assisted composition approach, and were enthused about it. We believe that this motivation is partially due to the benefits expected from service composition in terms of obtaining applications fine-tuned to the user needs, and partially due to the reduction of the perceived learning costs. The reduction in learning costs is attributed to our approach of hiding technical complexity using semantic reasoning, and the reuse possible by the template-based development process.

OneLab: Developing Future Internet Testbeds

Serge Fdida, Timur Friedman, and Sophia MacKeith

Laboratoire d'Informatique Paris 6, Université Pierre et Marie Curie (UPMC),
4 Place Jussieu, 75005 Paris, France
{Serg.Fdida,Timur.Friedman}@upmc.fr, Sophia.Mackeith@lip6.fr

Abstract. OneLab is an experimental facility developed by two European Commission research projects, OneLab (FP6, ran for 24 months) and OneLab2 (FP7, ran for 27 months). As the OneLab2 project will be coming to an end at the time of Ghent FIA, this would be a unique opportunity to present OneLab's key results to an interested audience. What is more, although OneLab as a European research project will have ceased to exist, the OneLab initiative will continue in its aim of developing Future Internet testbeds.

Keywords: Future Internet, testbed, wireless, measurement, network.

1 Introduction

OneLab's results offer a range of services to testbed users and owners, including an open federation of testbeds which supports network research for the Future Internet. Experimentally-driven research is key to success in exploring the possible futures of the Internet, and in this demonstration, we would like to present three of OneLab's testbeds.

In PlanetLab Europe, the NITOS wireless testbed, ETOMIC, and its other federated testbeds, OneLab provides an open, general-purpose, shared experimental facility, both large-scale and sustainable, which allows European industry and academia to innovate today and assess the performance of their solutions.

1.1 PlanetLab Europe: Gain Access to Over 1,000 Nodes Worldwide

PlanetLab Europe is OneLab's core testbed and is the European arm of PlanetLab, the world's most widely used research networking testbed. It gives European Internet stakeholders a means to experiment at the network and application layers and accelerate the design of advanced networking technologies for the Future Internet.

Based on the PlanetLab model, PlanetLab Europe has over 150 Europe-based member sites, currently hosting a total of over 200 nodes. Members have access not just to PLE nodes, but also many hundreds more on the wider PlanetLab system.

1.2 NITOS Wireless Testbed: Gain Access to Wireless Nodes in a Real-Life Environment

NITOS (Network Implementation Testbed using Open Source code) is a wireless experimental testbed that is designed to achieve reproducibility of experimentation,

E. Di Nitto and R. Yahyapour (Eds.): ServiceWave 2010, LNCS 6481, pp. 199–200, 2010.
© Springer-Verlag Berlin Heidelberg 2010

while also supporting evaluation of protocols and applications in real-world settings. It has been developed in the city of Volos, Greece by OneLab partner CERTH, in association with NITLab, the Network Implementation Testbed Laboratory of the Computer and Communication Engineering Department at the University of Thessaly. NITOS consists of nodes based on commercial Wi-Fi cards and Linux-based open-source platforms, which are deployed both inside and outside of the University of Thessaly's campus building. Currently, two kinds of nodes are supported: ORBIT-like nodes and diskless Alix2c2 PCEngines nodes.

NITOS is remotely accessible and gives users the opportunity to implement their protocols and study their behaviour in a real-case environment. Users can perform their experiments by reserving slices of the testbed though the NITOS scheduler. The control and management of the testbed is achieved by using cOntrol Management Framework (OMF) open-source software. OMF simplifies the procedure of experiment defining and offers a more centralized way of deploying experiments and retrieving measurements.

1.3   ETOMIC: A High-Precision Measurement Infrastructure

The European Traffic Observatory Measurement Infrastructure (ETOMIC) is a high-precision measurement infrastructure that is able to carry out analysis between specially-designed measurement boxes that are globally synchronized to a high temporal resolution (~10 nanoseconds).

It provides users with a dynamic, high-resolution, and spatially-extended picture of fast changes in network traffic. This opens up the possibility for a new kind of network tomography, where cross correlation between measurement flows can be measured on a precise timescale and the internal state of the network can be reconstructed and its time behaviour studied. This data can then be analyzed with methods developed in scientific publications produced by researchers working on ETOMIC.

The ETOMIC measurement infrastructure has been developed principally by OneLab lead partners ELTE, with UAM providing the expertise for additional advanced monitoring equipment, and is now hosted at over 20 different sites across Europe. ETOMIC hosts 18 first-generation nodes (based on DAG technology) and 20 second-generation nodes (consisting in the ARGOS measurement card, and APE and CoMo measurement boxes).

2   OneLab Video

A short introductory video about OneLab is available here: http:// www. dailymotion.com/video/x9s9j2_onelab-projcct-promo_tech?start=1#from=embed

Please note that this video is an introduction to OneLab, and not a representation of our planned FIA Ghent demonstration.

Coverage and Capacity Optimization of Self-Managed Future Internet Wireless Networks

Panagis Magdalinos, Dimitris Makris, Panagiotis Spapis, Christos Papazafeiropoulos,
Apostolos Kousaridas, Makis Stamatelatos, and Nancy Alonistioti

National & Kapodistrian University of Athens, Athens, Greece
{panagis,dmakris,pspapis,chrpap,akousar,makiss,nancy}@di.uoa.gr

Abstract. Future Internet network management systems are expected to incorporate self-x capabilities in order to tackle the increased management needs that cannot be addressed through human intervention. Towards this end, Self-NET developed a self-management framework based on the introduction of cognitive capabilities in network elements. In this paper, the experimentation platform for "Coverage and Capacity Optimization of Self-managed Future Internet Wireless Network", incorporating the self-management framework of Self-NET, is presented.

Keywords: Self-Management, Self-Organization, Coverage and Capacity Optimization, Future Internet, Wireless Networks, Cognitive Cycle.

1 Introduction

The management systems of Future Internet (FI) networks are expected to embed autonomic capabilities in order to face the increasing complexity of communication networks, reduce human intervention, and promote localized resource management. The Self-NET self-management framework is based on the Generic Cognitive Cycle, which consists of the Monitoring, Decision Making and Execution phases. The Network Element Cognitive Manager (NECM) implements the M-D-E cycle at the network element level, whilst the Network Domain Cognitive Manager (NDCM) manages a set of NECMs, implementing sophisticated M-D-E cycle features. In order to present and test the key functionalities of the proposed solution, we have addressed specific network management problems that lay under the umbrella of wireless networks coverage and capacity optimization family [1], [2].

2 Demonstration

In our testbed we have deployed a heterogeneous wireless network environment consisting of several IEEE 802.11 Soekris access points (AP, [4]) and an IEEE 802.16 base station (BS) [3], each embedding an NECM. Moreover, several single-RAT (i.e. WiFi) and multi-RAT (i.e. WiFi, WiMAX) terminals are located in the corresponding area, consuming a video service delivered by VLC-based service provider [5]. For the management of the underlying NECMs, an NDCMs is deployed. The cognitive network manager installed per network element undertakes a) the deductions about its

E. Di Nitto and R. Yahyapour (Eds.): ServiceWave 2010, LNCS 6481, pp. 201–202, 2010.
© Springer-Verlag Berlin Heidelberg 2010

operational status, b) the proactive preparation of solutions to face possible problems, and c) the fast reaction to any problem by enforcing the anticipated reconfiguration actions. The interaction of NECMs and NDCM enables the localized and distributed orchestration of the various network elements.

In this demonstration[1] we present the (re-)assignment of operating frequencies to wireless network elements and the vertical assisted handover of multi-RAT terminals. The demonstration scenario is divided into a) the optimal deployment of a new WiFi AP b) the Self-Optimization of the network topology through the assisted vertical handover of terminals from loaded to neighboring less loaded APs or BSs c) and the Self-Optimization of the network topology due to high interference situation. The M-D-E cycle is instantiated in both the NECM and the NDCM. The NECM periodically monitors its internal state and local environment by measuring specific parameters thus building its local view. All NECMs periodically transmit to the NDCM the collected information, which enables the latter to build the second level of situation awareness and have the domain level view.

The situation awareness inference engine is based on Fuzzy Logic Inference Systems (FIS). The latter consists of two parts: the "Fault and Optimization Opportunity Identification" and the "Configuration Action Selection". The first enables the identification of a symptom or an optimization opportunity by taking into account the monitored parameters, while the second uses the output of the first inference phase and deduces the most appropriate configuration action. When such a situation occurs the responsible cognitive manager proceeds to the Execution phase. In the presented scenario we implemented a channel (re-) allocation procedure, which triggered upon the deployment of an AP or in the case of high interference. Finally, the respective NECM undertakes to apply the configuration action.

3   Conclusion

The automation of network management systems and their ability to collectively address complex problems are key requirements for the FI networks. Self-NET proposes the software components (NECM, NDCM) for the engineering of an innovative self-managed FI system. Several benefits arise for both the Network Operator and the end user. This demonstration presented the software architecture for a realistic and implementable self-managed network system.

References

[1] Self-NET, E.U.: Project, http://www.ict-selfnet.eu
[2] Kousaridas, A., Nguengang, G., et al.: An experimental path towards Self-Management for Future Internet Environments (Book Chapter). In: Towards the Future Internet - Emerging Trends from European Research, pp. 95–104 (2010) [ISBN 978-1- 60750-539-6]
[3] AN-100U/UX Single Sector Wireless Access Base Station User Manual, RedMAX, Redline Communications (2008)
[4] Soekris Engineering net5501, http://www.soekris.com/net5501.htm
[5] VLC.: open-source multimedia framework, player and server, http://www.videolan.org/vlc

---

[1] The link for the video is: http://www.youtube.com/watch?v=EG_iSNrhwkE

Spectrum Sharing in Heterogeneous Wireless Networks: An FP7 CREW Use Case

Stefan Bouckaert[1], Lieven Tytgat[1], Sofie Pollin[2], Peter Van Wesemael[2],
Antoine Dejonghe[2], Ingrid Moerman[1], and Piet Demeester[1]

[1] Ghent University - IBBT,
Gaston Crommenlaan 8 bus 201 - 9050 Ghent - Belgium
[2] imec,
Kapeldreef 75 - 3001 Leuven - Belgium
firstname.lastname@intec.ugent.be
firstname.lastname@imec.be

1 Introduction

Cognitive radio (CR) techniques and cognitive networks [1] aim at optimizing the use of the wireless spectrum, by observing the wireless environment and intelligently configuring radio settings and network parameters. The aim of the FP7 CREW project [2] is to establish an open federated test platform in order to facilitate experimental research on advanced spectrum sensing, CR and cognitive networking strategies. The main goal of this demonstration is to showcase the possibilities of the Belgian branch of the CREW federation. A first aspect is the demonstration of the IBBT w-ilab.t testbed [3] which will be incorporated in the CREW federation, through an example CR set-up where Wi-Fi interference is avoided by an IEEE 802.15.4 network using distributed channel selection. Secondly, a high-performance advanced spectrum sensing design [4] by imec, based on reconfigurable analog and digital building blocks is demonstrated, showing the feasibility of spectrum sensing using low-cost low-power handheld devices. Within the CREW project, the integration of the advanced spectrum sensing component and the testbed (i) generates advanced possibilities for executing and monitoring reproducible testbed experiments, and (ii) allows the optimization of horizontal resource sharing between heterogeneous networks.

2 System Description and Novel Characteristics

(i) **Remote systems.** Since the IBBT testbed is deployed in an office building in Ghent, Belgium, it is accessed remotely. At each of the 200 nodes' locations, a Tmote Sky device, a routerboard with two Wi-Fi interfaces and an *environment emulator* (EE) are installed, thus supporting experiments with heterogeneous technologies. The generic integrated analysis and visualization tools ensure fast and accurate data analysis and representation. The custom built EE boards enable advanced logging of test data and physical node characteristics such as power consumption, and allow battery emulation and the manipulation of analog and/or digital input/output pins to emulate events at the sensor nodes. Within the scope of the CREW project, benchmarking strategies are being developed that will allow developers to obtain realistic and reliable performance indicators of CR concepts.

E. Di Nitto and R. Yahyapour (Eds.): ServiceWave 2010, LNCS 6481, pp. 203–204, 2010.
© Springer-Verlag Berlin Heidelberg 2010

(ii) Systems at the demonstration site. An example of the hardware mounted in the testbed will be available during the demonstration. Moreover, the low-power multi-band sensing solution is demonstrated locally. Where most existing platforms target a single technology and are based on laboratory equipment or limited sensitivity off-the-shelf demonstrators, the presented sensing solution is built out of an analog and digital front-end. The analog front-end consists out of the state-of-the-art imec SCALable raDIO (SCALDIO) chip, which is developed in order to support future flexible radios with a tuning range between $100MHz$ and $6GHz$ and supports cellular, WMAN, WLAN, WPAN and digital broadcast standards. During the demo, two antennas will be connected, allowing to scan the bands from $500\,MHz$ to $2.5\,GHz$, thus covering most relevant bands in the TV, cellular and GSM bands. The digital front-end contains an FPGA to buffer the samples, which are then fed to a PC for analysis.

3   Features to Be Demonstrated

Firmware images containing an interference avoidance scheme **are deployed** to sensor nodes in the testbed. Based on a local noise scan, each IEEE 802.15.4 node determines on which channel it wants to receive. This channel configuration is **visualized in real time** using the monitoring functions of the testbed. Next, a Wi-Fi access point is activated in the environment of the sensor nodes. In response, the sensor network reconfigures itself to avoid the generated interference, which is again visualized. Then, as an example, the **EE** is used to **emulate a depleting battery**. Using the **analyzer module**, the power consumption data acquired by the EE during the test is visualized. While the sensor nodes reconfigure themselves, this reconfiguration takes approximately 10 seconds due to delays caused by the scanning procedure at the nodes. This is where the imec **sensing solution** comes into action: assuming 1024 samples are needed at a sampling rate of $40\,Msamples/s$ for a bandwidth of $20\,MHz$, a $2\,GHz$ band can be sensed in $7.6\,ms$. To demonstrate this, the scanning procedure is started, which leads to a **periodogram**, plotting the signal power over time and frequency. For different configuration options, the **power consumption** of the scanning procedure **is estimated**. The influence of an access point on the spectrum is demonstrated, and it is indicated how the integration of such scanning functionality in the testbed within the CREW project will enable the development of advanced networking solutions and will provide invaluable information during testbed experiments.

References

1. Thomas, R.W.: Cognitive networks. PhD thesis, Blacksburg, VA, USA (2007)
2. CREW project. Home page, http://www.crew-project.eu/
3. Bouckaert, S., Vandenberghe, W., Jooris, B., Moerman, I., Demeester, P.: The w-iLab.t testbed. In: Magedanz, T., et al. (eds.) Tridentcom 2010. LNICST, vol. 46, pp. 141–150. Institute for Computer Sciences, Social Informatics and Telecommunications Engineering (2010)
4. Ingels, M.: et al. A 5mm^2 40nm LP CMOS 0.1-to-3ghz multistandard transceiver. Accepted for ISSCC 2010 (2010)

Demonstration for the 3DLife Framework

Qianni Zhang and Ebroul Izquierdo

Multimedia and Vision Research Group,
School of Electronic Engineering and Computer Science, Queen Mary,
University of London, Mile End Road, London E1 4NS, U.K.
{qianni.zhang,ebroul.izquierdo}@elec.qmul.ac.uk

Abstract. This paper describes a demonstration for the 3DLife framework, which embraces technologies developed in EU FP7 NoE project 3DLife - Bringing the Media Internet to Life. One of the key objectives in 3DLife is to build an open and expandable framework for collaborative research on Media interactive communication over the Internet[1]. This framework will be based on a distributed repository of software tools. Currently the 3DLife framework consists of four main modules: simulation of athlete body and motion, a virtual mirror and dressing room, autonomous virtual human, and sports activity analysis in camera networks. This demonstration will be organised in four parts according to the main modules in 3DLife framework.

Keywords: 3D body reconstruction, motion simulation, virtual human, virtual environment reconstruction, camera networks.

1 Demonstration for the 3DLife Framework and Its Modules

Athlete body and motion simulation

The objective of this module is to simulate a realistic virtual human body model in motion. Several advanced tools and computer graphics methods are used to achieve the visual realism. As a real case scenario, simulation of a tennis player in motion will be demonstrated. The production pipeline of this module consists of the following stages: Firstly a human model is scanned and post-processed to generate high quality mesh with texture. Secondly these models are processed for scalable rendering. Thirdly the resulting high quality mesh is mapped to an animation library. Fourthly, corresponding motion data is generated and finally the resulting model is streamed through network and rendered in an interactive environment for a visual demonstration. A diagram illustrating this process is given in Fig. 1.

Robust virtual mirror

The goal of this module is to work towards a virtual dressing room equipped with a *Virtual Mirror* and a *Clothing Advisor*. In conventional shopping, clothing is usually purchased by trying it on in front of a mirror. When buying customised and tailored clothes, people purchase something that has not been produced yet. An augmented

---

[1] A short video demonstration for the framework is available at:
http://dl.dropbox.com/u/9961943/3DLifeFrameworkDemo.wmv

E. Di Nitto and R. Yahyapour (Eds.): ServiceWave 2010, LNCS 6481, pp. 205–206, 2010.
© Springer-Verlag Berlin Heidelberg 2010

reality dressing room, equipped with a Virtual Mirror that shows the client wearing a virtual version of the customized product could assist the user in the selection of design, fabrics, textures and patterns, and thereby enhance the shopping experience on for customised and tailored clothes. Fig.2 shows the virtual mirror module structure.

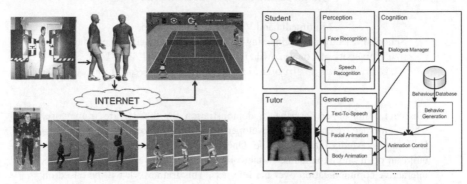

Fig. 1. Production pipeline of the athlete body and motion simulation module

Fig. 3. Overview of the autonomous virtual human module

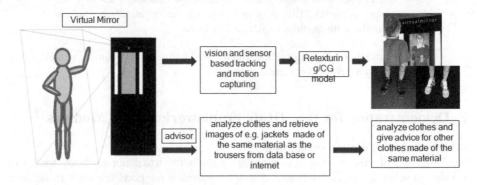

Fig. 2. The virtual mirror module in 3DLife framework

Autonomous virtual human

This module employs an Embodied Conversation Agent system by integrating its own technologies for 3D graphics, animation techniques and dialogue management. The dialogue management will accept text and speech based input and will react in speech with the appropriate facial expressions. Head and gaze movements of individual humans are recorded using a tracking device in a pre-defined dialogue. Based on this data, a model for facial gesture and eye-gaze controlled by specific dialogue events is defined. Fig. 3 presents an overview of this module.

Sports activity analysis in camera networks

3DLife is organising its challenge on Sports Activity Analysis in Camera Networks with ACM Multimedia Grand Challenges 2010. The 3DLife Challenge focuses on exploring the limits of what is possible in terms of 2D and 3D data extraction from a low-cost camera network for sports. In this part of the demonstration, technologies contributed by 3DLife consortium will be presented.

MICIE: An Alerting Framework for Interdependent Critical Infrastructures

Paolo Capodieci[1], Michele Minichino[2], Stefano Panzieri[3], Marco Castrucci[4], Alessandro Neri[1], Leonid Lev[5], and Paulo Simões[6]

[1] Selex Communications, Rome, Italy
Paolo.Capodieci@selex-comms.com
[2] ENEA, Rome, Italy
michele.minichino@enea.it
[3] Università di Roma Tre, Rome, Italy
panzieri@uniroma3.it
[4] SAPIENZA University of Rome, Rome, Italy
castrucci@dis.uniroma1.it
[5] Israel Electric Corporation, Haifa, Israel
leonid.lev@iec.co.il
[6] CISUC – DEI, University of Coimbra, Coimbra, Portugal
psimoes@dei.uc.pt

Abstract. In this demonstration we present the MICIE platform for on-line risk assessment in scenarios with heterogeneous interdependent Critical Infrastructures (CIs) such as power distribution networks, power plants, refineries, water distribution networks, transportation systems and telecommunication networks. These CIs are highly exposed to a large number of threats, including natural hazards, component failures and intentional attacks. Moreover, the increasing interdependence between CIs amplifies the effects of such threats and adds novel challenges to risk assessment tools. In this context, MICIE is the first systematic approach to integrate CI interdependence factors in on-line risk assessment, addressing both the development of on-line risk assessment models and the development of an information sharing platform for continuous exchange of relevant risk information between interdependent CIs.

Keywords: Critical Infrastructure Protection, On-line Alerting Systems.

1 Introduction

By their own nature, CIs have always been potentially weak points, exposed to a number of safety and security threats. Nevertheless, current CIs are more vulnerable than ever, as the need for efficiency and economic optimization pushes for increasingly complex systems with narrower safety margins, more complex technology and higher interdependency with external entities. CI sectors do not exist alone but interact each other, implying that protection needs to be cross sector and cross border: impacts occurring on one specific CI quickly propagate to others.

There is now a wide recognition of those risks, materialized in public initiatives such as the well-known Critical Infrastructure Protection Program, launched in 1998 by the US government, and the European Programme for Critical Infrastructure Protection. The alerting system we present is a core component of the MICIE FP7 Project

E. Di Nitto and R. Yahyapour (Eds.): ServiceWave 2010, LNCS 6481, pp. 207–208, 2010.

[1] and is in line with the European initiative to establish a Critical Infrastructure Warning Information Network (CIWIN).

2 The MICIE Framework

A complete and updated list of MICIE-related publications is available at [1]. In addition to the proposal of several off-line risk models able to integrate specialized risk assessment methods with generic interdependency models [2-3], MICIE proposes an on-line risk prediction tool able to provide CI operators with the estimated risk levels associated with each component or service of their infrastructure. This risk prediction tool, based on an evolution of the input-output interdependency model [3], is able to integrate low level details with high-level dependencies, whilst still keeping performance and scalability.

According to the MICIE framework each CI keeps its own risk prediction tool, fed by the monitoring of internal CI components and by metadata provided by interconnected CIs – with the risk of failure or degradation of the services outsourced to those CIs. The output of the risk prediction tool is then used by the operators of the CI and also to automatically feed the risk prediction tools of other infrastructures that consume services provided by that CI.

CI-to-CI communication is based on so-called Secure Mediation Gateways (SMGW) [4]. Interdependent CIs directly exchange relevant information, enhancing simplicity, privacy and scalability. According to the circumstances, multiple access models are available and multiple security and availability mechanisms can be applied, including trust-based mechanisms.

Overall, to the best of our knowledge, the MICIE Project is the first systematic approach to risk management in scenarios with interdependent CIs, addressing multiple levels: improvements to off-line CI-interdependency models and tools, a reference platform for on-line exchange of risk-level information between interdependent critical infrastructures, and the first prediction tool able to estimate risk levels based on monitoring data collected on-line from the internal components of the Critical Infrastructure and metadata received from other interconnected CIs providing outsourced services. This platform is now being integrated and evaluated in a real use-case scenario, provided by Israel Electric Corporation (IEC).

Acknowledgments. This research work has been carried out in the context of the MICIE Project, partially funded by the EU with the contract FP7-ICT-225353/2008. The authors would also like to thank all the project partners for their precious input.

References

1. MICIE Project Website, http://www.micie.eu
2. Ciancamerla, E., et al.: QoS of a SCADA system versus QoS of a Power Distribution Grid. In: Proc. of the 10th Int. Probabilistic Safety Assessment & Management Conference (PSAM 2010), Seattle, USA, June 7-11 (2010)
3. Oliva, G., Panzieri, S., Setola, R.: Agent Based Input-Output Interdependency Model. Int. Journal on Critical Infrastructure Protection 3(2) (July 2010)
4. Caldeira, F., et al.: Secure Mediation Gateway Architecture Enabling the Communication Among Critical Infrastructures. In: Proc. of the Future Network & Mobile Summit 2010, Florence, Italy, June 16-18 (2010)

A Management Framework for Automating Network Experiments and User Behaviour Emulation on Large Scale Testbed Facilities

Steven Latré[1], Filip De Turck[1], Dimitri Papadimitriou[2], and Piet Demeester[1]

[1] Ghent University – IBBT, Department of Information Technology,
Gaston Crommenlaan 8/201, B-9050, Gent, Belgium

[2] Alcatel-Lucent Bell Labs, Copernicuslaan 50, B-2018 Antwerpen, Belgium

Abstract. Generic test environments such as Emulab allow to perform large scale tests on different network topologies. While these facilities offer a tool to easily configure the topology, setting up realistic network scenarios afterwards is a manual and time consuming task involving the configuration of dozens of servers, including the installation of software suites and the emulation of subscriber behaviour. Also collecting the evaluation results afterwards can be complex and time consuming. This article discusses a management framework that allows both automating the configuration of networking experiments through a Graphical User Interface and automating the collection of measurements and visualisation of experimental results afterwards.

Keywords: experimental deployment, automation, validation.

A large number of intelligent components for managing the Future Internet have been proposed recently or are currently being investigated. However, before these network components can be deployed in real-life networks, they need to be thoroughly validated through realistic and large scale experiments. Testbed facility management tools such as Emulab [1] provide a means to set up large scale network topologies but offer only a limited functionality in managing the deployment of the experiment itself. As such, they are only a first step towards easily deploying large scale tests. From past experience we have observed that in implementing and deploying an algorithm on a test environment, the implementation of the algorithm takes only a fraction of the time. Configuring and deploying this algorithm is a manual and error prone process that can easily take a few hours. In this paper, we propose a management framework which automates the configuration and management of network experiments.

The management framework allows setting up a complete test scenario, starting with configuring a topology, collecting measurements, and ending with collecting the evaluation results in only a few minutes. All this is configured in one Graphical User Interface (GUI) as illustrated in Figure 1, that communicates with the iLab.t Virtual Wall testbed facility. The framework supports 4 different functions, that correspond with the 4 phases of running a network experiment.

E. Di Nitto and R. Yahyapour (Eds.): ServiceWave 2010, LNCS 6481, pp. 209–210, 2010.

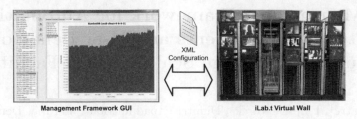

Management Framework GUI   iLab.t Virtual Wall

Fig. 1. Graphical User Interface for the management framework

First, the tool allows configuring the experiment, both on the network and application level. This configuration consists of (i) defining an appropriate network topology, (ii) plugging in the corresponding network components and (iii) emulating realistic user behaviour that emulates how users access the available services. Additionally, the management framework features two simplification mechanisms that allow to reduce the complexity of the experiment both spatially (i.e. by grouping nodes onto one physical node) and temporally (i.e. by speeding up the experiment).

Second, the experiment can be started with one click of the button. This one-button deployment phase automatically interfaces with the iLab.t Virtual Wall facility and consists of otherwise time consuming tasks such as the configuration of the network topology, the reservation of the needed physical hardware in the Virtual Wall and the separate configuration of each physical node separately. This automated configuration reduces the experimental setup time to a couple of minutes instead of hours compared to manual (and thus potentially error-prone) configuration.

Third, the tool provides real-time visualization of the experiment as it progresses. By showing continuously updating graphs containing network statistics such as total bandwidth on each link, a clear view is provided on the status and the results of the experiment as it progresses.

The fourth and final stage consists of automatically collecting the training sets containing realistic traffic patterns that are constructed during the experiment. For example, for a machine learning specific scenario, clustering algorithms that are under investigation are applied to the newly constructed data set and the performance can be evaluated through the automated generation of graphs that provide visualization of the clustering. For more information about the architecture and performance of the management framework itself, we refer to [2].

References

1. White, B., Lepreau, J., Stoller, L., Ricci, R., Guruprasad, S., Newbold, M., Hibler, M., Barb, C., Joglekar, A.: An integrated experimental environment for distributed systems and networks. In: Proceedings of the Fifth Symposium on Operating Systems Design and Implementation, pp. 255–270 (2002)
2. Latré, S., Van de Meerssche, W., Melis, S., Papadimitriou, D., De Turck, F., Demeester, P.: Automated management of network experiments and user behaviour emulation on large scale testbed facilities. In: Proc. of the 6th International Conference on Network and Service Management (CNSM 2010) (2010)

Environmental Service Infrastructure with Ontologies (ENVISION)

ENVISION Consortium

Arne J. Berre and Dumitru Roman

SINTEF, Oslo, Norway
`firstname.lastname@sintef.no`
`http://www.envision-project.eu`

Abstract. This demo paper briefly introduces the need for an open environmental service infrastructure for monitoring, managing and reporting about our environment, highlights an emerging architecture (ENVISION architecture) of such an infrastructure and presents the components of this architecture which will be demoed.

Keywords: environmental infrastructure, open architecture.

1 Top-Level Components of ENVISION

ICT have an essential role to play in the context of environmental information systems as they provide the necessary support in terms of tools, systems and protocols to establish a dynamic environmental space of collaboration in a more and more sophisticated digital world. Core challenges are not only related to providing seamless environmental data access to public authorities, businesses and the public at large, but also to allowing for interoperable environmental services based on Web technologies, and stimulating new market opportunities. The European Commission recently funded several projects[1] in the area of ICT for Sustainable Growth, with a core focus on ICT for Environmental Services and Climate Change aiming at providing the foundations for an infrastructure for monitoring, predicting and managing the environment and its natural resources. Current research problems addressed by such projects are centered on frameworks, methods, concepts, models, languages and technologies that enable enhanced environmental service infrastructures and platforms. Environmental Services Infrastructures with Ootologies (ENVISION)[2] is one of such projects focusing on architectural foundations of infrastructures and platforms supporting flexible discovery and chaining of distributed environmental services. The ENVISION consortium identified a set of components that have the potential to significantly improve the usability of environmental services (Figure 1). The components are grouped as follows:

---

[1] http://cordis.europa.eu/fp7/ict/sustainable-growth/environment_en.html
[2] http://www.envision-project.eu/

E. Di Nitto and R. Yahyapour (Eds.): ServiceWave 2010, LNCS 6481, pp. 211–212, 2010.

(1) Portal with a pluggable decision support framework, support for visual service chaining, and migration of existing environmental modeling applications to Model-as-a-Service (MaaS);

(2) Semantic annotation infrastructure to support visual semantic annotation mechanism and a multilanguage ontology management;

(3) Execution space that comprises a semantic discovery catalogue and semantic service mediator, and adaptive service chaining execution.

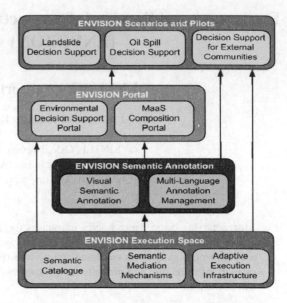

Fig. 1. Top-level Components of ENVISION

The *Execution Space* provides the basis for resource discovery and service chaining. Semantic interoperability is facilitated by the *Semantic Annotation* area, which contains ontologies, resource descriptions, and supporting tools. Both mentioned components provide input to the *Portal*. This area is also responsible for providing client components mechanisms for interfacing with the ontology and execution infrastructure. All areas in conjunction are applied to the *Scenarios and Pilots*. Concrete scenarios and pilots require application-specific decision support portals, and the overall framework provides means to generate such portals.

2 Demo

The proposed demo will present the following ENVISION tools (currently under development):

* Portlets-based ENVISION portal
* BPMN-based Web composition studio (visual composition of environmental services)
* Web OntoBridge (visual annotation of environmental services)
* Semantic querying and service discovery
* BPEL-based execution infrastructure for environmental services

A demo of the initial tools developed in the context of the SWING project (http://138.232.65.156/swing/) and which are currently being enhanced and further developed as components of the ENVISION platform can be found at http://138.232.65.156/swing/showcase.html.

MASTER as a Security Management Tool for Policy Compliance

Bruno Crispo[1], Gabriela Gheorghe[1],
Valentina Di Giacomo[2], and Domenico Presenza[2]

[1] University of Trento, Trento, Italy
name.surname@disi.unitn.it
[2] Engineering Ingegneria Informatica Roma, Italy
name.surname@eng.it

1 Short Description of the System

The problem of assessing security mechanisms in dynamic service-oriented architectures remains open. Assessment is particularly important in outsourcing scenarios to provide evidence on how policies across different providers are complied with. This evidence is essential to provide assurance to enterprise management that contractual agreements are satisfied, and if they are not, to what extend and in what conditions. The problem of assessing compliance with rules and regulations is difficult to solve, for several reasons. First, SOA are highly dynamic and distributed, which makes it difficult to monitor and aggregate evidence from different locations of interest. Second, the complexity of the requirements in the policies makes it difficult to associate these requirements with meaningful evidence. The reason is that high-level requirements may require evidence the collection of which needs to be broken down into low level evidence (i.e. operating system logs) that business constraints are satisfied as the application is running.

Most existing tools for security management are very high-level and with limited automated support: they leave to the security administrator the manual configuration of the required level of assessment and its monitoring. The security administrator needs to be aware of the semantics of the policies, which evidence to present to show the policies are met or are not met. More, the administrator needs to gather and correlate such evidence, and perform actions to compensate any misconfiguration or misbehaviour.

In trying to make the task of the security administrator easier, MASTER makes a step forward towards automatic security assessment. MASTER can (1) automatically monitor endpoints across the application, (2) gather policy relevant evidence, and (3) present this evidence to the security administrator. First, MASTER is able to do tasks (1) and (2) because it interposes itself in the communication of any services in the application. This is achieved by means of the MASTER Enterprise Service Bus (ESB) that is instructed to route messages among services based on low-level policy constraints. Secondly, the ESB is used as a ubiquitous monitoring tool able to report any application misbehaviours. The MASTER Control Cockpit interfaces between the administrator and the evidence of misbehaviours.

For MASTER, the infrastructure is the middleware that performs communication mediation in a SOA enterprise. This mediation is transparent for the service clients.

E. Di Nitto and R. Yahyapour (Eds.): ServiceWave 2010, LNCS 6481, pp. 213–214, 2010.
© Springer-Verlag Berlin Heidelberg 2010

Using this approach, MASTER can monitor any application, irrespective of its implementation, as long as it is deployed on the MASTER ESB.

The picture below shows the components of our tool: the MASTER ESB, which comprises a rule engine and a local enforcer in charge with monitoring and enforcing policies at the infrastructure level. MASTER ESB can support both access and usage control policies. The Control Cockpit provides the main administration features: the policy management via the Policy Manager, and the interface to the evidence needed to assess if the policies are satisfied.

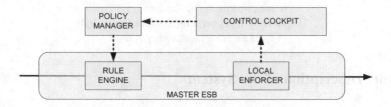

Fig. 1. The architectural components of the MASTER tool. Dashed lines represent control flows, the continuous line shows the message flow.

In this demonstration, we will show the automatic monitoring of the traffic flowing in the ESB and the enforcement of usage control policies. We used a health care scenario, and in particular a drug dispensation process, and we will show how MASTER detects and reacts to compliance violations to this process. We also show the features of the management interface that the administrator is presented with and possible ways in which this evidence can be aggregated for analysis.

2   Summary of Novel Characteristics

The main innovations in this demonstration are: the support to the traffic analysis using the trust level of log events, a preventive enforcement to usage control policies violations, and the possibility to involve the supervisor in the enforcement process. The MASTER ESB has full visibility to perform complete mediation that is transparent to application users. Also, the MASTER Control Cockpit can be seen as a stateful cross-service control panel, that the administrator can use to tune the enforcement mechanisms according to the application context and runtime

3   Functions and Features to Be Demonstrated

- Enforcing message-level policies across service endpoints, on the MASTER ESB (MASTER ESB: Extended Apache Servicemix 3.3.1 running on Windows XP, Java6. Policy Decision Point running on OpenBSD)
- Configuring monitoring and reporting on certain service endpoints
- Presenting runtime evidence to the security administrator

Link to demonstration video: http://www.master-
fp7.eu/index.php?option=com_docman&task=doc_download&gid=88&Itemid=60

Future Internet Monitoring Platform for Computing Clouds

Stuart Clayman[1], Alex Galis[1], Giovanni Toffetti[2], Luis M. Vaquero[3],
Benny Rochwerger[4], and Philippe Massonet[5]

[1] University College London – U.K.
{s.clayman,a.galis}@ee.ucl.ac.uk
[2] University de Lugano –Switzerland
toffettg@lu.unisi.ch
[3] Telefonica – Spain
lmvg@tid.es
[4] IBM Haifa Research Lab
rochwer@il.ibm.com
[5] CETIC - Belgium
philippe.massonet@cetic.be

Abstract. This paper presents a monitoring platform and demonstration enabling effectively operation of service clouds. It is designed for monitoring resources and services in virtualized environments. It provides data on the actual usage and changes in resources of the cloud and of the services running in the cloud.

Keywords: Service Clouds, Monitoring Platform.

1 Monitoring Service Clouds

A service cloud, such as RESERVOIR (www.reservoir-fp7.eu) operates by acting as a platform for running services in virtual execution environments (VEEs), which have been deployed on behalf of a service provider. Within each service cloud site there is a Service Manager (SM) and a VEE Manager (VEEM) which provide all the necessary management functionality for both the services and the infrastructure. The Virtual Execution Environment Host (VEEH) is a resource that can host a certain type of VEEs. In a service cloud hosting site there is likely to be a considerable number of VEEHs organised as a cluster. These three main components of the service cloud architecture interact with each other using well defined interfaces, namely SMI, VMI, and VHI, within a site and also use the VMI interface for site-to-site federation via the VEEM. In figure 1 the relationship between these components and interfaces is shown.

The Lattice developed as part of the RESERVOIR project and issued as open source (http://www.reservoir-fp7.eu/) provides a framework from which various monitoring systems in federated environments can be built to that can it collects all the relevant data in an effective way [1-3]. It provides the building blocks and the

E. Di Nitto and R. Yahyapour (Eds.): ServiceWave 2010, LNCS 6481, pp. 215–217, 2010.
© Springer-Verlag Berlin Heidelberg 2010

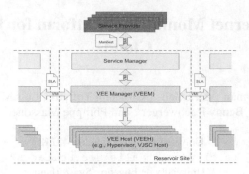

Fig. 1. RESERVOIR Service Cloud Architecture

glue from which specific monitoring elements can devised, including the following features:

- *Minimal runtime footprint* and not be intrusive, so as not to adversely affect the performance of the network itself or the running service applications. *Filtering* and control of the relevant probes, so that the management components only receive data that is of relevance.

- *Scalability* - ensure that the monitoring can cope with a large numbers of probes; *Elasticity* - so that virtual resources created and destroyed by expanding and contracting networks are monitored correctly.

- *Migration* - so that any virtual resource, which moves from one physical host to another is monitored correctly. *Adaptability* - so that the monitoring framework can adapt to varying computational and network loads in order to not be invasive.

- *Autonomic* - so that the monitoring framework can keep running without intervention and reconfiguration. *Federation* - so that any virtual resource, which reside on another domain is monitored correctly.

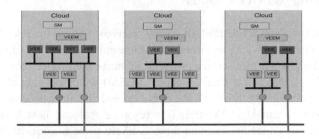

Fig. 2. Monitoring a Federation of Virtual Execution Environments for Multiple Service

The LATTICE platform was developed, integrated with the rest of the RESERVOIR systems and validated on a testbed enabling experimentation with thousands of virtual machines: V^3 – UCL's Experimental Testbed located in London. It consists of 80cores with a dedicated 10 Gbits/s infrastructure. Video of the full RESERVOIR service cloud demonstration is available at: http://www.youtube.com/

v/hHsFQ9u2fvQ. It shows how : 1. the deployment of virtual machines in a federated cloud can be monitored; 2. the cloud provider monitors the infrastructure enabling also the service provider to monitor the services/applications deployed on the cloud.

Acknowledgments. The work presented in this paper is partially supported by the EC.

References

[1] Clayman, S., Galis, A., Chapman, C., Merino, L.R., Vaquero, L.M., Nagin, K., Rochwerger, B.: Monitoring Future Internet Service Clouds. In: Towards the Future Internet. IOS Press, Amsterdam (April 2010), http://www.iospress.nl/
[2] Chapman, C., Emmerich, W., Galn, F., Clayman, S., Galis, A.: Software Architecture Definition for On-demand Cloud Provisioning. In: ACM HPDC, Chicago, June 21-25 (2010), http://hpdc2010.eecs.northwestern.edu/
[3] Clayman, S., Galis, A., Mamatas, L.: Monitoring Virtual Networks. In: 12th IEEE/IFIP NOMS 2010 /ManFI 2010, Osaka, April 19–23 (2010), http://www.man.org/2010/

Enhanced Privacy and Identity Management for Community Services – Demo of the PICOS Project

Christian Kahl, Katja Böttcher,
Markus Tschersich, Stephan Heim, and Kai Rannenberg

Goethe University Frankfurt, Chair of Mobile Business & Multilateral Security
Grüneburgplatz 1
60629 Frankfurt am Main, Germany
{Christian.Kahl,Katja.Boettcher,Markus.Tschersich,Stephan.Heim,
Kai.Rannenberg,picos}@m-chair.net

Abstract. As online communities get increasingly mobile, enabling new location based community services, including privacy and trust for their users gets more important. Within the PICOS project we investigated and elaborated innovative concepts to improve the privacy of users within mobile communities based on three exemplary communities.

Keywords: Privacy, Identity Management, Mobile Communities, Social Networks, Mobility, Application Prototype.

1 Introduction

Online communities get increasingly mobile, enabling new and enhanced (location based) community services. However, when users participate in such communities, they leave private information traces they may not be aware of. The project PICOS[1] has the goal to develop a new approach to identity management, for enhancing the trust, privacy and identity management aspects of (mobile) community services.

In a first step to address this challenge, we analysed contemporary research and investigated the context of communities (e.g., legal, technical and economic aspects). In a next step, we gathered requirements from exemplary mobile communities (anglers, gamers, taxi drivers) in a bottom-up approach and designed a community platform architecture including concepts to address the gathered requirements and enable open, privacy-respecting identity and trust management. The architecture and concepts were prototypically implemented in a community platform and community applications, which have been tested in user trials and evaluated concerning trust, privacy, usability, ergonomics and legal issues.

---

[1] PICOS - Privacy and Identity Management for Community Services. The project PICOS is receiving funding from the European Community's Seventh Framework Programme (FP7/2007-2011) under Grant Agreement n° 215056.

E. Di Nitto and R. Yahyapour (Eds.): ServiceWave 2010, LNCS 6481, pp. 218–219, 2010.

2 Novelty

PICOS gathered requirements from exemplary mobile communities in a bottom-up approach and designed a community platform architecture including cutting-edge concepts and tools for managing the privacy and identity to address the requirements.

Especially novel concepts such as partial identities, which allow users to use different identities in different usage contexts, and privacy policies, which allow a fine-grained adjustment of privacy settings, support users to preserve their privacy while being an active member of the community. Further concepts are location blurring, which helps users to obfuscate their exact location and selectively share it with others and the privacy advisor, which provides guidance to users regarding the disclosure or sharing of personal information (e.g. location information). The Privacy Advisor provides context sensitive hints in situations when personal information of users is involved.[2]

3 Functions and Features

The architecture and concepts were prototypically implemented in a community platform (server) and community applications (client)[3]. The PICOS community applications are state-of-the-art mobile applications, based on a Symbian touch-screen handset. The applications were developed in close collaboration with end users from our focused exemplary angling and gaming communities as well as usability experts, to ensure that user requirements are continuously considered.

In our presentation we provide an interactive demo of the prototype application to the visitors. The visitors will be introduced to the application by scheduled live presentations and guided by PICOS representatives. As the application basically works like similar community applications it is relatively easy to understand and use. Visitors can enter the demo-community ad-hoc at the stand, make use of the prototype features and thereby try out the unique PICOS concepts. E.g. they can create partial identities, manage their privacy policies and interact with other users. Thereby users will be enabled to experience how the unique features of PICOS help to enhance their privacy and trust in mobile communities.

Furthermore complementing background information in form of posters and flyers will be available, which gives users the possibility to obtain a holistic picture of the PICOS work and to learn more about our motivation, the approach and our achievements. Visitors will be able to learn why research with regard to privacy, trust and identity management in mobile communities is needed and how we want to achieve an improvement of such aspects.

---

[2] Kahl, C., Boettcher, K., Tschersich, M., Heim, S., Rannenberg, K.: How to enhance Privacy and Identity Management for Mobile Communities: Approach and User driven Concepts of the PICOS Project. In: Rannenberg, K., Varadharajan, V., Weber, C. (eds.) SEC 2010. IFIP AICT, vol. 330, pp. 277–288. Springer, Heidelberg (2010)
[3] The PICOS Concepts and Features website provides a detailed overview and demo videos of the unique PICOS features (http://www.picos-project.eu/index.php?id=204).

Future Internet Architectures and Scenarios by Means of Opportunistic Networks and Cognitive Management Systems

Panagiotis Demestichas[1], Jens Gebert[2], and Markus Mueck[3]

[1] University of Piraeus, Dep. of Digital Systems, Piraeus, Greece
[2] Alcatel-Lucent, Stuttgart, Germany
[3] Infineon Technologies, Munich, Germany
pdemest@unipi.gr, Jens.Gebert@alcatel-lucent.com,
MarkusDominik.Mueck@infineon.com

Abstract. Our work showcases Future Internet oriented technologies: (i) operator governed opportunistic networks; (ii) cognitive management systems and control channels for their cooperation. The demonstration of these technologies shows enhanced service provision capabilities, higher resource utilization, lower transmission powers, and "green" network operation.

Keywords: Scenarios, architectures, opportunistic networks, cognitive management, cost-efficiency.

1 Introduction

Main requirements defining the Future Internet (FI) motivate our work: (i) Demand for a wide range of diversified applications and expanded use of wireless, which set the networks under a serious stress for resources. (ii) Need for increased cost-efficiency in resource provisioning.

In response to these requirements, our work showcases a FI architecture that includes the following elements [1,2]: (i) Opportunistic networks and heterogeneous network infrastructures; (ii) Cognitive systems for managing the opportunistic network and the infrastructure, and control channels for their cooperation. This solution enables the cost efficient provision of applications and the realization of important (technical and business) *scenarios* of the FI.

2 Short System Description – Features Demonstrated

Opportunistic networks are operator-governed, temporary, coordinated extensions of the infrastructure. They are dynamically created, in places and for the time they are needed to deliver multimedia flows to mobile users, in a cost-efficient manner. Operator governance is materialized through the designation of resources (e.g., spectrum, transmission powers, etc.) that can be used, and the provision of policies,

E. Di Nitto and R. Yahyapour (Eds.): ServiceWave 2010, LNCS 6481, pp. 220–221, 2010.
© Springer-Verlag Berlin Heidelberg 2010

information and knowledge. They can comprise nodes of the infrastructure, and terminals/devices potentially organized in an ad-hoc network mode.

Cognitive management systems are required for managing the opportunistic networks and for coordinating the infrastructure. Their role will be to provide the functionality for determining the suitability, creating, modifying and releasing of opportunistic networks. *Control channels* [3] convey information and knowledge on context, profiles, policies, and decisions.

The features demonstrated are related to important scenarios: (i) Enhanced application delivery by expanding the coverage of the infrastructure; (ii) Application delivery, by resolving cases of congested access to the infrastructure, through opportunistic networks.

3   Summary of Novel Characteristics

The following novel characteristics are included: (i) Increased cost-efficiency in the provision of main applications envisaged in the FI context; (ii) Distributed cognitive functionality and interfaces.

Sample facts that prove the cost-efficiency are: (i) the higher utilization of resources, and therefore, the achievement of higher capacity levels, without the need for new investment in the infrastructure; this means lower capital expenditures; (ii) the use of lower transmission powers, and therefore, the lower energy consumption in the infrastructure; this means lower operational expenditures; (iii) the "green" footprint of the application delivery model.

4   Conclusions

Our work showcases technologies of an architecture that enables the support of important (technical and business) scenarios and lead to the cost-efficient application provision in a Future Internet context.

Acknowledgments. This work is performed in the project OneFIT which is partially funded by the European Community's 7th Framework programme. This paper reflects only the authors' views. The Community is not liable for any use that may be made of the information contained herein. The contributions of OneFIT colleagues are hereby acknowledged.

References

1. OneFIT (Opportunistic networks and Cognitive Management Systems for Efficient Application Provision in the Future Internet) project, http://www.ict-onefit.eu
2. E^3 (End-to-End Efficiency) project, http://www.ict-e3.eu
3. European Telecommunication Standardization Institute (ETSI), Technical Committee on Reconfigurable Radio Systems (RRS),
   http://www.etsi.org/website/technologies/RRS.aspx

Enabling Interoperability for SOA-Based SaaS Applications Using Continuous Computational Language*

Yehia Taher[1], Dinh Khoa Nguyen[1], Willem-Jan van den Heuvel[1],
and Ali Ait-Bachir[2]

[1] European Research Institute in Service Science (ERISS), Tilburg University
[2] LIG Laboratory, University of Grenoble
{Y.Taher,D.K.Nguyen,wjheuvel}@uvt.nl, ali.ait-bachir@imag.fr

Abstract. Today there still exist many interoperability issues concerning the communications between Web Services (WSs). Most of the existing approaches can only solve either the structural or behavioural interoperability conflicts between SOAP messages that are exchanged by heterogeneous WSs. Furthermore, they are usually ad-hoc approaches that are too costly and not reusable elsewhere. In this demonstration we present a novel prototype tool that allows encoding adaptation rules in the Continuous Query Language (CQL) for SOAP messages on both structural and behavioural levels, and then deploying and managing the rules on a rule engine in a predictable and repeatable manner.

1 Motivation

Software-as-a-Service (SaaS) is an "on-demand" application delivery model in which users access software over the Internet, from anywhere, at any time. Through the SaaS model, distributed and globally networked software services can be seamlessly integrated in many cross-organizational settings. However, the benefit of SaaS can only be fully exploited if they follow the "true spirit" of *Service Oriented Architecture* (SOA). SOA promotes highly standardized, loosely coupled and Web-enabled Services to foster rapid, low-cost and easy composition of distributed enterprise applications [1]. Hence, SOA-enabling SaaS applications results in a mixing and matching of external WS with on-premise ones. This combination makes it possible to efficiently develop and manage loosely coupled composite *SOA-based SaaS applications*.

Unfortunately, solving incompatibilities between the structures (contents) and behaviours (protocols) of the exchanged messages still remains an acute problem and gives rise to many new

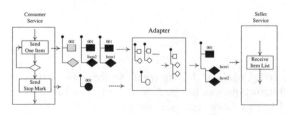

Fig. 1. Incompatibility example

* The research leading to these results has received funding from the European Community's Seventh Framework Program FP7/2007-2013 under grant agreement 215483 (S-Cube).

E. Di Nitto and R. Yahyapour (Eds.): ServiceWave 2010, LNCS 6481, pp. 222–224, 2010.

research challenges. A practical example of this problem (see Figure 1) is that a customer WS submits a Purchase Order that specifies every item separately while the Online Sales WS expects a comprehensive list of all items together. Such a simple broken scenario may significantly damage the whole costly transaction.

As a straightforward approach, ad-hoc adapters may be built for resolving interoperability conflicts between the SOAP messages that are exchanged between WSs. However, they are typically too costly and not reusable elsewhere. There exist also other generic and repeatable approaches for WS adaptation. Unfortunately, they only target either the structural or the behavioural interoperability problem.

2 Tool Demonstration

Inspired by our previous work in [3] our aim is to provide a generic and automated solution for interoperability conflicts both on the message structure and behaviour level in a repeatable and predictable manner. Our approach leverages the Continuous Query Language (CQL) [2], a special continuous computational language, to encode the adaptation rules at the structural and behavioural level. CQL codes are fed into a rule engine that is able to interpret the rules, listen to the incoming messages, and restructure the messages according to the predefined loaded CQL rules. A set of generic operators (Merge, Split, Match, etc.) are supported in the rule engine to enable the message restructuring. Figure 2 visualizes our prototype tool in some more detail.

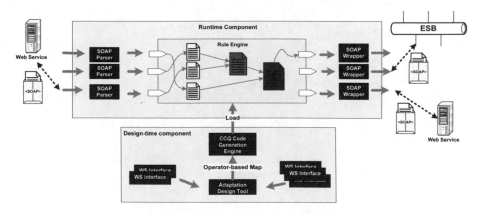

Fig. 2. Architecture of the Prototype Tool

The prototype tool we introduce here has two main components: the design-time component and runtime component. The design-time component is endowed with templates that users may customize to specify adaptation logic that is tailored towards the structural and behavioural properties of WSs. Moreover, the design-time component has a CQL generation engine that takes the users' adaptation logic specification as input and then generates and feeds the CQL rules to the runtime component. The Rule Engine inside the runtime component is able to interpret the encoded CQL rules and act accordingly to treat the incoming SOAP messages. As depicted in the Figure 2 for instance, it may compose the many source SOAP messages to a single target message for the outgoing SOAP. For a live demonstration of our prototype tool please visit http://www.youtube.com/watch?v=g05ciEPZ_Zc .

References

1. Papazoglou, M.P., van den Heuvel, W.J.: Service-oriented Design and Development Methodology. Int. Journal of Web Engineering and Technology 2, 412–442 (2006)
2. Arasu, A., et al.: The CQL continuous query language: semantic foundations and query execution. The VLDB Journal 15(2), 121–142 (2006)
3. Taher, Y., et al.: Diagnosing Incompatibilities in Web Service Interactions for Automatic Generation of Adapters. In: AINA 2009, pp. 652–659 (2009)

NinSuna: Metadata-Driven Media Delivery

Davy Van Deursen*, Wim Van Lancker, Erik Mannens, and Rik Van de Walle

Ghent University – IBBT, ELIS – Multimedia Lab, Belgium
davy.vandeursen@ugent.be

1 Platform Overview

Today, delivery of multimedia content introduces a number of important challenges due to the growing amount of multimedia content on the one hand and the growing diversity in usage environments on the other hand. Furthermore, we need to deal with a growing amount of media formats used for compressing and packaging multimedia content.

In order to deal with such a heterogeneous multimedia landscape, we developed NinSuna [3], which is a fully integrated metadata-driven media delivery platform. Its basic design is inspired by the principles of XML-driven content adaptation techniques, while its final design and the implementation thereof are based on Semantic Web technologies such as the Resource Description Framework (RDF), Web Ontology Language (OWL), and SPARQL Protocol And RDF Query Language (SPARQL). Furthermore, a tight coupling exists between the design of the media delivery platform and a model for describing structural, content, and scalability information of media bitstreams, enabling a format-independent adaptation and packaging approach [1].

2 Features

Our media delivery platform is characterized by a number of features. First of all, the core software modules of the platform (i.e., selection, adaptation, and packaging of media bitstreams) are fully **independent of media formats** (i.e., both coding and delivery formats). Therefore, the platform is highly **extensible**, since new media formats can be added by means of plugins. Also, the different platform modules can be distributed over different machines, which makes the platform **scalable**.

NinSuna uses a central **multimedia ontology** which couples the served media resources with any available metadata. Hence, the metadata is stored into a fully **RDF-based storage backend** for descriptive metadata which is accessible through a SPARQL endpoint. Also, a number of **metadata parsers** are provided for importing and converting XML-based metadata to an enhanced

* The research activities as described in this paper were funded by Ghent University, the Interdisciplinary Institute for Broadband Technology (IBBT), the Institute for the Promotion of Innovation by Science and Technology in Flanders (IWT), the Fund for Scientific Research Flanders (FWO-Flanders), and the European Union.

E. Di Nitto and R. Yahyapour (Eds.): ServiceWave 2010, LNCS 6481, pp. 225–226, 2010.

RDF representation (e.g., NewsML) while parsers for other metadata schemes can be added as plugins.

The platform supports various forms of **content adaptation**: scenes or shots can be extracted from any media resource to facilitate fine-grained search queries, requested media fragments can be adapted depending on the scalability provisions in the media stream, and track combinations can be selected (e.g., audio/video stream selection based on bit rate). Further, the platform supports the most common **media delivery formats** on the Web: streaming media delivery through RTSP and RTMP, HTTP progressive download (MP4, Ogg, 3GPP, MPEG-2 TS), and HTTP Live streaming.

Finally, NinSuna is a server-side reference implementation of the **W3C Media Fragments URI** 1.0 specification [2], which mission is to address media fragments on the Web using Uniform Resource Identifiers (URIs). Having global identifiers for arbitrary media fragments allows substantial benefits, including linking, bookmarking, caching, and indexing.

3   Demonstration

We built two front-end applications to demonstrate our media delivery platform. The first demonstration consists of a faceted browser facilitating the retrieval of news fragments[1]. More specifically, media resources representing news broadcasts are annotated on a scene level, by using NewsML metadata serialized in RDF. Hence, we can use the faceted browsing paradigm to let the end-user obtain his/her desired news fragments. Once a news fragment is chosen, the selected media fragment is extracted, packaged, and sent to the client. Additionally, dynamic frame rate adaptations are demonstrated as well.

The second demonstration shows the interaction between NinSuna and Media Fragment 1.0 URIs[2]. More specifically, we show which HTTP requests/responses are sent to/from our platform and how the user agents can visualize such media fragment URIs.

References

1. Van Deursen, D., et al.: Format-independent and Metadata-driven Media Resource Adaptation using Semantic Web Technologies. Multimedia Systems 16(2), 85–104 (2010)
2. Van Deursen, D., et al.: Implementing the Media Fragments URI Specification. In: 19th International Conference on World Wide Web, WWW 2010, Raleigh, North Carolina, USA, pp. 1361–1364 (April 2010)
3. Van Deursen, D., et al.: NinSuna: a Fully Integrated Platform for Format-independent Multimedia Content Adaptation and Delivery based on Semantic Web Technologies. Multimedia Tools and Applications – Special Issue on Data Semantics for Multimedia Systems 46(2-3), 371–398 (2010)

---

[1] Screen cast available at `http://ninsuna.elis.ugent.be/NinSunaFacets#demo`
[2] Screen cast available at
`http://ninsuna.elis.ugent.be/MediaFragmentsServer#screencast`

SOA4All in Action:
Enabling a Web of Billions of Services

Maurilio Zuccalà (on behalf of the SOA4All Consortium)

http://www.soa4all.eu

Abstract. SOA4All aims at realizing a world where billions of parties expose and consume services via advanced Web technology. The main objective of the project is to provide a comprehensive framework that integrates complementary and evolutionary technical advances (i.e., SOA, Context Management, Web Principles, Web 2.0 and Semantic Technologies) into a coherent and domain-independent service delivery platform. The demonstration will focus on the SOA4All Studio, a user-friendly holistic platform that provides users with a unified view covering the whole lifecycle of services. Through the SOA4All Studio interface, users will be invited to discover available services and compose their own. I.e., they will be able to find services, semantically annotate them, compose them in processes and finally monitor their execution. They will see results immediately without any pre-knowledge required.

Keywords: SOA, Services, Semantic Web, Web 2.0, Context Management, Web Principles, Future Internet.

1 SOA4All Project

Service Oriented Architectures for All (SOA4All) [1] is a Large-Scale Integrating Project funded by the European Seventh Framework Programme, under the Service and Software Architectures, Infrastructures and Engineering research area (project ref. 215219). SOA4All is endorsed by the NESSI Initiative [2] and is contributing significantly to the NESSI Open Framework, which is one of the main challenges of the European Platform on Software and Services.

SOA4All aims to enable a world where billions of parties are exposing and consuming services via advanced Web technology. To this end, SOA4All aims to bear SOA, Context Management, Web Principles, Web 2.0 and Semantic Technologies as the core principles able to provide the power, flexibility and simplicity that is necessary for a wider uptake of service-oriented technologies in the Web. One major contribution of the project is the SOA4All Studio [3] [4], a fully-fledged Web-based framework that supports users throughout the entire life-cycle of services.

2 Demonstration

The "SOA4All in Action" demonstration will illustrate the SOA4All Studio and bring it to end users. Through the intuitive graphical user interface of the

E. Di Nitto and R. Yahyapour (Eds.): ServiceWave 2010, LNCS 6481, pp. 227–228, 2010.

SOA4All Studio, users will be invited to compose and connect their own services in a Future Internet scenario. In particular, they will be able to:

- Discover existing services in a distributed service space, through the SOA4All Studio browser interface, where services can be browsed by category, by tag etc.,
- Annotate services with semantic information or extend current annotations, so to enhance service descriptions and simplify operations such as composition and adaptation,
- Combine services into processes in a visual, mashup-like way through the SOA4All Studio process editor,
- Monitor and analyze service execution,
- See results immediately, without any pre-knowledge required, through the SOA4All Studio interface.

People with different backgrounds (e.g., SOA, semantics, business) will get an immediate insight into the novelties and potentialities of the SOA4All integrated solution from their own perspectives.

A short video illustrating a sample usage session of the SOA4All Studio for composing a new business service can be found at the following address: http://coconut.tie.nl/video. This video covers only a part of the SOA4All Studio features and potentialities that will be shown in the demonstration.

More details about the SOA4All service delivery platform, the SOA4All use cases, the underlying technologies developed or used in the project, and other resources are available on the SOA4All Web site [1]. For more information about the SOA4All vision and approach, see, e.g., [5] and [6].

3   Conclusion

The "SOA4All in Action" demonstration will present the SOA4All approach to a global service delivery platform, and make it available to end users thanks to the SOA4All Studio. The SOA4All solution can be seen as a key pillar in achieving a Web that allows everyone to easily create and access services, and to turn the "Web of billions of services" into reality.

References

1. SOA4All Web site, http://www.soa4all.eu
2. NESSI Web site, http://www.nessi-europe.eu
3. SOA4All public deliverables about the SOA4All Studio, http://www.soa4all.eu/file-upload.html?func=select&id=7
4. SOA4All Studio Core Dashboard, http://coconut.tie.nl:8080/dashboard
5. Domingue, J., Fensel, D., Gonzalez-Cabero, R.: SOA4All, Enabling the SOA Revolution on a World Wide Scale. In: International Conference on Semantic Computing, pp. 530–537. IEEE Computer Society, Los Alamitos (2008)
6. Krummenacher, R., Norton, B., Simperl, E., Pedrinaci, C.: SOA4All: Enabling Web-scale Service Economies. In: International Conference on Semantic Computing, pp. 535–542. IEEE Computer Society, Los Alamitos (2009)

Demonstrating Distributed Virtual Networks

Alexandru Paler, Andreas Fischer, and Hermann de Meer

University of Passau, Passau 94032, Germany
{alexandru.paler,andreas.fischer,hermann.demeer}@uni-passau.de

Keywords: future internet, virtual networks, virtual network deployment.

1 Introduction

The current internet is commonly perceived as being too inflexible. Network Virtualization has been recognized lately as a method to overcome these limitations. Previous implementations of Virtual Network (VN) deployment software either provided limited access to the network layer (like PlanetLab), or focused only on specific application scenarios (like VNUML or VLAN). A first step toward the expected flexibility, with a solution that is both universal and thorough, is the implementation of network virtualization using system virtualization approaches [2].

We present a system that is constructing an underlying VN in a universal, scalable and flexible way. This was developed as part of the Autonomic Internet project[3]. A video demonstrating the software can be found at [1].

2 Controlling Distributed Virtual Networks

This demonstration features a software for the on-demand deployment and management of VNs distributed on physical infrastructures. Applications running on top of it are supported transparently and have full access to the VN layer. From a hardware perspective, a VN is composed of virtual routers (VRs) and virtual links (VLs). The routing service (RS) supported by the VN can also be viewed as an intrinsic component.

The software architecture is based on two loosely coupled components. The first component translates the description of a VN topology into a set of commands. The commands are then forwarded to and processed by the second component, and as a result, a VN is constructed or modified. The description of a VN contains names for both VRs and VLs. Moreover, the VLs can be configured, allowing the user to assign network addresses. The software is designed to be protocol agnostic (e.g. IPv4, IPv6, ATM), making future extensions possible.

The chosen physical test bed consists of four physical hosts interconnected with Gigabit Ethernet. The current version is using XEN for the VRs, OpenSSH for supporting the VLs and Quagga as a basis for the RS. The functionality of the software is demonstrated by constructing a VN with a linear topology distributed across all the physical hosts of the test bed. We use this particular

E. Di Nitto and R. Yahyapour (Eds.): ServiceWave 2010, LNCS 6481, pp. 229–230, 2010.

virtual topology because it eases the visual presentation, but this fact does not limit the generality of our software.

To construct a VN, the following steps are executed on each physical host:

1. Receive a complete set of commands
2. For each VR command start the VR_i and the corresponding RS_i
3. For each VL command (between VR_1 and VR_2)
   (a) Add a virtual network interface to the VR_1
   (b) Connect to the remote physical host to create a link-segment
   (c) Add a virtual network interface to the VR_2
   (d) Create a link (tunnel) between VR_1 and VR_2
   (e) Instantiate VL_i and configure the RS in VR_1 and VR_2

A VL is constructed between two existing VRs and consists of three segments: one is connecting the physical hosts, and the other two are connecting each VR with its host. All three segments are aggregated to a VL by two software bridges. If the linked VRs are hosted on the same host, then Step 3b is optional.

Once a VN is built, third-party applications can monitor it by using a request/response mechanism implemented in the software. Collecting monitoring data about the infrastructure helps taking management decisions like the migration of VRs (together with corresponding VLs) or the change of topology. Such decisions can increase the resilience of the VN in the face of faults or attacks. The modification of topology is transparently affecting the RS, thus leading to an automatic reconfiguration.

3   Conclusion

A major goal of the Future Internet is to enable very flexible and scalable topologies. The presented software proves this to be possible. Future work will be targeted on improving the performance and the responsivenes to live-migration scenarios.

Acknowledgements. The research leading to these results has received funding from the European Community's Seventh Framework Programme ([FP7/2007-2013] [FP7/2007-2011]) in the context of the AutoI project, grant agreement no. 216404.

References

1. Distributed Virtual Networks - Video Demonstration (August 2010),
   http://www.net.fim.uni-passau.de/demo_ghent
2. Fischer, A., Berl, A., De Meer, H.: Virtualized networks based on system virtualization. In: Proc. of the 2nd GI/ITG KuVS Workshop on The Future Internet (2008)
3. Rubio-Loyola, J., Astorga, A., Serrat, J., Chai, W.K., Mamatas, L., Galis, A., Clayman, S., Cheniour, A., Lefevre, L., Mornard, O., Fischer, A., Paler, A., de Meer, H.: Platforms and Software Systems for an Autonomic Internet. In: Proc. IEEE Global Communications Conference (GLOBECOM 2010), Miami, USA (December 2010)

A Middleware Infrastructure for Multi-rule-Engine Distributed Systems

Pierre de Leusse, Bartosz Kwolek, and Krzysztof Zieliński

Distributed System Research Group,
AGH University of Science and Technology, Krakow, Poland
{pdl,bkwolek,kz}@agh.edu.pl

Abstract. The rule technological landscape is becoming ever more complex, with an extended number of specifications and products. It is therefore becoming increasingly difficult to integrate rule-driven components and manage interoperability in multi-rule engine environments. The described work presents the possibility to provide a middleware infrastructure for rule-driven components in a distributed system. The authors' approach leverages on a set of middleware, discovery protocol, rule interchange and user interface to alleviate the environment's complexity.

Keywords: Rule-Based Distributed Systems, middleware, rule interchange, RIF.

1 Introduction

In recent years, rule-based systems have become increasingly popular. This evolution has been mostly attributed to three factors, 1) better separation of concerns between the knowledge and its implementation logic in contrast to a hard-coded approach; 2) rule repositories that increase the visibility and readability of the knowledge and 3) graphical user interfaces that render rules more usable while bridging the gap between users (e.g. domain experts) and IT specialists.

Influenced by this increased interest, the technological landscape of rules is becoming more and more complex. This is partly due to the number of technologies being developed and the frequency in which they appear. In particular, the amount of platforms implemented as well as the various specifications related to rule expression and enactment have rendered this domain more opaque.

This abundance of technologies and products can be beneficial as different approaches attempt to address a variety of problems (e.g. production, reaction). However, it greatly impacts the usability of distributed systems that leverage on rule engines in order to automate managed components behavior. The behavioral and functional complexity reduced by rule engines at the component level translates into management and interoperability issues in the distributed application plane. The main contribution of this paper and the demonstration system it presents, is a middleware infrastructure for multi-rule-engine distributed systems. This demonstration addresses challenges in the domains of rule-driven component discovery, rule interchange and multi-rule-engine usability.

E. Di Nitto and R. Yahyapour (Eds.): ServiceWave 2010, LNCS 6481, pp. 231–232, 2010.

2   Anatomy of a Middleware Infrastructure for Multi-rule-Engine Distributed Systems

In order to simplify the demonstration, in this experiment the authors assume that no semantic translation is needed – i.e. an "Order" in one rule engine has the same meaning in the others. The describe work does not investigate acquisition of the knowledge between different systems.

Component discovery: In order to allow for the discovery and storage of the different artifacts (e.g. rule engines, translators) the authors make use of a central repository. In this experiment, the repository is implemented using the Atom Publication Protocol (APP) and eXist DB. Thus, different atoms feeds are used to store data about rule engines and translators.

Rule engine interoperability: The two rule engines experimented upon present similarities that allowed the authors to design one single model of middleware interface. Thus two soap services for each rule engine are provided, allowing to control and evaluate the state of the engines' working memories. The *'Management'* service allows administration type operations and the *'Functional'* service allows operations on rules and facts in specific sets of knowledge (i.e. instance of a working memory).

It is noticeable that the authors do not make the assumption that a single model of middleware is possible for every rule engines and anticipate that further experimentation will make use of different types of interfaces. The Drools project, for instance, already proposes a RESTful middleware.

Rule interchangeability: For the purpose of this experiment, the authors have chosen to investigate rule interchange between Drools and Jess using the Rule Interchange Format (RIF) core language as platform neutral language. Drools and Jess were chosen for their popularity and similarities.

It is not possible to provide in this short document a full description of the translation mechanisms used in the demonstration.

At the time of writing, the interchange soundness is verified by a specific *'validate'* function of the *'functional'* service. This function makes use of the target rule engine specific mechanism for rule validation and attempt to validate both the grammatical validity of the rule and its relevance in the current context (e.g. presence of concordant fact types in the working memory). The authors understand the limitations of such approach and further work will investigate more appropriate techniques to evaluate the soundness of the interchange.

System usability: The authors have designed a web user interface for the demonstration software using Adobe Flex technology. Using this interface, the user can browse through and make use of different rule engines and their rules.

Acknowledgements

This work is part of the IT SOA project founded by the European Union and the Polish Minister of Higher Education. More details on this project can be found at: http://www.soa.edu.pl

SRLG Inference in OSPF for
Improved Reconvergence after Failures

Bart Puype[1], Dimitri Papadimitriou[2], Goutam Das[1], Didier Colle[1],
Mario Pickavet[1], and Piet Demeester[1]

[1] University of Ghent, Department of Information Technology (INTEC),
Gaston Crommenlaan 8 bus 201, B-9050 Gent, Belgium
{bart.puype,gdas,dcolle,mpick,demeester}@intec.ugent.be
[2] Alcatel-Lucent Bell, Copernicuslaan 50, B-2018 Antwerpen, Belgium
dimitri.papadimitriou@alcatel-lucent.com

Abstract. The ECODE FP7 project researches cognitive routing functions in
future networks. We demonstrate machine learning augmented OSPF routing
which infers SRLGs from network failure history. Inferred SRLGs are used to
improve OSPF convergence and recovery times during subsequent (multiple)
network failures.

Keywords: OSPF, machine learning, cognitive routing, network recovery.

1 Overview

As part of the Future Internet Research and Experimentation (FIRE) initiative, the
ECODE FP7 (Experimental COgnitive Distributed Engine) project [1] designs and
experiments cognitive routing system functionality. For this purpose, online
distributed machine learning techniques are developed to improve network
performance. Specifically for this demonstration, the Open Shortest Path First (OSPF)
link state routing protocol [2] and its functionality to recover from network failures
using IP re-routing are considered. A machine learning component was developed and
implemented, which allows the OSPF to anticipate multiple network failures, and
speed-up routing convergence and recovery of connectivity.

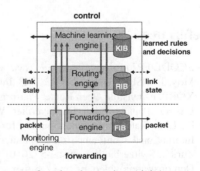

Fig. 1. IBBT ilab.t facility (left); routing system functional overview (right)

E. Di Nitto and R. Yahyapour (Eds.): ServiceWave 2010, LNCS 6481, pp. 233–234, 2010.
© Springer-Verlag Berlin Heidelberg 2010

This functionality was developed and tested on the IBBT ilab.t facility (Fig. 1, left), a network emulation platform allowing for easy setup and execution of networking experiments. The ECODE cognitive routing platform uses the eXtensible Open Routing Platform [3], with the machine learning component implemented as a XORP process (Fig. 1, right). The machine learning engine augments control plane functionality, and interacts with the routing and forwarding engine.

2 SRLG Inference

Layered networks suffer from multiple concurrent upper layer failures caused by failure of a lower layer resource. A set of network links relying on a lower layer resource is called a shared risk link group (SRLG). The SRLG inference algorithm running in the machine learning engine receives link failure event information from the OSPF protocol running in the local routing engine. From the failure history, the algorithm can learn and identify SRLGs [4]. These are then passed to the OSPF instance. When the OSPF protocol receive a link state update indicating a link failure, it can anticipate further link failures from SRLG information, leading to faster network recovery.

3 Demonstrated Functions

We demonstrate SRLG inference by running the machine learning augmented OSPF on an emulated network. Each node runs a separate augmented OSPF instance, demonstrating distributed machine learning. The setup visualizes network connectivity by displaying a graph model of the network, as well as showing several video streams transported over the network, allowing spectators to verify the impact on network connectivity of multiple link failures. We compare standard OSPF which offers slow, piece-wise recovery of connectivity, versus SRLG inference augmented OSPF operation which reroutes and recovers for all links in an entire SRLG at once. A short video overview of the demonstration setup is available at [5].

Acknowledgments. This research work is (partially) funded by the European Commission (EC) through the ECODE project (INFSO-ICT-223936) part of the European Seventh Framework Programme (FP7).

References

1. ECODE FP7 project, http://www.ecode-project.eu/
2. Moy, J.: OSPF Version 2, RFC 2328, Internet Engineering Task Force (IETF) (April 1998)
3. XORP, eXtensible Open Router Platform, http://www.xorp.org/
4. Das, G., Papadimitriou, D., Tavernier, W., Colle, D., Dhaene, T., Pickavet, M., Demeester, P.: Link State Protocol data mining for shared risk link group detection. In: Proc. of 19th International Conference on Computer Communications and Networks (ICCCN 2010), Zurich, Switzerland, August 2-5 (2010)
5. Demonstration video, http://users.ugent.be/~bpuype/pub/fia-ghent/

Future Internet Management Platforms for Network Virtualisation and Service Clouds

Alex Galis[1], Stuart Clayman[1], Andreas Fischer[2], Alexandru Paler[2],
Yahya Al-Hazmi[2], Hermann De Meer[2], Abderhaman Cheniour[3],
Olivier Mornard[3], Jean Patrick Gelas[3], Laurent Lefevre[3],
Javier Rubio Loyola[4], Antonio Astorga[5],
Joan Serrat[5], and Steven Davy[6]

[1] University College London – U.K.
{a.galis,s.clayman}@ee.ucl.ac.uk
[2] University of Passau – Germany
{andreas.fischer,paler,yahya.al-hazmi,
hermann.demeer}@uni-passau.de
[3] INRIA- France
{abderhaman.cheniour,olivier.mornard,
jean-patrick.gelas,laurent.lefevre}@ens-lyon.fr,
[4] CINVESTAV Tamaulipas - Mexico
jrubio@tamps.cinvestav.mx
[5] Universitat Politècnica de Catalunya – Spain
{aastorga,serrat}@nmg.upc.edu
[6] Waterford Institute of Technology
sdavy@tssg.org

Abstract. This paper presents a number of service-centric platforms and demonstrations that have been developed by the FP7 Autonomic Internet project with the aim to create a flexible environment for autonomic deployment and management of Virtual Networks (VN) and Services as validated on large-scale testbeds.

Keywords: Service and Virtual Networks deployment and management.

1   Autonomic Internet Platforms

AutoI (http://ist-autoi.eu/autoi/) [3] advocates for an architectural model for Future Internet consisting of a number of distributed management systems, which are described with the help of five abstractions - the OSKMV (Orchestration, Service, Knowledge, Management and Virtualisation) planes.

OP governs and integrates the behaviours of the management systems distributed across the network, in response to changing context. *SP* consists of functions for the automatic (re)deployment of new management services, as well as resource and end-user facing services (e.g. service computing clouds). *KP* provides knowledge and expertise to enable the network to exhibit self-* functionality. *MP* consists of

E. Di Nitto and R. Yahyapour (Eds.): ServiceWave 2010, LNCS 6481, pp. 235–237, 2010.
© Springer-Verlag Berlin Heidelberg 2010

236   A. Galis et al.

Fig. 1. Autonomic Internet Planes

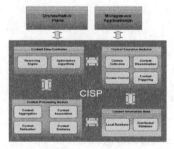

Fig. 2. vCPI Conceptual View

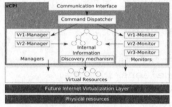

CISP

Fig. 3. Context and Information

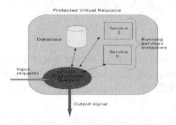

Fig. 4. ANPI Conceptual View

Autonomic Management Systems, which are designed to implement autonomic control loops. The *VP* consists of software mechanisms to treat selected physical resources as a programmable pool of virtual resources.

A set of integrated service-centric platforms and supporting systems have been developed [1], [2] and issued as open source in the AutoI project, which aims to create a highly open and flexible environment for Future Internet. VP's main component is a common management of the heterogeneity of virtual resources and enabling programmability of network elements.

vCPI (virtual Component Programming Interface). In each physical node there is an embedded vCPI, which is aware of the structure of the virtual resources, which are hosted in the physical node.

KP's main component is **CISP** *(Context Information Service Platform)* supported by a distributed monitoring platform for resources & components. CISP has the role of managing the context information, including its distribution to context clients/consumers.

Context clients are context-aware services, either user-facing applications/services or network management services, which make use of or adapt themselves to context information. **SP**'s main component is **ANPI** *(Autonomic Network Programming Interface)* that enables large-scale autonomic services deployment on virtual networks. **MBT** *(Model-Based Translator)* platform, which takes configuration files compliant with the AUTOI Information Model and translates them to device specific commands.

APE *(AutoI Policy-based Engine)* supports context-aware policy-driven decisions for management and orchestration activities. **XINA** is a modular scalable platform that enables the deployment, control and management of programmable or active sessions over virtual entities, such as servers and routers. **RNM** *(Reasoning and Negotiation Module)*, which mediates and negotiates between separate federated domains.

The AutoI platforms were developed, integrated and validated on 2 testbeds enabling experimentation with thousands of virtual machines: V^3 – UCL's Experimental Testbed located in London consisting of 80 cores with a dedicated 10 Gbits/s infrastructure; **Grid5000** - an Experimental testbed located in France consisting of 5000 cores and linked by a dedicated 10 Gbits/s infrastructure. Five videos with AutoI demonstrations are available at: http://clayfour.ee.ucl.ac.uk/demos/ and they are used for: 1. Autonomic deployment of large-scale virtual networks (*VN Provisioning*); 2. Self – management of virtual networks (*VN Management*); 3. Autonomic service provisioning on virtual networks (*Service Clouds*).

Acknowledgments. The work presented in this paper is partially supported by EC.

References

[1] Results of the Autonomic Internet Approach (D6.3) (June 2010),
    http://ist-autoi.eu/autoi/
[2] Rubio-Loyola, J., et al.: Platforms and Software Systems for an Autonomic Internet. In: IEEE Globecom 2010, Miami, USA, December 6-10 (2010)
[3] Galis, A., et al.: Management Architecture and Systems for Future Internet Networks. In: Towards the Future Internet. IOS Press, Amsterdam (April 2009)

Author Index